DEFEATING TERRORISM

Shaping the New Security Environment

Russell D. Howard
Colonel US Army

Reid L. Sawyer
Major US Army

Foreword by Wayne A. Downing
General US Army (Ret.)

The **McGraw·Hill** Companies

Book Team

Vice President and Publisher   *Jeffrey L. Hahn*
Managing Editor   *Theodore Knight*
Director of Production   *Brenda S. Filley*
Developmental Editor   *Ava Suntoke*
Designer   *Charles Vitelli*
Typesetting Supervisor   *Juliana Arbo*
Typesetting   *Jocelyn Proto, Cynthia Powers*
Proofreader   *Julie Marsh*
Permissions Editor   *Rose Gleich*

McGraw-Hill/Dushkin

A Division of The McGraw-Hill Companies

530 Old Whitfield Street, Guilford, Connecticut 06437

Cover © 2002 AFP/CORBIS

Cover Design *Michael Campbell*

The credit section for this book begins on page 158 and is considered an extension of the copyright page.

Library of Congress Control Number 2003106504

Howard, Russell D.
    Defeating terrorism: Shaping the new security environment / Russell D. Howard
and Reid L. Sawyer. Guilford, CT: McGraw-Hill, © 2004
    176p.; cm.

ISBN 0-07-287302-7

Discusses Islamic terrorist movements, global financing, and how businesses and military intervention can combat terrorism, weapons of mass destruction, cyberterrorism, and SARS.

1. Terrorists—Religious aspects—Islam. 2. War on Terrorism, 2001—3. Qaeda (Organization)—Finance. 4. Weapons of Mass Destruction. 5. Terrorism—Prevention—United States. 6. Islam and terrorism. 7. Information warfare. 8. Cyberterrorism. 9. Suicide bombing. I. Sawyer, Reid L. II. Title.

Printed in the United States of America

10 9 8 7 6 5 4 3 2 1

Visit the Online Learning Center With PowerWeb at

http://www.dushkin.com/terrorism/

Contents

For Vincent Viola—unsung hero
in the global war on terrorism

About the Authors

Colonel Russ Howard, a career Special Forces officer, is now a professor and department head at the United States Military Academy. As a Special Forces officer, Colonel Howard served at every level of command, including: A Detachment Commander in the 7th Special Forces Group to Group, B Detachment Commander in the 1st Special Forces Group, Battalion Commander in the Special Warfare Center and School, and Commander of the 1st Special Forces Group. In preparation for his academic position, Colonel Howard earned degrees from San Jose State University, the University of Maryland, the Monterey Institute of International Studies, and Harvard University. Presently, he is finishing a Ph.D. in international security studies at the Fletcher School of Law and Diplomacy. During the course of his career Colonel Howard has had antiterror and counterterror responsibilities, and has taught and published articles on terrorism subjects.

Major Reid Sawyer, a career Military Intelligence officer, is an instructor of political science at the United States Military Academy. As an Intelligence officer, Major Sawyer served in counternarcotics and special operations assignments. Major Sawyer earned his undergraduate degree from the United States Military Academy and holds a master's degree from Columbia University. Major Sawyer has lectured on terrorism to various groups and is currently working on a research project for the Institute of National Security Studies on the efficacy of counterterrorism measures. Major Sawyer is the current director of terrorism studies at West Point.

Foreword

Two years after September 11, 2001, the world continues to face an imminent and dangerous threat from terrorism. Attacks ranging from those in Bali to the near simultaneous car bombings in Saudi Arabia remind us of the resolve and strength of those terrorist groups that are committed to destroying the United States and its interests. The transformation of terrorism since the end of the cold war has created an enemy that is resilient, well armed, better trained than terrorists of old, and exceptionally dangerous. The new terrorism of today presents greater challenges to governments around the world than ever before. As terrorism continues to transform itself in new and different ways, so too will it transform the world around us. While our survival as a nation may not be at risk, there is little doubt that America will remain a prime target of terrorists for the foreseeable future.

The issues underlying terrorism are far ranging and diverse. No single solution or sole instrument of national power can hope to resolve these questions alone. Instead, we must search out new and different solutions that challenge our traditional assumptions. The United States must focus on the prevention of terrorist attacks by disrupting the terrorists' means to conduct their operations whether through attacking their revenue sources or limiting their available "safe havens." Moreover, the aggressive pursuit of terrorism calls for the redefinition of the problem. The old manner of thinking, planning, and reacting to terrorism simply does not work in this new security environment. Compounding all of this is a world where international travel is easier than ever, national borders are more porous than ever, and information on almost any subject is widely available.

This volume, edited by Colonel Russ Howard and Major Reid Sawyer, uniquely features a wide range of experts who present forward thinking solutions to the different facets of this pressing problem. The authors featured in this work are a diverse group of leaders in their respective fields, who combine here to present some of the best and truly innovative thinking on defeating terrorism. This distinguished group ranges from the Global Crisis Manager of Goldman Sachs to the world's leading expert on al-Qaeda. Together, this collection of policy makers, academics, military officers, and business leaders offer a range of concrete measures to reduce this growing threat. The goal of this excellent collection is to heighten the reader's awareness of the critical issues surrounding terrorism and to present a diverse range of solutions to these issues.

Colonel Russ Howard, the Director of West Point's Combating Terrorism Center, and Major Reid Sawyer, Director of Terrorism Studies at West Point, combine impressive academic credentials with an extensive background in special operations. Through their teaching of the future leaders of our Army in terrorism and security courses at West Point and their contributions to the war on terrorism, Colonel Russ Howard and Major Reid Sawyer are able to draw upon some of the best thinking being done in this arena. It is at this intersection of theory and practice from which we can derive the most effective approach to address the broad range of issues that terrorism raises.

The challenges posed by terrorism will not be solved easily or quickly. Instead, we must recognize that this is a multigenerational problem that requires flexible and adaptive policy. Policies must reach beyond military solutions and look to address the root causes of terrorism. The complexity of this problem is overwhelming, yet it is sound, reasoned thinking like the articles in this volume that will contribute to finding a solution.

—Wayne A. Downing

Preface

In much the same way that many Cold Warriors miss the predictability and transparency of the U.S.-Soviet confrontation, many intelligence professionals, military operators, pundits, and academics miss the familiarity of a type of terrorism that was quite dangerous, but was, in the end, merely a nasty sideshow to the greater East-West conflict.[1] There is no question that the commando-style, predominantly state-sponsored terrorism waged by the likes of Andreas Baader and Ulrike Mainhof of the German extreme left Rote Armee Fraction or by Abu Nidal of the Fatah National Council (who was killed in Baghdad last August) was brutal. However, it was not nearly as deadly as the threat the world faces today[2] from a religiously and ethnically motivated terrorism that "neither relies on the support of sovereign states nor is constrained by the limits on violence that state sponsors observed themselves or placed on their proxies."[3]

Bruce Hoffman, head of terrorist research at the Rand Corporation and arguably one of the world's leading experts on the subject, puts it this way, "I don't mean to sound perverse, but there may be a certain nostalgia for the old style of terrorism where there wasn't the threat of loss of life on a massive scale…. It's a real commentary on how much the world has changed."[4]

This new terrorism has a much greater potential to cause harm to America, the West, and all secular countries, including those in the Muslim world. Led by al Qaeda and Osama bin Laden, it "is built around loosely linked cells that do not rely on a single leader or state sponsor."[5] The new terrorism is transnational, borderless, and prosecuted by non-state actors. Also, it is very, very dangerous.[6]

The "old" and "new" terrorism can be distinguished in six different ways:

First, the "new terrorism" is more violent. Under the old paradigm, terrorists wanted attention, not mass casualties. Now they want both. Al Qaeda is responsible for the most lethal terrorist attack in history and has achieved the highest ever rate of lethality per attack.[7]

Second, unlike their Cold War counterparts, who were primarily sub-state actors trying to effect change in local politics, the most dangerous terrorists today are transnational, non-state actors who operate globally and want to destroy not only the West, but all Islamic secular state systems. While earlier terrorist organizations had local aspirations, al Qaeda has global reach and strategic objectives. Its operators are transnational, non-state actors who hold allegiance to a cause, not a state. This is problematic because the traditional forms of state interaction—diplomatic, economic, and military—to solve differences prior to conflict are difficult to apply in a non-state actor context. When things get testy, whom do you negotiate with, whom do you sanction, and whom do you threaten with force? And if a transnational, non-state actor like bin Laden uses a weapon of mass destruction against you, whom do you nuke?

Third, the new terrorists are much better financed than their predecessors, who relied mainly on crime or the largesse of state sponsors to fund their activities. Today's terrorists have income streams from legal and illegal sources and are not accountable to state sponsors—or anyone else. Al Qaeda is a wealthy, multinational organization with numerous income streams. It has investments and concealed accounts worldwide, many in the Western societies bin Laden most despises.[8] Osama bin Laden and his followers will use their wealth to continue to coerce governments for access and safe haven, just as they have done in Sudan and Afghanistan. They also pay to subcontract and franchise the services of like-minded terrorist organizations, all for the purpose of killing Americans.

Fourth, today's terrorists are better trained in the arts of war and the "black arts" than those in past decades. We know this from the materials captured in al Qaeda's training camps in Afghanistan and from very similar training materials of other Muslim extremist groups found in Europe and Central Asia. Al Qaeda operatives are well trained in military, special operations, and intelligence functions. Notwithstanding the coalition's victory in Afghanistan, the allies soon learned that the al Qaeda global terrorist network is "a relatively sophisticated, well-trained and financed organization that drew on ongoing grass-roots support and a fanatical willingness to fight to the death," making it a daunting foe.[9]

Fifth, this generation's terrorists, particularly the religious extremists, are more difficult to penetrate than terrorists of previous generations. The networked, cellular structure used by al Qaeda and its allies is particularly difficult to penetrate, especially for a hierarchical security apparatus like that in the United States. The al Qaeda model, which is composed of many cells whose members do not know one another, have never met in one place together and use strict communication discipline, is more than a match for Western intelligence agencies that rely mainly on technical means of intelligence collection.[10] "America's new enemies can't be bought, bribed, or even blackmailed."[11] They want to kill Americans and will do so at any cost. While bribes and sex traps could help catch terrorists for prosecution and information in the old days, it is difficult to "turn" religious extremists now using the same methods. Today, the $25 million reward on bin Laden has yet to be collected, and it is unclear how successful other methods have been in getting bin Laden's followers to talk.

Sixth, and most insidious, is the availability of weapons of mass destruction (WMD). Back in the 1980s, when I was first became engaged in counterterrorism, we were concerned about small arms, explosives (particularly plastique), rocket-propelled grenades, and the occasional shoulder-fired anti-aircraft missile. Today, the concern is about nuclear, radiological, chemical, and biological weapons—all of which are potentially catastrophic, with massive killing potential. In addition, the possibility of acquiring these weapons is greater because of globalization, information technology, and the increased availability of shady suppliers. Indeed, terrorism today has a global reach that it did not have before the information generation and globalization. It can ride the back of the Web, use advanced communications to move immense financial flows from Sudan to the Philippines or from Australia to banks in Florida.[12] And for $28.50, any Internet surfer can purchase *Bacteriological Warfare: A Major Threat to North America*, which will show you how to grow deadly bacteria. Shady suppliers come from many countries, particularly Russia, which cannot offer employment to many scientists and weaponeers, who were among the elites in the old Soviet Empire. In fact, there are many reports of some of them peddling plutonium across Eastern Europe and of scientists who once worked in Soviet labs linked to germ warfare now selling their services for hefty fees in the Middle East.[13]

As a tactic, suicide bombing has been a weapon in the terrorist's arsenal for decades. It is not new, but it has never been used with such frequency and intensity as it is now. Suicide bombing—"martyr operations" in Islamic extremists' lexicon—is the one aspect of the terrorism threat we (Americans and those in the West) really do not get. We know from the McVeigh, Oklahoma City episode, that Americans can be terrorists and perform horrific acts of wanton murder. McVeigh, however, had a getaway strategy, which suicide bombers obviously do not. Not having a getaway strategy is counterintuitive in Western culture; counterintuitive to our law enforcement officials too, who solve crimes and capture perpetrators based on evidence collection. But suicide bombers, such as the al Qaeda terrorists on September 11, destroy themselves and much of the evidence during the crime, leaving little to analyze.

As envisioned by al Qaeda, the "perfect new warfare" day would combine multiple attacks against America that would produce the greatest number of casualties. For maximum effect, these would take place nearly simultaneously and at geographically separated locations, much like the attacks of September 11 in New York City, and Washington D.C.[14] When, where, and how will the new terrorists hit the United States again? No one knows for sure, but the odds are they will, possibly when and where it is least suspected.

One might say that America's war against the new terrorism is far colder than the Cold War ever was—"cold" as in the "cold-blooded murder" of September 11.[15] At least with the Soviets we always knew who was in charge and that we couldn't be attacked without his orders. In fact, the U.S. president had a direct line to the Soviet leaders and he could personally work through difficult moments with them.[16] By contrast, we lost thousands of people on September 11, 2001; and even though we know Osama bin Laden ordered the killing, we have no direct line to him or anyone else in his leadership. We also know that he and his followers will continue to hit the United States and its allies, including secular Islamic states, again and again, until he and his network are stopped.

It has been said that generals always make the mistake of preparing to fight the last war instead of the next one. This book illustrates the changes that have taken place in the terrorist threat since Cold War. More importantly, it offers suggestions on how to defeat the new terrorism, so that today's generals and their civilian masters understand how to fight the current war, not the past, and in hopes that we will not have to fight a war like this ever again.

Reid Sawyer and I were asked to edit this book after the favorable response to our first book *Terrorism and Counterterrorism: Understanding the New Security Environment*. Some of the contributors in this book were featured in our first effort, some are new. All are forward thinking and have looked at ways to combat and defeat terrorism, not just recalculate the "terrorism problem." All but two of the articles are original contributions. Bruce Hoffman's "The Logic of Suicide Terrorism," was first published in the *Atlantic Monthly* in June 2003, and Audrey Kurth Cronin's "Behind the Curve—Globalization and International Terrorism" first appeared in the winter 2002/03 edition of *International Security*. Both articles are superbly written and add great value to this work.

The first seven articles in this book are sequenced to compliment the "six differences" and "suicide bombing" in this introduction. The remaining articles suggest alternative, and perhaps provocative, means of defeating the "new terrorism." Al Qaeda is the principal threat to defeat in most, but not all, of the articles. It is, after all, America's clear and present danger.

Rohan Gunaratna

Dr. Rohan Gunaratna is arguably one of the world's most knowledgeable al Qaeda watchers. His contribution to this book, "Defeating al Qaeda—The Pioneering Vanguard of the Islamic Movements," initially describes why al Qaeda's "network of networks" is so difficult to defeat. According to Dr. Gunaratna, al Qaeda has indeed suffered formidable losses since September 11, but despite the U.S.-led global campaign against terrorism, it continues to present an unprecedented threat. Failing to destroy the core leadership of al Qaeda was the Coalition's greatest failure. Developing a multipronged, multidimensional, multi-agency and multinational response to al Qaeda and its associate groups, writes Gunaratna, is the only way to destroy the threat's continuity and its opportunities for escalation.

Audrey Kurth Cronin

Audrey Kurth Cronin, in "Behind the Curve—Globalization and International Terrorism," argues that the current wave of international terrorism is characterized by unpredictable and unprecedented threats from nonstate actors. According to Dr. Cronin, terrorism is not only a reaction to globalization but is facilitated by it, while the U.S. response to the terrorist threat has been reactive and anachronistic. Furthermore, she explains, the combined focus of the United States on state-centric threats and its attempt to cast twenty-first century terrorism into familiar strategic terms avoids and often undermines effective responses to the current nonstate terrorist phenomena. Military power, writes Cronin, is an important but supporting instrument in the campaign against terrorism. More effective, however, will be nonmilitary instruments such as intelligence, public diplomacy, and cooperation with allies.

Patrick D. Buckley and Michael J. Meese

The bottom line of "The Financial Front in the Global War on Terrorism," written by Pat Buckley and Michael Meese is to hit terrorists where it hurts—in the pocketbook. Al Qaeda must raise, move, and use money for its operations, explain the authors, so pursuing their finances makes good sense. According to Buckley and Meese, the major ways to disrupt terrorists, financial networks are by freezing and blocking assets, following financial transactions for intelligence purposes, and prosecuting terrorists and their supporters for financial crimes. Because the vast majority of al Qaeda's assets are located outside the United States, the authors insist international cooperation is essential to be victorious on the "financial front."

Robert Mandel

In "Fighting Fire with Fire: Privatizing Counterterrorism," Dr. Robert Mandel contends that there is a vital need for unorthodox counterterrorist strategies to defeat the new terrorism, as traditional responses have been less than effective, particularly with regard to intelligence gathering and preemptive coercive measures against well-trained nonstate terrorist groups. Western democracies, argues Mandel, are handicapped by their own civility in confronting terrorists; he therefore advocates suborning transnational criminal organizations to help gather intelligence on terrorists and employing private security firms to help fight them. In raising this "somewhat novel" approach, Mandel does not recommend replacing conventional mechanisms for fighting terror but believes unorthodox means must be considered, given the military sophistication of today's terrorist adversaries.

James S. Robbins

In "Defeating Networked Terrorism," Dr. James S. Robbins has a more optimistic view than Rohan Gunaratna. Robbins argues that the U.S.-led coalition has moved significantly toward the goals of its antiterror strategy. According to Robbins, the al Qaeda global network, which was spawned in an era of Western inattention, was well adapted to the conditions prevailing before 9/11. However, it has not shown itself to be as adaptive as first thought, and examining key measures of network activity—such as initiative, finances, cohesion, and ability to wage war on the West—shows a terrorist organization that is unable to prosecute sustained offensive operations and is fighting mainly for survival. The war against al Qaeda is being won, says Robbins, but it is far from over.

Michael Eastman and Robert Brown

"Security Strategy in the Gray Zone" by Michael Eastman and Robert Brown assesses three potential strategies for keeping weapons of mass destruction out of terrorists' hands: deterrence, prevention, and preemption. After analyzing the strengths and weaknesses of each, the authors conclude that "preventing" hostile states from acquiring WMD in the first place is the "best of three bad options" for safeguarding the nation against WMD terrorist attacks.

Bruce Hoffman

As Dr. Bruce Hoffman explains in "The Logic of Suicide Terrorism," the tactics of terrorists, particularly suicide bombing, are quite logical. Written in easily understood, cost-benefit terms, Hoffman's article posits that "the fundamental characteristics of suicide bombing, and its strong attraction for the terrorist organizations behind it, are universal: "Suicide bombings are inexpensive and effective." Hoffman's syntax forces one to rethink modern warfare's technological jargon. Hoffman considers suicide bombers the ultimate smart bomb: they guarantee media coverage and are less complicated and compromising than other kinds of terrorist operations. Hoffman uses Israel as the case study for his article because it has had more experience with suicide bombers than any other place and its experience is instructive. Hoffman notes that Israel is not the United States, but he believes Americans can take precautions based on the Israeli experience to substantially reduce the threat of suicide bombing in America.

Kelly J. Hicks

In "How Business Can Defeat Terrorism," Kelly Hicks asks his readers to first imagine that a terrorist group has just deployed a deadly, highly infectious disease in a densely populated financial capital: "By the time three days pass, hundreds of people worldwide are infected with and dying from a virus of unknown type, with no known cure." While Hicks could be describing a deadly terrorist scheme of attack, it is instead a realistic description of how the Severe Acute Respiratory Syndrome (SARS) pandemic brought Hong Kong to its knees. Hicks uses the Hong Kong response to SARS as a case study to explain both how a bio-terrorist attack could unfold and, more importantly, how business, government, and the international community can respond successfully.

Russell D. Howard

In "Preemptive Military Doctrine—No Other Choice Against Transnational, Non-State Actors," I argue that deterrence and containment, the previous foundations of U.S. strategy, are no longer valid when confronting transnational, non-state terrorists. I agree with President Bush that the United States must identify and destroy the terrorist threat before it reaches our borders and, if necessary, act alone and use preemptive force. In my view, the traditional economic, political, diplomatic, and military applications of American power used to leverage and influence states in the past are not effective against non-state actors. Whom do you sanction or embargo? With whom do you negotiate? How do you defend against or deter Osama bin Laden? You don't. The only effective way to influence the bin Ladens of the world is to preempt them before they can act.

Brian M. Jenkins

In "Counter al Qaeda," Brian Jenkins argues that while the initial goal of defeating al Qaeda has been achieved, the United States now faces a more complex phase of the war against terrorism, one in which the United States will find it more difficult to coordinate its response, as the tasks for waging the war are dispersed among numerous departments, agencies, and offices. Jenkins's strategy for prosecuting this complex second phase consists of thirteen "key elements," one of which is "that the second phase of the war on terrorism cannot be accomplished unilaterally—international cooperation is a prerequisite for success."

Wayne A. Downing

General Wayne Downing (Retired), like most of the other contributors to this book, agrees that a multinational and multilateral approach is the only way to defeat al Qaeda and other terrorist groups. In "The Global War on Terrorism: Focusing the National Strategy," Downing states that "the world will never be free of all terrorism. A more realistic goal is to eliminate terrorists' global reach, render them less lethal—and reduce their capabilities—to the point they are a regional threat, then a state threat, then a provincial or local threat that can be handled as ordinary crime by local law enforcement. Downing further explains that the root causes of terrorism must be identified and addressed if there is to be any long-term progress on the war against terrorism.

—Russell D. Howard

Notes

1. John Mearsheimer, "Why We Will Soon Miss the Cold War," *Atlantic Monthly*, August 1990. See also, Glenn Sacks, "Why I Miss the Cold War," Internet: www.glennsacks.com
2. Brian Murphy, "The Shape of Terrorism Changes," *Fayetteville Observer*, Aug. 21, 2002, p. 9A.

3. Steven Simon and Danier Benjamin, "America and the New Terrorism," *Survival*, vol. 42, no. 1, Spring 2000, p. 69.
4. Quoted frequently from several sources, Dr. Hoffman has mentioned this to me personally on two occasions.
5. Brian Murphy.
6. Ibid.
7. Bruce Newsome, "Executive Summary," Mass-Casualty Terrorism: Second Quarterly Forecast by the University of Reading Terrorism Forecasting Group, June 13, 2003, p. 3. Internet: http://www.rdg.ac.uk/GSEIS/University_of_Reading_Terrorism_Forecast_2003Q2.pdf
8. Robin Wright, *Sacred Rage* (New York: Simon & Schuster, 2001), p. 253.
9. Ann Tyson, "Al Qaeda, Resilient and Organized," *Christian Science Monitor*, Mar. 7, 2002, p. 1.
10. Rohan Gunaratna, *Inside Al Qaeda: Global Network of Terror* (New York: Columbia University Press, 2002), p. 76.
11. Glenn Sacks, "Why I Miss the Cold War," July 1, 2003, www.glensacks.com.
12. Paul Mann, "Modern Military Threats: Not All They Might Seem?" *Aviation Week & Space Technology*, April 22, 2002, p. 1. (Gordon Adams quote)
13. Doug Gavel, "Can Nuclear Weapons Be Put Beyond the Reach of Terrorists?" *Kennedy School of Government Bulletin*, Autumn 2002.
14. "A Military Assessment of the al Qaeda Training Tapes," Jun 28, 2003, Internet: http://www.strategypage.com/articles/tapes/5.asp
15. Glen Sacks.
16. Ibid.

Rohan Gunaratna, 2003

Defeating Al Qaeda—The Pioneering Vanguard of the Islamic Movements[1]

Introduction

Since the emergence of the contemporary wave of terrorism in the Middle East in 1968, the world has witnessed three categories of terrorist organisations: ideological (left and right wing), ethnonationalist (irredentist, separatist, autonomy), and politico-religious groups. Two landmark events—the Islamic revolution in Iran and Soviet intervention in Afghanistan—both in 1979 marked the emergence of the contemporary wave of Islamist guerrilla and terrorist groups.[2] While Iran's clerical regime held 66 Americans as hostages for 444 days in Tehran, the anti-Soviet multinational Afghan campaign checkmated the world's largest army, the Soviet army, in a protracted guerrilla campaign that lasted a decade. While an Islamic regime defied one superpower in the Middle East, an Islamic movement defeated another superpower in Afghanistan. In response to the Soviet occupation of Afghanistan (December 1979–February 1989), U.S. presence in the Arabian Peninsula (December 1990), Gulf War I (January 1991) and the U.S.-led coalition occupation of Iraq (March 2003–present), Islamism grew in strength, size and influence. As a result, virulent and extremist ideologies found greater acceptance, existing Islamist political parties and terrorist groups became more influential, and new Islamist organisations proliferated.

Since its founding in March 1988, one year before Soviet troop withdrawal from Afghanistan, Al Qaeda built a "network of networks."[3] By co-opting leaders of like-minded Islamic movements, Al Qaeda built an umbrella of which Osama bin Laden gradually assumed the leadership. In its earlier life as Maktab-il-Khidamat (Afghan Service Bureau), established in 1984, it built a global network that channeled resources and recruits to Afghanistan from around the world. After defeating the Soviet Army, the largest land army in the world, and stripping the Soviet Empire of its superpower status, the Islamists aimed their sights at the remaining superpower—the United States of America. As the vicious by-product of the anti-Soviet multinational Afghan campaign, Al Qaeda had inherited a state-of-the-art training infrastructure, wealthy sponsors, proven trainers, experienced combatants and a vast support base stretching from Australia throughout the Muslim world into Canada.

After its victory against the Soviet army in Afghanistan in the 1980s, Al Qaeda transformed itself from a guerrilla group to a terrorist group capable of operating in urban terrain and targeting civilians after its headquarters relocated from Peshawar, Pakistan, to Khartoum, Sudan, in December 1991. After the 1993 meeting in Khartoum between Osama bin Laden and Imad Mugneyev, the head of the Special Security Apparatus of Hezbollah, the most dangerous terrorist group at that time, Al Qaeda members and recruits received terrorist instruction in Sudan and Southern Lebanon.[4] The camps in Sudan were sponsored and conducted by the Iranian Ministry of Intelligence and Security Affairs (MOIS) and the

Iranian Revolutionary Guards Corps (IRGC). As the Taliban regime perceived the clerical regime in Iran as inimical, Iranian sponsorship declined after Osama bin Laden relocated from Sudan to Afghanistan in May 1996.[5] After U.S. occupation of Iraq in March 2003, Iran became the immediate neighbour of the United States of America. In conducting its operations from Afghanistan, a landlocked country, Al Qaeda has to rely either on Pakistan or Iran as a launching pad. With severe losses on its Pakistan front, since October 2001, Al Qaeda has opened a new staging area, the Iranian front. Is Iran turning a blind eye to Al Qaeda or actively supporting it, and if so, exactly which agency of Iran, a fractured government, is supportive of Al Qaeda? There are early signs of covert Iranian sponsorship of Al Qaeda, but it may be from one segment of the fractured government. As an immediate neighbour, both Iran and Syria, sponsors of the Lebanese Hezbollah, perceive the United States of America as a severe threat as well as their number one enemy, a notion shared by Al Qaeda and Hezbollah, the leading Shiite and Sunni terrorist groups today.

The Context

Al Qaeda has suffered formidable losses since September 11, 2001. Over 3,200 leaders, members and key supporters of Al Qaeda have been killed or captured in 102 countries since the United States of America's declared "War on Terrorism."[6] Nonetheless, the robust Islamist milieu, in which Al Qaeda operates, has enabled the group to replenish its human losses—members captured and killed, and material wastage—assets seized and funds frozen. Furthermore, having imparted guerrilla and terrorist training to several tens of thousands of Islamists from around the world in its camps in Afghanistan, Al Qaeda built sufficient strategic depth worldwide for the generation of support and recruits. As a well-endowed and well-resourced group from its inception, Al Qaeda invested in creating a cadre of highly dedicated and committed fighters willing to kill and die in the name of religion. Whether they live in the West or the East, Al Qaeda supporters and sympathizers believe in the often repeated Al Qaeda dictum: "It is the duty of every Muslim to wage jihad."

Despite the U.S.-led intensive and sustained global hunt, Al Qaeda continues to present an unprecedented threat. Its unique historical origins, religious character, and organizational structure guarantee its sustenance and survival. When compared with all the other terrorist groups we have been studying since the emergence of the contemporary wave of terrorism in 1968, Al Qaeda is different in composition, diversity, and reach. With the exception of Aum Shinrikyo of Japan, Al Qaeda is the first multinational terrorist group of the 21st century.[7] It has recruited from the Muslim territories of Asia, Africa, Middle East, Caucuses and the Balkans as well as the Muslim migrant and diaspora communities of Europe, North America and Australia. In contrast to other groups that recruited from one single nationality[8] or groupings of nationalities from one particular region,[9] Al Qaeda is truly multinational. Despite global efforts to detect, disrupt, degrade and destroy Al Qaeda, the group has survived because it has a global presence. Periodically it has attacked symbolic, strategic and high profile targets across geographic regions to make its presence known to its support base and to its enemies. Its capacity to survive is largely due to its loosely networked structure, diverse composition and universal ideology. To counter and evade the growing threat to Al Qaeda, the group itself has transformed structurally, strategically and geographically. Al Qaeda is global in reach, from Asia to Canada; multinational in composition, from Uigurs in Xingjiang to American Hispanics, and therefore enjoys diverse capabilities, access to resources, and multiple modus operandi. There is no standard textbook for fighting Al Qaeda. As such, to effectively destroy a group like Al Qaeda, a global approach and a global strategy are prerequisite.

Post–9-11 Al Qaeda

Today, Al Qaeda is in a period of transition. It has lost its base, Afghanistan, and its host, the Islamic Movement of the Taliban, the ruling party of the Islamic Emirate of Afghanistan. More significantly, the death or capture of at least half its operational leaders, members and key supporters has dented its operational effectiveness. Despite the dismantling of its training and operational infrastructure in Afghanistan, Al Qaeda remains a serious, immediate and a direct threat to its enemies. Although Al Qaeda's physical and personnel infrastructure worldwide has suffered, its multi-layered global network still retains sufficient depth to plan, prepare and execute operations directly and through associated groups. By ideologically and physically penetrating a number of regional conflicts where Muslims participate, Al Qaeda's decentralized network works with like-minded groups. With sustained action by the United States, its allies and its friends in Afghanistan and Pakistan, the core of Al Qaeda, its organisers of attacks, trainers, financiers, operatives and other experts are moving to lawless zones of Asia, Middle East, Horn of Africa and the Caucuses.

Like a strike on a hive of bees, Al Qaeda members are seeking new bases in Mindanao in the Philippines, Bangladesh-Myanmar border, Yemen, Somalia, Pankishi Valley in Georgia and Chechnya. Like sharks rapidly moving in search of new opportunities, post–9-11 Al Qaeda cells survive and strike on opportunity. After identifying the weaknesses and the loopholes of the new security architecture, a constantly probing Al Qaeda is likely to infiltrate. While retaining a presence in Afghanistan, post–9-11 Al Qaeda members are active and its fresh recruits train in the conflict zones. For Al Qaeda, regional conflicts are healthy greenhouses to rebuild, regroup, and strike.

Although Al Qaeda as an organization per se has suffered, it is still retaining its pioneering vanguard status of the Islamic movements. In keeping with its founding charter authored by its founder/leader Dr Abdullah Azzam, Al Qaeda remains the spearhead of the Islamic movements. Despite repeated high quality losses, Al Qaeda is still able to set the ideological and operational agenda for three-dozen foreign Islamist groups it trained and financed during the last decade. Al Qaeda is able to preserve its global status by relying on its associated groups to sustain its fight against the United States, its allies and its friends. To compensate for the loss of its state-of-the-art training infrastructure in Afghanistan, Al Qaeda is exploiting the Islamic movements within its ideological, military and financial spheres of influence. Until U.S. intervention in October 2001, the international neglect of Afghanistan turned the country into a "terrorist Disneyland" with about 40 Islamist groups receiving both guerrilla and terrorist training throughout the 1990s. These Asian, Middle Eastern, African and Caucasian groups, hitherto fighting local campaigns, influenced by Al Qaeda's vision of a global jihad, today pose a threat comparable to Al Qaeda.

The post–9-11 trajectory of Al Qaeda operations demonstrates its staying power. With sustained U.S. and allied action in Afghanistan and Pakistan, Al Qaeda has an infinite capacity to change its shape. In the coming months, Al Qaeda will fragment, decentralise, regroup in lawless zones of the world, work with like-minded groups, select a wider range of targets, focus on economic targets and population centres, and conduct most attacks in the global South. Although the group will be constrained from conducting coordinated simultaneous attacks against high profile, symbolic or strategic targets in the West, Al Qaeda together with its regional counterparts will attack in Asia, Africa, Middle East, and even in Latin America, a region where it has only a limited presence. Despite the likely capture or death of its core and penultimate leaders, Al Qaeda's anti-Western universal jihad ideology inculcated among the politicised and radicalised Muslims will sustain support for Al Qaeda.

While its organisers of attacks will remain in Pakistan and Iran, its operatives and messengers will travel back and forth coordinating with Al Qaeda nodes in safe zones such as Yemen, Somalia, Bangladesh, Philippines and Chechnya. To make its presence felt, Al Qaeda will increasingly rely on its global terrorist network of groups in Southeast Asia, South Asia, Horn of Africa, Middle East, and the Caucuses to strike at its enemies. Already attacks in Kenya, Indonesia, India, Pakistan, Kuwait and Yemen seek to compensate for the loss and lack of space and opportunity to operate in the West. Its operatives are currently working together with Jemmah Islamiyah (JI: Southeast Asia), Al Ithihad al Islami (Horn of Africa), Al Ansar Mujahidin (Caucuses), Tunisian Combatants Group (Middle East), Jayash-e-Mohammad (South Asia), Salafi Group for Call and Combat (GSPC, North Africa, Europe and North America) and other Islamist groups it had trained and financed in the past decade. As Al Qaeda has a very small number of cells in the West, the group will operate through the GSPC and Takfir Wal Hijra—two groups it had infiltrated in Europe and North America.[10] With the transfer of terrorist technology and expertise from the centre to the periphery, the attacks by the associated groups of Al Qaeda pose a threat comparable to Al Qaeda.

The fragmentation of Al Qaeda support and operational infrastructure under sustained military and law enforcement action is making it rely on its strategic linkages, diversity, and global reach. The decentralisation of Al Qaeda has contributed to its flexibility of targeting. Despite being the most hunted terrorist group in history, its cellular structure, rigid compartmentalization, and the robust Islamist milieu ensure its resilience to destruction. With sustained military action in Afghanistan, the threat of terrorism has diffused, increasing the threshold for political violence worldwide. The new threshold terrorism is a multidimensional, complex, and global challenge. Despite sustained attrition of Islamist networks since October 2001, their high capacity for replenishing losses by regenerating fresh support and recruits has ensured the continuity of the intellectual and operational capabilities of Al Qaeda. As such, many governments and publics will have to live with a medium-to-high threat index for several years in different parts of the world.

Current Situation

In response to the high threat to Al Qaeda, the group is becoming more creative and lethal. The group is adapting dual technologies—airplanes and commercially available chemicals, agricultural fertilizers, liquid petroleum gas, and liquid nitrogen gas—as its new weapons. The group is also searching for new weapons such as chemical and biological agents, especially contact poisons easy to conceal and breach security. Both Osama's statement in February 2003 to "think intelligently and kill the Americans secretly" and in May 2003 Sheikh Nasr bin Hamid al Fahd's fatwa legitimizing the use of chemical, biological, radiological and nuclear weapons demonstrate its intent and lethality.[11] Although an attempt to pervert Islam, it is likely that the Saudi Sheik presented Koranic justifications, a requirement in Islam, as a prelude to an attack. Reflecting the existing and emerging threat, Eliza Manningham-Buller, the head of the British Security Services (MI5) said in London on July 17, 2003, that a terrorist attack on a Western city using chemical, biological, radiological and nuclear (CBRN) technology is "only a matter of time."[12] She added: "We know that renegade scientists have cooperated with al Qaeda and provided them with some of the knowledge they need to develop these weapons."[13] The Al Qaeda associate group—the Salafi Group for Call and Combat (GSPC)—successfully developed ricin, one of the contact poisons found in the Al Qaeda manuals, and its rudimentary manufacturing apparatus in London in January 2003. The ricin network in Europe, especially in London, Manchester, East Anglia and Edinburgh in the UK, worked together with Al Qaeda experts in the Pankishi Gorge in Georgia, the border of Chechnya.

In the current environment, terrorist groups will continue to recruit and incite its members and supporters living in the West to support and conduct attacks. With the exception of the bombing of the Federal Building in Oklahoma in 1995, almost all the major terrorist attacks in the West have been conducted by members of diaspora and migrant communities. The 9-11 coordinator Ramzi bin al Shibh and the suicide pilots were migrants living in the West. As foreign terrorist groups based in North America, Western Europe, and Australia did not pose a direct and an immediate threat to Western security until 9-11, these host governments tolerated their activity and presence. Even after 9-11, due to the reluctance of Europe, Canada, and Australia to disrupt terrorist support networks, terrorist organizations continue to target émigré communities for recruits and support. Other than Al Qaeda front, cover and sympathetic groups, Islamist groups are aggressively politicizing, radicalizing and mobilizing their migrants and diaspora. Assif Mohammed Hanif, 21, and Omar Khan Sharif, 27, two British suicide bombers of Asian origin from Derbyshire, UK, infiltrated Israel and attacked Mike's Place, a nightclub, on April 30, 2003. While Hanif detonated his bomb, killing two musicians and one waiter and injuring 60, Sharif's explosives device failed to detonate. Since the 31-month uprising in Israel, Hanif's bombing was the first suicide attack by a foreigner. Similarly, in Asia, the first suicide bomber who targeted the State Assembly in Srinagar, Kashmir, was a British Muslim, also of Asian origin. The émigré communities remain vulnerable to ideological penetration, recruitment, and provision of financial support. Despite stepped-up government surveillance, disenfranchised segments of the émigré communities in Western countries still identify themselves with the struggles in their homelands. Until and unless host governments develop a better understanding of the threat and target terrorist propaganda, both its tools and its ideologues, the threat to the West from within will persist.

As illustrated by the statements of both Osama bin Laden and his successor and deputy Dr Ayman Al Zawahiri, although Al Qaeda's capability to attack the West has diminished, its intention to attack has not. On October 6, 2002, Osama bin Laden, the Emir-General of Al Qaeda said: "I am telling you, and God is my witness, whether America escalates or de-escalates this conflict, we will reply to it in kind, God willing. God is my witness, the youth of Islam are willing [and] are preparing things that will fill your hearts with tears. They will target the key sectors of your economy until you stop your injustice and aggression or until the more short-lived of the U.S. die."[14] Ayman Al Zawahiri said on Al Jazeera on October 8, 2002: "Our message to our enemies is this: America and its

Allies should know that their crimes will not go unpunished, God willing. We advise them to hasten to leave Palestine, the Arabian Peninsula, Afghanistan, and all Muslim countries, before they lose everything. We addressed some messages to America's Allies to stop their involvement in its crusader campaign. The Mujahid youths have addressed a message to Germany and another to France. If these measures have not been sufficient, we are ready with the help of God, to increase them."[15] In many ways their periodic pronouncements and statements are the best guide to future Al Qaeda actions.

Targeting Trends

Having recruited from a cross section of society—the rich, the poor, the educated and the less educated—Al Qaeda has developed a reasonably good understanding of Western security measures and countermeasures. After the bombing of the U.S. embassies in East Africa in August 1998, the U.S. government enhanced the perimeter security of its land targets. Then Al Qaeda attacked USS *Cole*, a maritime target in October 2000. When the U.S. government enhanced the perimeter of its land and maritime targets, Al Qaeda attacked America's icons from the sky. The tactical trajectory of Al Qaeda suggests a cunning foe always keen to harass, hurt, and humiliate the enemy by deception.

Al Qaeda's tactical repertoire was deeply influenced by the Iranian-sponsored Lebanese Hezbollah. Hezbollah's modus operandi of coordinated simultaneous suicide attacks influenced Al Qaeda's modus operandi in a big way. As Al Qaeda's aim was also to force the withdrawal of U.S. troops from the Arabian Peninsula, the group emulated the success of Hezbollah in Beirut where the group forced the U.S.-led multinational peacekeeping force to withdrew from Lebanon in 1983, following coordinated simultaneous suicide attacks on U.S. and French targets. In the attack on its Marine barracks, the United States lost 243 personnel, the single biggest loss since Vietnam. As a result, for several years, the United States disengaged itself from the politics of the Middle East. With the exception of the attack on the USS *Cole*, all the mega attacks by Al Qaeda have been coordinated simultaneous suicide attacks. For instance, Al Qaeda attacked the U.S. embassies in Kenya and Tanzania in August 1998; attempted to destroy the Los Angeles international airport; Radisson Hotel in Amman; Jewish and Christian holy sites in Jordan; and the USS *Cole*; *The Sullivans* in Aden, Yemen, on the eve of the Millennium; and attacked America's most outstanding economic and military symbols and attempted to attack its political landmark on 9-11. Similarly Al Qaeda influenced its associated groups to conduct coordinated simultaneous attacks. For instance, Jemmah Islamiyah successfully attacked 16 churches in Indonesia on Christmas Day in 2000 and five targets in Manila, Philippines, on December 30, 2000.

In the early 1990s, Al Qaeda's aim was to create Islamic states in the Middle East by targeting the false Muslim rulers and the corrupt Muslim regimes. After suffering significant losses, both its operatives and material, in the Middle East, Al Qaeda decided to abandon its policy of targeting near targets in favour of targeting the distant enemy—the West—especially the "head of the poisonous snake"—the United States. Gradually, Al Qaeda attacks escalated in intensity and sophistication—East Africa in August 1998, USS *Cole* in October 2000, and America's mainland on 9-11. The two wave attacks in October 2001 and May 2003 are major turning points. Today, Al Qaeda is returning to its near-targets in the Middle East, Asia, Africa and the Caucuses. Having suffered significant losses to its support and operational infrastructure in North America, Western Europe and Australasia, the primary target countries, in the last two years, Al Qaeda is aggressively seeking Western and Jewish targets in the Muslim World.

Although attacking inside North America, Europe, Australasia and Israel remains a priority, Western security measures and countermeasures have made it expensive and difficult for Al Qaeda to mount an operation on Western soil. Nonetheless, Al Qaeda and its associate groups will attack Western targets outside the West where security is largely in the hands of foreign governments. Al Qaeda finds it less costly to operate in parts of Asia, Africa, and the Middle East, where there is lack of security controls. Therefore, most attacks will be against Western targets located in the global South such as the attack in Saudi Arabia. While focusing on Western targets, Al Qaeda will continue to conduct operations against Muslim rulers and regimes supporting the U.S.-led "war on terror." The physical security of the Saudi royalty, Pakistani and Afghan leaders Musharraf and Karzai, respectively, will remain particularly vulnerable and their regimes will come under sustained political challenges in the coming years.

With the hardening of U.S. targets, the threat is shifting to both government and population targets of allies and friends of the United States. Similarly, Al Qaeda is increasingly looking for opportunity targets. For instance, when Al Qaeda failed to target a U.S. warship off Yemen, it targeted a French oil supertanker in October 2002. The hardening of government land and commercial aerial targets has shifted Al Qaeda targeting to both soft land and maritime targets. Although the primary intention of Al Qaeda is to target inside the United States, it lacks the quality operatives of the Mohammad Atta caliber to operate inside the United States. Therefore, Al Qaeda is focusing on U.S. land, sea, and aviation targets overseas. Increased hardening of U.S. military and diplomatic targets after 9-11 is steadfastly shifting the threat to other classes of targets. For instance, Al Qaeda cells in Morocco attempted to target both British and U.S. shipping in the Straits of Gibraltar in mid-2002. Due to perimeter and structural hardening of Israeli and U.S. embassies in Europe and Asia, Al Qaeda decided to target friends and allies of Israel and the U.S. More than ever before, today, the allies and the friends of the United States are vulnerable to Al Qaeda attack.

Hardening of government targets will also displace the threat to softer targets, making civilians prone to terrorist attack. For instance, Al Qaeda planned to attack U.S. diplomatic targets in Bangkok, Singapore, Kuala Lumpur, Phnom Penh, Hanoi and Manila, American Institute in Taiwan, and the U.S. consulate in Surabaya in September 2002,[16] but visible security presence made the group consider soft targets. Although not in all cases, hardening of targets works but as the world witnessed with horror, countermeasures make terrorists creative and innovative. As the traditional explosives-laden vehicle was a non-option to breach the hardened perimeter security of America's most outstanding landmarks, Al Qaeda was forced to develop an aerial airborne capability. Similarly, hardening of military and diplomatic targets in Southeast Asia prompted Jemmah Islamiyah to seek entertainment targets such as Bali. The reality is that government countermeasures have increased the vulnerability of population centres and economic targets. As Islamist groups weaken they are likely to hit soft targets, killing civilians, if possible in large number. As it is impossible to prevent bombing of public places, civilian and civilian infrastructure targets will remain the most vulnerable to terrorist attack in the immediate, mid- and long term.

Hardening of land and aviation targets will shift the threat to sea targets, particularly to commercial maritime targets. As any aviation incident attracts significant attention, Al Qaeda assigns a high priority to aviation-impact terrorism. Due to the difficulty of hijacking aircraft to ram them against targets, Al Qaeda will increasingly invest in conducting stand-off attacks and use hand-held Surface to Air Missiles (SAMs). For instance, an Al Qaeda Sudanese member fired an SA-7 missile at a U.S. military transport plane at the Prince Sultan base in Saudi Arabia in mid-2001. His arrest in Khartoum in December 2001 led the Saudi authorities to recover another complete missile system buried in the Riyadh desert. If appropriate and immediate countermeasures are not taken to target the Al Qaeda shipping network, SAMs under Al Qaeda control held in the Pakistan-Kashmir-Afghanistan theatre, the Arabian Peninsula, and the Horn of Africa will find their way to Far Asia and to Europe, and possibly even to North America. Protective measures, especially target hardening of vulnerable government personnel and infrastructure, by law enforcement and protective services are a temporary solution. To reduce the threat, governments have no option but to hunt terrorists and prevent public support and sympathy for terrorism.

The post–9-11 robust security architecture has forced Al Qaeda to transform its targeting strategy. Al Qaeda's capacity to conduct spectacular or theatrical attacks has diminished due to three factors. First, heightened human vigilance. The high state of alertness of the public and law enforcement authorities has led to the disruption of several operations. For instance, the alert passengers and crew prevented the bombing of the transatlantic flight by Richard Reid, the Al Qaeda shoe bomber on board American Airlines Flight 63 on December 22, 2001. Second, unprecedented law enforcement, security and intelligence cooperation and coordination. As a direct result of inter- and intra-agency cooperation, a large number of suspects have been detained and arrested, and over 100 attacks by Al Qaeda and its associated groups have been interdicted, prevented or abandoned since 9-11. Cooperation beyond the Anglo-Saxon countries, Europe and Israel, especially with the Middle East and Asia, has led to significant arrests. For instance, José Padilla, who intended to mount surveillance and reconnaissance to detonate a radiological dispersal device in Washington DC, en-route from Pakistan via Zurich, was arrested at Chicago's O'Hare international airport in the United States on May 8, 2002. Third, hunting Al Qaeda and its associate groups has limited their time, space and resources to conceptualise, plan and prepare elaborate terrorist strikes. As long as the international community can maintain the public vigilance, anti- and counterterrorism cooperation and coordination worldwide, and maintain sustained pressure on the group, Al Qaeda will not be able to mount large-scale coordinated simultaneous attacks on symbolic, strategic and high profile targets. Large attacks require long-term planning and preparation by several operatives and across several countries. In the current security environment, where there are periodic desertions, arrests, and penetration, a terrorist group can only plan, prepare and execute medium- to small-scale operations. Preventing complacency from setting in especially after a long period of Al Qaeda inactivity is difficult but it is a must if we are to prevent the next attack.

The nature of the Al Qaeda threat has clearly changed since 9-11. In comparison, the post–9-11 threat to the United States, its allies and its friends is fragmented and diffused. Although it has no resources to carry out theatrical or spectacular attacks, it has a clandestine network to move experts, messages and money to associate groups. All indications are that Al Qaeda is not deserting from the 1,520-mile long Pakistan-Afghanistan border but its leadership is actively and aggressively tasking its membership and ideologising associate groups.[17] From the centre of Afghanistan and Pakistan, Al Qaeda's technical experts and financiers, organizers of attacks and operatives are gravitating to lawless zones in Asia, Horn of Africa, Caucuses, Balkans and the Middle East, widening the perimeter of the conflict. The regional groups, such as Jemmah Islamiyah, and local groups, such as Islamic Army of Abyan Aden, are providing a platform for Al Qaeda to plan, prepare, and execute operations against targets of the West and Muslim countries friendly to the West. For instance, the attack on the French tanker *Limburg* was staged by Al Qaeda working with the Islamic Army of the Abyan in Aden. Similarly, the Bali bombing was staged by Jemmah Islamiyah, working together with Al Qaeda experts. Likewise, in Pakistan, a dozen attacks have been conducted by Al Qaeda through individual members of Jayash-e-Mohammad, Lashkar-e-Jhangvi, Harakat-ul-Jihad-I-Islami, Lashkar-e-Tayyaba, and Harakat-ul Mujahidin.[18] A decentralised Al Qaeda working with Islamist and other groups worldwide is a force multiplier. In the years ahead, Al Qaeda—that has a long history of providing experts, trainers and funds to other groups—is likely to operate effectively and efficiently through their associates. To compensate for the losses suffered by the group, post–9-11 Al Qaeda operatives are heavily reliant on the social and familial contacts in associate groups. Therefore, mapping the family and social trees of leaders, members, supporters and sympathizers is key to understanding the deepening operational nexus between Al Qaeda and its associate groups. The nexus has manifested in tactical and opportunity targeting as well as the globalisation of the terrorist strategy, developments that call for closer political, diplomatic, law enforcement, military, security and intelligence cooperation and coordination.

Wave Attacks

Today, Al Qaeda conducts two types of attacks—stand-alone attacks and wave attacks. For maximum impact and effect, Al Qaeda prefers to conduct attacks in waves. The first wave of attacks by Al Qaeda after 9-11 was in October and November 2003, when Al Qaeda, working together with the Islamic Army of the Abyan in Yemen, Jemmah Islamiyah in Indonesia (Islamic Group), Al Ansar Mujahidin in Chechnya (The Supporters of the Warriors of God); Shurafaa al-Urdun (The Honourables of Jordan); Al Ittihad Al Islami (Islamic Union), staged five attacks. A suicide boat meant for a U.S. warship attacked the French oil supertanker *Limburg* off Mukalla, Yemen, on October 6; gunmen killed two U.S. Marines on exercises in Failaka, Kuwait, on October 8; multiple suicide bombings in Bali, Indonesia on October 12, 2003; hostage taking in a theatre in Moscow on October 24; assassination of USAID official Laurence Foley in Amman, Jordan on October 28; suicide bombing of an Israeli-owned Kikambala Paradise hotel; and Surface-to-Air Missile attack on Israeli Arkia Flight 582 on November 28.

After maintaining a year of silence Al Qaeda presented Koranic justifications in October 2002, immediately before launching the coordinated multiple attacks in the Middle East and Asia. The attacks in Yemen, Kuwait and Jordan indicated the ability of Al Qaeda and its associated groups to function amidst security countermeasures. Islamist groups in Chechnya and Thailand also conducted terrorist operations in Russia and in Southern Thailand, respectively. On October 6, an explosives-laden suicide boat rammed the 157,833-ton French oil supertanker *Limburg* before mooring at al Shihr off the coast of Yemen. The explosion killed one Bulgarian and injured one crew member, spilling 90,000 barrels of crude oil.[19] Although the time and the place of the attack could not be determined, governments in Asia and in the Middle East anticipated maritime suicide attacks on military and commercial shipping in the Straits of Malacca and in the Persian Gulf by Al Qaeda.[20] Based on debriefing of Al Qaeda operatives detained in the Middle East and in Asia, the U.S. intelligence community warned of impending attacks. For instance, before U.S. and Indonesian joint military and naval exercises were held May 30–June 3, 2002, Al Qaeda's former Southeast Asian representative Omar Al Faruq was trying to source terrorists to conduct suicide attacks against U.S. warships in Surabaya in Indonesia's second largest city in May 2002.[21] Two days after the *Limburg* attack, two terrorists in a pickup truck attacked a marine unit of the U.S. military on training maneuvers on Failaka, an island 10 miles east of Kuwait City.[22] The October 8 attack killed Lance Corporal Antonio J. Sledd, 20 years old, from Hillsborough County, Florida. The terrorists drove to a second location to attack again but were killed by U.S. Marines.

Al Qaeda, operating through Jemmah Islamiyah (JI), its Southeast Asian network, staged the worst terrorist attack in Indonesia's tourist resort of Bali, killing 202 and injuring over 300 people, mostly Australian tourists, on October 12, 2002, also the anniversary of the USS *Cole* attack.[23] Before and after the mass casualty bombing at the Sari Club, Bali at 23.15 Hrs, small bombs exploded near other targets reflecting both Al Qaeda and JI modus operandi and widespread capability to conduct coordinated simultaneous or near-simultaneous attacks. The targets were the Philippine Consulate, Manado City, North Sulawesi, at 18.45, 23.00 Hrs at the Paddy Restaurant, Kuta Beach Strip in Bali, and 23.25 Hrs near the U.S. Consulate in Denpasar, Bali.[24] Bali, a predominately Hindu city where 22,000 Australians were holidaying, was the ideal target for JI–Al Qaeda. The neighbouring Philippines witnessed five bombings killing 22 including a U.S. serviceman and injuring over 200 in October 2002. Although the perpetrators have not been identified, the Philippines intelligence community suspects that the bombings were carried out by the Al Qaeda–affiliated Abu Sayyaf Group, a group that has suffered significantly as a result of post–9-11 U.S. assistance to the Armed Forces of the Philippines. On October 28, a terrorist opened fire on Laurence Foley, a 60-year old U.S. diplomat in Jordan working as an administrator for the U.S. Agency for International Development (USAID).[25] Foley was shot point blank seven times in his chest when he was heading for his car parked in his garage at his house in Amman. The Shurafaa al-Urdun (The Honourables of Jordan), a suspected front for Al Qaeda, claimed that Foley was killed in protest of U.S. support for Israel and the "bloodshed in Iraq and Afghanistan."[26] The attack came amidst a warning in August 2002, when the U.S. government stated that Al Qaeda was planning to kidnap U.S. citizens in Jordan.

Following the tradition of Prophet Muhammad of calling its enemies to convert to Islam before subduing them, Al Qaeda launched multiple attacks in Kuwait, Yemen, and Bali, all in the second week of October 2002. Bin Laden said: "In the name of God, the merciful, the compassionate; a message to the American people: peace be upon those who follow the right path. I am an honest advisor to you. I urge you to seek the joy of life and the afterlife, and to rid yourself of your dry, miserable, and spiritless materialistic life. I urge you to become Muslims, for Islam calls for the principle of 'There is no God but Allah,' and for justice and forbids injustice and criminality. I also call on you to understand the lesson of the New York and Washington raids, which came in response to some of your previous crimes. The aggressor deserves punishment. However, those who follow the movement of the criminal gang at the White House, the agents of the Jews, who are preparing to attack and partition the Islamic World, without you disapproving of this, realize that you have not understood anything from the message of the two raids.... We beseech Almighty God to provide us with his support. He is the protector and has the power to do so. Say: O People of the Book! Come to common terms as between us and you: That we worship none but Allah; that we associate no partners with him; that we erect not from among ourselves lords and patrons other than Allah. If then they turn back, say ye: bear witness that we at least are Muslims bowing to Allah's will."[27]

To assess the statements of bin Laden and Zawahiri, the CIA approached the most senior Al Qaeda leaders in U.S. detention, Abu Zubaidah, former head of Al Qaeda's external operations, and Ramzi bin Al Shibh, the chief logistics officer of the 9-11 operation. They interpreted with dead accuracy that bin Laden would not make such a statement unless the organisation was "ready and able to carry out such attacks" and according to Abu Zubaidah, "bin Laden's modus operandi consisted of reviewing operational plans, weighing the consequences of each, selecting targets, and finally releasing his message regarding an impending attack. The plan has been approved and the timing is now determined by the operatives and the local security situation."[28] They said that the same way the prophet urged his opponents to embrace Islam before being subdued by his army, Osama was calling his opponents to convert to Islam before attacking them. Although the tape was meant for an external constituency, Osama was trying to justify Koranically his course of action to his internal constituency.

Diffusion of Threat

Both the spreading out of Al Qaeda cells and the conduct of spectacular attacks have certainly made anti- and counterterrorism initiatives difficult and complex. As terrorists are copycats, the direct and indirect influence of Al Qaeda is reflected in the changing behaviour of several groups. As terrorist groups closely guard their foreign linkages, often it has become difficult even by government intelligence agencies to identify the exact nature of their external relationships. While the Russian secret service is convinced of the Al Qaeda–Chechen terrorist nexus, there has been a grave reluctance in the Western press to call Chechen groups that practice terrorism as "terrorists."[29] On October 23, 2002, 53 male and female suicide terrorists from Chechnya, 600 miles away from Moscow, stormed the 1,163 seat auditorium of Act II screening *Nord-Ost* (North-East), a popular musical.[30] After mining the theatre with 850 hostages, they wanted Russian forces to withdraw from Chechnya. The next day, they sent a video tape to Al Jazeera where a hostage taker said: "I swear by God we are more keen on dying than you are keen on living.... Each one of us is willing to sacrifice himself for the sake of God and the independence of Chechnya."[31] On October 26, after the terrorists began to execute their hostages, Spetsnaz commandos in the elite Alfa and Vympel antiterror squads of the Federal Security Service rescued the hostages after injecting sleeping gas though the ventilation system and holes bored underneath the auditorium. Of the 119 dead hostages, only two died of gun-shot injuries—others perished from the gas, due to lack of timely medical care. The Moscow operation was conducted by 25-year-old Movsar Baraye, the nephew of Arbi Barayev, the Chechen Islamic Special Units leader who oversaw the beheading of three British and one New Zealand telecommunication workers in Chechnya in 1998.[32] The deputies of the Chechen rebel President Aslan Maskhadov were Shamil Basayev, leader, and Ibn ul-Khattab, military leader,

Majlis ul-Shura of Mujahidin of Ichkeria and Dagestan respectively.[33] Khattab, the then commander of the Al Ansar Mujahidin (Islamic International Brigade) and a protégé of bin Laden, was assassinated by the Russian secret service on March 19, 2002. Movsar was close to Khattab, who remained a part of the Al Qaeda network until his death.[34] Khattab was succeeded by Mohammad al Ghamdi, alias Abu Walid, the cousin/brother of two 9-11 hijackers, the Ghamdi brothers. The Moscow operation bore the first four hallmarks of Al Qaeda: (1) grandiose operations, (2) suicide, (3) targeting the heart, and (4) coordinated simultaneous attacks.

Second Wave

The post–9-11 second wave targeted Riyadh, Casablanca, Chechnya and Karachi in May 2003. Demonstrating that the group remains a resilient threat, Al Qaeda coordinated its attack in Riyadh with its associated groups' timings of the bombings in North Africa, Caucuses and Asia. To compensate for the loss of significant personnel and physical infrastructure, Al Qaeda is relying on its associate groups to conduct operations.

Despite being hunted by the Saudi intelligence and its law enforcement agencies, Al Qaeda was able to plan, prepare and execute an operation in the heart of the Kingdom on May 12, 2003. Amidst domestic and foreign intelligence, both technical and human, that Al Qaeda was in the final phases of an operation, Saudi authorities failed to detect and disrupt the operation that destroyed three poorly protected foreign residential complexes in Riyadh at 11.25 p.m. on May 12, 2003. The triple suicide attacks killed in Al Hamra, Coroval, and Jedawal 34 including nine bombers and injured 194 people. A fourth explosion hit the offices of Siyanco, a Saudi maintenance company, a venture between Frank E. Basil, Inc., of Washington and local Saudi partners, but there were no casualties.

In Morocco, suicide bombers attacked Casa de España, a Spanish social club; Hotel Farah; a Jewish community center and cemetery; and a restaurant next to the Belgium consulate in Casablanca, all within 20 minutes, on May 16. In addition to 12 bombers who perished in the raid, the attacks killed 27 and injured 100. Of the 14-man attack team, one failed suicide bomber was captured, and later one bomber was arrested. The attacks in Saudi Arabia and Morocco bear the hallmarks of Al Qaeda. Al Qaeda in Saudi Arabia and its associated group Assirat al-Moustaquim (The Straight Path) in Morocco conducted the coordinated simultaneous suicide attacks against Western and Jewish targets with the aim of inflicting maximum fatalities.

In Chechnya, Al Ansar Mujahidin, an associate group of Al Qaeda, mounted suicide operations on Znamenskoye killing 59 and injuring 200 also on May 12 and Iliskhan-Yurt killing 18 and injuring 100 on May 14. The bombings in Chechnya were aimed at producing mass fatalities and fear—offices and homes in Znamenskoye, northern district of Nadterechny, and an assassination of Akhmad Kadyrov, the Chechen administration leader near a shrine in Iliskhan-Yurt where 15,000 Muslims gathered to mark the birth of Prophet Muhammed. Al Ansar Mujahidin is led by Abu Walid alias Mohammad al Ghamdi, the successor of Ibn Omar al Khattab, Afghan veterans and protégés of Osama bin Laden. Abu Walid is the cousin of the 9-11 hijackers—Ahmed and Hamza al Ghamdi—all from the Southern Saudi Province of Asir.

In Pakistan, Muslim United Army (MUA) simultaneously bombed 19 Shell and two Caltex gasoline stations in Nazimabad, Joharabad, SITE, Sharea Faisal, Gulshan-I-Iqbal, all in Southern Karachi between 4 and 5 a.m. on May 15. MUA is believed to be Lashkar-e-Jhangvi, an Al Qaeda associated group in Pakistan. The improved explosives devices, weighing 200 grams, with 15-minute timers, were placed inside garbage cans beside fuel pumps by motorcyclists. The bombings damaged the Pakistani infrastructure owned by Anglo-Dutch and American companies and injured one customer, three station attendants, and one security guard. To prevent such attacks, Pakistan had increased security of food chains—Pizza Hut, McDonalds, KFC—but the group had selected its tactic and targets creatively. The bombing was in revenge of Pakistan hunting Al Qaeda and its associate members in Pakistan.

Middle East—Striking the Heartland

For those who believed that Al Qaeda is dead, the attack in Riyadh on May 12, 2003, demonstrated that Al Qaeda remains a significant threat in the coming months, if not years. Despite recurrent indications and warnings, including from the CIA that "they are coming for you," the Saudis were defiant stating that "everything was under control."[35] Two weeks before the attack, it was very clear to both the American and the Saudi authorities that Al Qaeda was in the final phases of launching an operation.

There were multiple indications and at least one warning the week preceding the attack. This included a U.S. government warning of the likelihood of attack in Saudi Arabia. Although the warning was not target specific, it was country specific. Under the no-double-standards policy, the United States was mandated to place all general and specific warnings to its citizens both at home and overseas in the public domain. On April 29, the U.S. Embassy in Riyadh requested Saudi authorities to increase the security of the residential complexes. On May 1, the U.S. State Department issued a travel warning requesting private U.S. citizens in Saudi Arabia to consider departing and Americans to defer non-essential travel. On May 6, nineteen members of Al Qaeda escaped after a firefight with the Saudi security forces. During the confrontation, demonstrating their willingness to kill and to die, one member exploded a device killing himself. The 19 had fought with Osama bin Laden in the Tora Bora battles in Afghanistan. They were the same members who conducted the operation. One Al Qaeda member surrendered and provided information about the Al Qaeda organization in Saudi Arabia but not about the attack. The Saudis released the identities of the 19 wanted men requesting public assistance. On May 7, a spokesman for Al Qaeda, Thabet bin Qais, stated that Osama bin Laden's forces were gearing up for a series of attacks. On May 7, the U.S. Embassy in Riyadh again requested Saudi authorities to increase the security of the residential complexes. On May 8, Saudi authorities seized 800 lbs of explosives, automatic weapons, grenades, ammunition, computers, communication equipment and money from both a house and a vehicle about a quarter-mile from Jedawal, one of the complexes later attacked. On May 10, the U.S. Embassy in Riyadh requested Saudi authorities to increase the security of the residential complexes. The U.S. Embassy specifically requested the Saudi authorities for additional protection for the Jedawal complex. On May 11, an Al Qaeda member Abu Mohammed Ablaj wrote to the London-based *Al-Majalla* magazine that the armed martyrdom squads were about to attack. "Beside targeting the heart of America, among the strategic priorities now is to target and execute operations in the Gulf countries and allies of the United States," Ablaj wrote in an email the day before the attack.

Even prior to these indications, the intelligence reports suggested that Saudi Arabia was coming under increasing threat. Both the CIA and the FBI informed their Saudi counterparts nearly a year before the attack that Abdel Rahman Jabarah, a Canadian Al Qaeda member of Kuwait origin, had entered the Kingdom. Together with Mohammed al-Johani, who led the operation, Abdel Rahman, one of the organizers of the bombing, was the elder brother of Mohamad Mansour Jabarah, a 21-year-old Al Qaeda operative in U.S. custody. After the Al Qaeda operation to destroy the U.S. and Israeli diplomatic targets in Manila and the U.S., British, Australian and Israeli diplomatic targets in Singapore were thwarted on December 2001, its operations coordinator Mohammad Mansour fled to the Middle East and was arrested in Oman in March 2002. Both the operations commander Mohammad al-Johani and the Canadian brothers who worked under Khalid Sheikh Mohammad, the head of the Military Committee of Al Qaeda, and his successor and Deputy Tawfiq Attash, were arrested in Rawalpindi and Karachi in Pakistan in March 2003. Al-Johani, who left Saudi Arabia when he was 18, returned to Saudi Arabia on a forged passport in March 2003 to conduct the operation. Operating under the Al Qaeda front "The Mujahideen in the Peninsula," al-Johani built the organization to conduct attacks in the region starting with Saudi Arabia. Thirty-six hours after the attack, Al-Muwahhidun (Those who profess the oneness of God), a front for Al Qaeda, claimed responsibility for the attack. The new front operated under the leadership of three fugitives—Ali bin Khudair Al-Khudair, Nasir bin Hamd Al-fahd, and Ahmad bin Hamd Al-Khalid—and 19 wanted individuals.

As the attack was intended against the Westerners and the first against a Western target after the United States intervened and occupied Iraq, it will be viewed with mixed feelings within the Kingdom and the Middle East. The elite who want to retain their power and status will want to control the group. However, the suppression and repression of the Islamists of the Al Qaeda brand is likely to generate a fresh wave of recruits and support for Al Qaeda and its associated groups in the Gulf. While the Saudi over-reaction is likely to decrease the threat in the short term, it will increase Saudi public support for Al Qaeda in the long term. Unless Saudi Arabia reforms the education system of the country, Osama bin Laden, the popular hero of all the Saudis who oppose the House of al Saud, will remain their symbol of resistance.

Outside the Middle East, Al Qaeda members are concentrated in the Horn of Africa, the Caucuses (Chechnya and Pankishi Gorge in Georgia) and in Asia. In the international intelligence community, the Achilles heel has always been Africa, especially the Horn. Intelligence on the Horn has improved since August 1998 but not appreciably. While based in Sudan (December 1991–May 1996) and having made significant inroads to the countries in East Africa, Al Qaeda continues to operate in the Horn. While the Russian military has sustained heavy losses in Chechnya, the U.S. Special Operations Forces working with the Georgian forces are conducting operations to clear the gorge. In Djibouti, there are several hundred U.S. personnel engaged in activities in the Horn of Africa and Yemen. In addition to Afghanistan and Pakistan, Al Qaeda elements have a presence throughout Asia. For instance, Al Qaeda members regularly infiltrate Kashmir and Bangladesh in South Asia. In addition to the Middle East, when it comes to regions, the Horn of Africa and Southeast Asia present the biggest challenges. Even before the gravity of terrorism moved from the Middle East to Asia in the early 1990s, the Middle Eastern groups were active in Southeast Asia.

Southeast Asia: A New Theatre

Of the two-dozen Islamist terrorist groups active in Southeast Asia, JI presents the biggest threat. There are about 400 Al Qaeda–trained JI members in Southeast Asia. With the exception of Afghanistan and Pakistan, Southeast Asia is the home of the single largest concentration of Al Qaeda–trained active members in any given region. The presence of 240 million Muslims, emerging democracies, corrupt governments, weak rulers, and lack of security is making Southeast Asia emerge as a new centre for Al Qaeda activity. Historically, Southeast Asia has featured prominently in all Al Qaeda operations including 9-11, when Khalid Sheikh Mohammad, the head of the Al Qaeda military committee convened a meeting of 12 Al Qaeda operatives in Kuala Lumpur from January 5–12, 2000, to coordinate both the USS *Cole* and the 9-11 operation. Immediately before 9-11, bin Laden dispatched the key financier Mohammed Mansour Jabarah (a Kuwaiti of Canadian citizenship), alias Sammy, to Malaysia to plan and prepare the attacks against U.S. and Israeli diplomatic targets in Manila, Philippines. After visiting the embassies with an Al Qaeda suicide bomber, Ahmed Sahagi, Jabarah concluded that "the attack on the U.S. Embassy in Manila would have been much more difficult" and that "a plane would be needed to attack this building because the security was very tough."[36] Therefore, Al Qaeda decided to shift the operation to Singapore where the "embassy is very close to the streets and did not have many barriers to prevent the attack."[37] Due to the difficulty of shipping the explosives from Singapore to the Philippines, Nurjaman Riduan Isamuddin alias Hambali, a 36-year-old Indonesian serving both on the Al Qaeda and JI Shura (Consultative) Councils, decided to cancel the Singapore operation of destroying U.S., British, Australian and Israeli diplomatic targets—and pick "better" targets in the Philippines. The detection and disruption of the Singapore operation by Singapore's Internal Security Department led to the discovery of Al Qaeda's JI regional network in December 2001. Although the Malaysian and the Philippine governments arrested JI members, Indonesia's President Megawatti Sukarnoputri was reluctant to follow suit, and as a result about 180 JI members moved to Indonesia and Thailand. In Southern Thailand, Hambali together with Jabarah discussed bombings in "bars, cafes, or nightclubs frequented by westerners in Thailand, Malaysia, Singapore, Philippines and Indonesia."[38] Although Hambali's original plan was to conduct a number of small bombings in line with the in-house capability and modus operandi of JI, the arrival of bomb-making experts and finances from Al Qaeda into the region improved JI technical expertise to conduct large-scale bombings.

The Moro Islamic Liberation Front (MILF), an associate group of Al Qaeda, provided training to JI recruits in Mindanao, Philippines. After Camp Abu Bakar was overrun in April 2000, MILF and JI established training camps in Indonesia: Poso, Sulawesi and in Balikpapan and Sampit in Kalimanthan.[39] Even after MILF–Manila government resumed peace talks, MILF camps in Vietnam, Hudeibiya and Palestine continue to provide facilities to over a hundred foreign nationals including Arab members of Al Qaeda. The arrest in Indonesia in January of Muhammad Saad Iqbal Madni, a Pakistani, and in June 2002, Omar Al Farook, alias Mahmoud bin Ahmed Assegaf, a Kuwaiti, the former leader of Camp Vietnam, provided insight into MILF-JI linkages and future Al Qaeda plans.[40] Omar Al Farook also divulged attack plans and information of financial transfers, including US$73,000 from Sheikh Abu Abdallah Al Emarati of Saudi Arabia to Abu Bakar Bashir in Indonesia to purchase explosives. An Indonesian intelligence report states: "In the absence of an Internal Security Act, it is almost impossible for the Indonesian government to take legal action against anybody involved in Al Qaeda unless he has committed a crime. Therefore, Farook was deported on immigration grounds and the illegal acquisition of documents. He was arrested on June 5 [2002]. On June 8 [2002], he was deported to the U.S. Air Force base in Baghram, Afghanistan."[41] The JI spiritual, ideological and political leader is Abu Bakar Bashir (who also had an operational role), and Hambali, the operational commander of JI and Al Qaeda in Southeast Asia. Unlike Indonesia and Thailand, which have denied the existence of a terrorist network, the Philippines has steadfastly fought terrorism. However, it has lacked the resources of the United States, support of European governments, and cooperation of its neighbours, and as a result forced to negotiate even with MILF, a group that has failed to condemn bin Laden and Al Qaeda.

The lack of a zero tolerance terrorism policy in the region and beyond facilitated the spawning and sustenance of a robust terrorist support and operational network. When the JI network was discovered in December 2001, Indonesia permitted the continued operation of a fully-fledged JI infrastructure. This was despite the Al Farook and Jabarah debriefings implicating the continued use of Indonesia and Thailand by JI and Al Qaeda. These governments as well as the neighbouring governments failed to engage in sustained targeting of terrorist operatives and assets. Despite the U.S. intelligence community providing strategic intelligence including the threat to "bars, cafés, or nightclubs," there was a failure on the part of the regional governments to develop the ground, contact or tactical intelligence by technical and human source penetration. The Australian government should have invested sufficient resources in its immediate neighbourhood to dampen Islamism and use the JI infrastructure in Perth, Sydney, Melbourne, and Adelaide to penetrate the network. Despite a dozen Australian citizens and residents participating in JI and Al Qaeda training camps from Mindanao, Philippines to Afghanistan,[42] the government assessment and operational agencies did not believe that the threat was "significant" until Bali.[43]

Liberal Democracies: North America, Europe, Australasia

Examination of terrorist support and operational infrastructure worldwide reveals that liberal democracies offer the ideal conditions for foreign terrorist groups to establish their support networks in the West. For terrorism to flourish, prerequisites are terrorists, who conduct attacks, and non-terrorists, who provide support. To defeat terrorism, both these categories must be targeted. During the past two decades, Asian, Middle Eastern and Latin American terrorist groups established open offices or secret cells for disseminating propaganda, raising funds, specialized training, procuring and transporting supplies in the West. For instance, Australia became the home of several foreign terrorist groups: Palestinian Hamas, Lebanese Hezbollah, Chechen mujahidin, Kurdish Workers Party (Turkey), Euzkadi Ta Askatasuna (Spain), Liberation Tigers of Tamil Eelam (Sri Lanka), Babbar Khalsa International (India), International Sikh Youth Federation (India), and dissident factions of the Irish Republican Army. The foreign terrorist groups disseminate terrorist propaganda, recruit, raise funds, procure and transport technologies from the West to perpetrate terrorism elsewhere. As these groups did not pose a direct and an immediate threat to host countries, Western security and intelligence agencies monitored these groups without disrupting their propaganda, fund raising, procurement and transportation infrastructure. As a result, several terrorists, their supporters and sympathisers infiltrated Western society and governments. These foreign terrorist groups diverted the resources raised in the West to attack target countries in the global South.

In addition to establishing Al Qaeda cells, the group also co-opted the leaderships of two European networks. As a result, both Takfir Wal Hijra and GSPC in Europe and to a lesser extent in North America present a significant threat to Western security. These two networks are fed by migrants from North Africa and ideologically fuelled by the developments in the lands of jihad especially of their home countries. As Europe witnessed a spillover of terrorism from the Middle East, the developments in Southeast Asia have increased the threat to Australia, New Zealand and their interests overseas. Australia has been an Al Qaeda target since 1999 but certain events increased the threat to the country since 2000, for example, Australia's high profile participation in the U.S.-led anti-terrorist campaign in Afghanistan in October 2001, and the angry reaction of Australian Muslims; bin Laden's claim in early November 2001 that Australia conspired and led a crusade against the Islamic nation to dismember East Timor in November 2001, and so on. A grenade was lobbed from a motorbike into the garden of the Australian International School in Jakarta in November 2001; large firecrackers were hurled into the Australian Embassy in Jakarta in November 2001; an Arab Al Qaeda suicide bomber in an explosives-laden truck planned to destroy the Australian High Commission in Singapore in early 2002.[44] Al Qaeda and Taliban detainee and prisoner interrogation in Afghanistan, Pakistan, Camp Delta and in the United States revealed that Australian Muslims trained in Camp Al Farooq in Afghanistan and elsewhere were tasked to conduct terrorist operations against Australian targets.

Before Al Qaeda targeted Australians overseas, Al Qaeda established a support network in Australia using its Southeast Asian arm—JI. At the invitation of the JI Australia, JI founder/leader, the late Abdullah Sungkar, his successor Abu Bakar Bashir and operations commander Hambali visited Australia a dozen times. Furthermore, JI penetration of local Muslim groups led to a significant generation of propaganda within Australia aimed at politicising and radicalising Australian Muslims. Sungkar spoke of the "obligation of jihad within the framework of aiming to re-erect dawlah islamiyyah" by applying the strategies of faith and its expression in word and action and jihad.[45] He added: "In this, quwwaatul musallaha or military strength is essential."[46] The JI leaders said Indonesian Muslims have two choices: "life in a nation based upon the Koran and the sunnah or death while striving to implement, in their entirety, laws based on the Koran and the sunnah."[47] Bin Laden gave an exclusive interview to his supporters in Australia that was published on a Website in Australia. JI also raised funds in Australia and funds were transferred from Australia, first to JI Malaysia and then with the disruption of the JI network in Malaysia, to JI Indonesia.[48] Furthermore, Australia features prominently in the JI regional structure. The JI network in the Asia-Pacific is divided into four geographic regions, which includes Australia. JI's Area 4 or Mantiqi 4 (M4) covers Irian Jaya and Australia. As such, Australia has no option but to work jointly with the Southeast Asian countries to detect, disrupt, degrade and destroy the JI organisation. Its failure to do so will result in further attacks both in Australia and in its neighbourhood.

Another reason the terrorist threat is rising in Australia is that several terrorist groups in its immediate neighbourhood—notably in the Philippines, Indonesia and Malaysia— have stepped up their activities at home and abroad. In addition, half a dozen groups with links to Al Qaeda perceive Australia as an enemy. Australia and the Southeast Asian region do need to improve cooperation toward strengthening security in the Asia-Pacific. Until

Bali, there was definitely a very poor understanding of the threat in Australia. The Australian malaise is one of not being sufficiently educated on the Asia-Pacific region with a poor understudying of the culture, politics and economics of its neighbours.[49] When you factor in a serious transnational terrorist threat, it seems the 'she'll be right' or 'it can't happen to us' attitude prevails.[50] In the task ahead, Australia lacks the expertise and capacity but it may require a shift of thinking on how its finite resources will be deployed. As a technologically advanced country with significant economic, political, diplomatic and military capability, Australia could also assist countries in Southeast Asia, especially Indonesia, to improve its capability to fight terrorism. Australia can make a significant contribution to the ensuing criminal investigation to assist Indonesia. Australia should take a leadership role in the region as a whole, especially with its Southeast Asian friends in moving Indonesia into action. This tragic event could see a rapid maturation of cooperation in the region spurred on by Australia.

To meet the current threat, the Australian Security Intelligence Organisation (ASIO) (Australia's counter-intelligence and anti-terrorist agency) and the Australian Security and Intelligence Service (ASIS) (its overseas intelligence service) need to double their strength without loss of quality and resources as well as increase their powers to operate effectively and efficiently. To improve the security of Australia and New Zealand, Australian agencies must work closely with their New Zealand counterparts.

Afghanistan-Pakistan-Iran

With U.S. intervention in Afghanistan in October 2001, Osama bin Laden requested the bulk of the Al Qaeda members to travel to their home countries and await instructions. Those who had come to the adverse attention of their home security and intelligence agencies were asked to remain in Pakistan. Al Qaeda's operational leaders Abu Zubaidah and Khalid Sheikh Mohammad relocated to Pakistan and coordinated the global terrorist campaign until their arrests in March 2002 and May 2003 respectively. After the arrest of Khalid Sheikh Mohammad's successor Tawfiq bin Attash, Osama bin Laden appointed his Chief of Security Seif Al-'Adel as the new operations chief in April 2003. The May 2003 operations were executed by Seif Al-'Adel, a former officer of the Egyptian military, and thereafter a member of the Egyptian Islamic Jihad. After fighting against the Soviet army, he joined Al Qaeda and thereafter trained with the Hezbollah in Southern Lebanon. Seif Al-'Adel was joined in the Riyadh operation by another senior member, Abu Khaled, and Osama bin Laden's son Sa'ad bin Laden, a bodyguard of the Al Qaeda leader. Although the extent of Iranian sponsorship is unclear, the operational leadership that coordinated the Riyadh bombing and dispatched experts to Casablanca, Morocco, to advise Assirat al-Moustaquim was located in Iran. Due to the loss of a large number of Al Qaeda leaders and operatives in Pakistan, Al Qaeda is increasingly looking toward Iran. An Iraqi Islamist group Ansar al-Islami, another Al Qaeda associate group, is also operating on the Iran-Iraq border.

The international community has gravely failed to rebuild Afghanistan and to transform the war-ravaged state into a modern state of the 21st century. Al Qaeda has reinvented itself in Afghanistan by working with Mullah Omar's Taliban and Gulbaddin Hekmatiyar's Hezbi-e-islami. Similarly, Al Qaeda continues to work with Sipai Sahaba, Lashkar-e-Jhangvi, Lashkar-e-Toiba, Jayash-e-Mohammad, Harakart-ul-Mujahidin and a number of other Pakistani groups. With U.S. security forces and the intelligence community targeting Al Qaeda's nerve centre in Afghanistan-Pakistan, Al Qaeda will decentralise even further. While its organisers of attacks will remain in Pakistan and its immediate neighbourhood, its operatives will travel back and forth coordinating with Al Qaeda nodes in the south. To make its presence felt, Al Qaeda will increasingly rely on its global terrorist network of like-minded groups in Southeast Asia, South Asia, Horn of Africa, Middle East, and the Caucuses to strike its enemies. Already attacks in Kenya, Indonesia, India, Pakistan, Kuwait, and Yemen seek to compensate for the loss and lack of space and opportunity to operate in Afghanistan. With the transfer of terrorist technology and expertise from the centre to the periphery, the attacks by the associated groups of Al Qaeda will pose a threat as great as Al Qaeda.

Impact on Separatist Conflicts

Although Al Qaeda is waging a universal jihad, the influence of Al Qaeda on Muslim separatist groups active in their territories is growing. It is a worrying trend as Islamists tend to "hijack" the resources of the ethnonationalists. There is very little governments can do to arrest the trend. Whether it is in the Moroland in the Philippines, Aceh in Indonesia, Pattini in Thailand, Kashmir in India-Pakistan, or Chechnya in Russia, Muslim secessionist conflicts have been penetrated by Islamist groups to different degrees. Either by emulation or direct contact, factions, splinters and main groups of the separatist category are learning from Al Qaeda tactics, techniques and styles. Al Qaeda did not engage in kidnapping, hostage taking or assassination frequently, but its camps in Afghanistan and elsewhere taught these tactics to several tens of thousands of youth.[51] Even before 9-11, it has been observed that Al Qaeda has been attempting to develop alliances with non-Islamist Muslim groups. Rabitat-ul Mujahidin is an alliance of Islamist and Muslim separatist groups from the Philippines, Indonesia, Malaysia, Myanmar and Thailand.[52] Thailand, especially Bangkok and Narathiwat Province, a safe haven for Jemmah Islamiyah, is the home of a number of other groups. The Pattani United Liberation Organisation (PULO) formed in 1967, New PULO formed in 1995, Barisan Revolusi Nasional Malayu Pattani (BRN) formed in 1960, Gerakan Mujahideen Islam Pattani (GMIP) formed in 1986, and Bersatu (Unity) formed in 1997.[53] GMIP has members, such as Wae Ka Raeh, who trained in Afghanistan and fought for Al Qaeda.[54] In spite of the successes of the Thai government of bringing the secessionist violence to an end in the 1980s, there has been a revival in 2001. On October 29, 2002, a series of arson incidents and bombs exploded in Southern Thailand. Five schools were set on fire in Songkhla Province and bombs damaged both My Garden Hotel and a Buddhist temple in the neighbouring Pattani Province in 2001. Since April 2001, about two-dozen law enforcement officers have been killed in southern Thailand, but the authorities in Bangkok have dismissed the violence as criminal and not terrorist. After Bali, the threat to popular tourist destinations, including to Pukhet and Pataya in Thailand, has increased. Furthermore, the Al Qaeda network in Thailand, where two of the 9-11 hijackers were launched after a meeting in Malaysia in January 2000, remains uninterrupted. After living in denial for one and a half years, Thailand was forced to arrest Thai JI members in June 2003, after a Singaporean JI member was arrested in Bangkok. As a result, an attack being planned by JI Thailand on diplomatic targets in Bangkok and two tourist resorts was disrupted.

Ideological Threat

More than an organization, the ideology of Al Qaeda remains a resilient threat. Although Al Qaeda can still mount operations, with the increase in pressure, Al Qaeda will become relegated to an ideology. As Al Qaeda increasingly depends on like-minded groups to conduct attacks, other Islamist groups will become like Al Qaeda. For instance, Mas Salamat Kasthari, the Chief of Jemmah Islamiyah (JI) of Singapore, was planning to hijack an Aeroflot plane from Bangkok and crash it into the Changi International Airport in Singapore in 2002. The tactic of using an air vehicle as a weapon was clearly an Al Qaeda invention. When asked by his interrogators why he chose to hijack an Aeroflot plane, he responded that JI had decided to teach Russia a lesson for killing civilians in Chechnya. Furthermore, the killing of 202 civilians in Bali by the same group was not Southeast Asian in character. Southeast Asia had never witnessed a mass fatality terrorist attack before. Likewise, the JI attack in Bali witnessed the first suicide attack by a Southeast Asian terrorist.[55] During the past decade, JI and other associated Islamist groups had come under Al Qaeda influence in a substantial way.

Traditionally, Al Qaeda with better trained, more experienced and highly committed operatives wanted to attack more difficult targets—especially strategic targets—and leave the easier and tactical targets to its associated groups. With Al Qaeda decentralizing, its operatives are working closely together at a tactical level with other groups. As a result, the lethality of the attacks conducted by the associate groups of Al Qaeda is increasing. As Bali in 2002 and Casablanca in 2003 demonstrated, the attacks conducted by the associate groups of Al Qaeda can be as lethal as the attacks conducted by the parent group itself. With attacks conducted by Al Qaeda's associated groups posing a threat as great as Al Qaeda, the theatre of war will widen. Government security and intelligence agencies will be forced to monitor the technologies, tactics and techniques of a wide range of groups.

Although the United States is under severe pressure to withdraw from Saudi Arabia, the United States will prefer to remain in the Kingdom because withdrawal after the recent attack will mean defeat in the eyes of its opponents. Nonetheless, U.S. visibility in the Middle East, U.S. assistance to Israel, and continued U.S. presence in Iraq will generate wide-ranging reactions from the Islamists, both terrorist groups and political parties. Especially after U.S. and Coalition troops intervened in Afghanistan on October 7, 2001, Iraq is an attractive base for Al Qaeda. The Islamists desperately need a new theater to produce psychologically and physically war-trained Islamists.

Successes and Failures

Although branded a "War against Terrorism" by the United States, the fight is against a radical ideology producing Muslim youth willing to kill and die, and wealthy Muslims willing to support and suffer incarceration. For the Al Qaeda umbrella—the World Islamic Front for Jihad Against the Jews and the Crusaders—the fight is against a civilisation. The reality is that it is a fight between the vast majority of progressive Muslims and the miniscule percentage of radical Muslims. It is not a clash of civilisations but a clash among civilisations—a fight that must essentially be fought within the Muslim world. While the immediate (1–2 years) consequences are apparent, the mid- (5 years) and long-term (10 years) consequence of fighting primarily an ideological campaign militarily are yet to be seen. All indications are that Islamism—whether it is in Turkey, Pakistan, Malaysia, or in Indonesia—is moving from the periphery to the centre. U.S. intervention in Iraq has spiked the ideological fuel prolonging the strength, size and life of Islamist political parties and terrorist groups.

The greatest failure of the U.S.-led coalition is its lack of capability to neutralise the core leadership of both Al Qaeda and the Islamic Movement of the Taliban. While preparations for protracted guerrilla operations against the coalition forces inside Afghanistan are coordinated by the Taliban leader Mullah Mohammad Omar, terrorist operations world-wide including in Afghanistan are coordinated by Osama bin Laden and his deputy, principal strategist and designated successor Dr Ayman Zawahiri. Multiple sources, including the CIA reveal that both bin Laden and al-Zawahiri are alive.[56] Furthermore, Zawahiri refers to suicide attacks on the oldest Jewish synagogue in North Africa in Djerba, Tunisia, killing 21, including 14 German tourists on April 11, 2002 and the killing of 14, including 11 French naval technicians working on the submarine project outside the Sheraton Hotel in Karachi, Pakistan, on May 9, 2002. He states, "Thank God, America could not reach the leaders of Al Qaeda and Taliban, including Mullah Muhammad Omar and Shayak Osama bin Laden, who enjoy good health and, alongside the rest of the patient mujahidin, are managing the battle against the U.S. crusader raid on Afghanistan."[57] Members of the former Army of the Islamic Emirate Afghanistan loyal to Mullah Omar and Al Qaeda's 055 Brigade that survived death or capture are supporting or engaged in guerrilla and terrorist operations against the U.S.-led coalition both inside and outside Afghanistan respectively. Mullah Omar is building a clandestine network slowly and steadily in Afghanistan, utilizing its vast and porous borders to wage a protracted campaign of sustained urban warfare. Bin Laden and Zawahiri are developing targets overseas, especially soft targets with a twin focus on population centres and economic targets.

Change of Mindset

To make it difficult for its enemies, Al Qaeda has constantly innovated its military tactics, financial methods, and propaganda techniques in the past year. Al Qaeda—focusing on strategic targets prior to 9-11—is operating across the entire spectrum targeting both strategic and tactical targets. Although the West seized US$150 million of terrorist money in the first four months after 9-11, with the transformation of Al Qaeda financial practices only about US$10 million has been seized. With the targeting of the above ground open banking system, the underground unregulated banking network (*hawala*) has grown bigger. With mosques, madrasas, charities and community centres that disseminate Islamist propaganda coming under threat, Al Qaeda is increasingly relying on the Internet. As Al Qaeda is a learning organisation, the law enforcement and security and intelligence forces fighting it must be goal-oriented and not rule-oriented.

With the terrorists adapting to the threat posed by government law enforcement authorities, government security and intelligence agencies are increasing their human and technical source penetration. Capabilities for terrorist tracking, pre-emption, and disruption of terrorist operations are increasing. For instance, an Al Qaeda team travelling in their vehicle in Yemen's northern Province of Marib was attacked by a Hellfire missile from the CIA-controlled unmanned Predator drone on November 4, 2002. The attack killed Ali Senyan al-Harthi, alias Qaed Senyan al-Harthi, alias Abu Ali, the mastermind of the

USS *Cole* operation and a key Al Qaeda leader in the region. To meet the current threat, the Pentagon has increased its intelligence capability and the CIA has increased its paramilitary capability. In the foreseeable future, human intelligence and covert strike forces will remain at the heart of fighting secret and highly motivated organisations like Al Qaeda. It is critical for the United States to increase its sharing of intelligence especially with their Middle Eastern and Asian counterparts. Traditionally, the United States has been averse to sharing high-grade intelligence, especially source-based intelligence, with the Muslim World. This has changed since 9-11 but not adequately.

If Al Qaeda is to be defeated a change in the thinking of the U.S.-led "War on Terrorism" is paramount. Despite a U.S.-led coalition campaign worldwide, the Al Qaeda alliance—the World Islamic Front for Jihad Against the Jews and Crusaders—has managed to repair the damage to their support and operational infrastructure. As no serious international effort has been made to counter the Islamist ideology (the belief that "every Muslim's duty is to wage jihad") the robust Islamist milieu is providing recruits and financial support for Islamist groups worldwide to replenish their human losses and material wastage. Today, two to four Al Qaeda and Taliban members per week are captured or killed in Afghanistan but at the end of the week the Islamists are successful in attracting a dozen recruits as members, collaborators, supporters, and sympathisers.[58] To put it crudely, the rate of production of Islamists is greater than the rate of their kill or capture. Into the counterterrorism toolbox, the powerful message that Al Qaeda is not Koranic but heretical has not been integrated. As such there is popular support for the Al Qaeda model of Islam among the politicised and radicalised Muslims. As there is no effort to counter or dilute the ideology of extremism, the military campaign against Al Qaeda even if pursued single-mindedly and unrelentingly is likely to take decades. The "deep reservoir of hatred and a desire for revenge"[59] will remain unless the United States can start to think beyond the counterterrorist military and financial dimensions.

The international community must seek to build a zero tolerance level for terrorist support activity. The tragedies of 9-11, Bali, Moscow, Riyadh, Casablanca and several other attacks demonstrate that contemporary terrorists are indiscriminate. As terrorists do not recognise and respect ethnicity, religion or national borders, terrorism irrespective of location should be fought. There is no appeasement with those who seek to advance their political aims and objectives using violence. Like Indonesia, countries that condone, tolerate or fail to take tough action against terrorism will be touched by it. It is not only the countries in the South but even countries in the North have been complacent in the fight against terrorism. Within four months of 9-11, Western governments froze US$150 million of terrorist money in Europe and North America, indicative of the magnitude of terrorist wealth in liberal democracies. Although the Al Qaeda support network has suffered in the United States, its propaganda, recruitment, and fundraising activities are still continuing in Europe. Despite efforts to the contrary, segments of Muslims in the migrant communities of North America, Western Europe and Australasia and territorial communities of the Middle East and Asia continue to provide support to Al Qaeda and other Islamist groups. As Europe has not suffered a large-scale attack, Europeans do not perceive Al Qaeda as a high threat. As a result, Islamist support activities are continuing in Western Europe. With the increase in threat, both governments and their publics that do not take threat information seriously are bound to suffer.

Managing the Threat

Al Qaeda has had a head start of ten years. Until one month after U.S. diplomatic targets in East Africa were destroyed by Al Qaeda in August 1998, the CIA did not even know the correct name of Osama bin Laden's group.[60] However, during the past two years the understanding of the U.S. intelligence community of its principal enemy—Al Qaeda—has grown dramatically. The tragedy of 9-11 has empowered the Counter Terrorism Center at the CIA to develop the much-needed organisation and more importantly the mindset to hunt Al Qaeda. Largely due to detainee debriefings, the West today understands the threat it faces much better than ever before. The U.S. government, especially its security and intelligence community, has learnt at a remarkable pace. There is a remarkable improvement in collection and analysis both by the CIA and the FBI. For instance, immediately before the Yemeni, Kuwaiti and Bali attack, the CIA and FBI alerted friendly counterpart agencies and the U.S. State Department issued worldwide alerts. The West together with its Middle Eastern and Asian counterparts seriously started to fight Al Qaeda only after 9-11, and Al Qaeda has suffered gravely. The global strategy of the West to meet the global threat posed by Al Qaeda is taking shape slowly but steadily. As it contained the Soviet threat in the second half of the 20th century, it will develop the organisation and a doctrine to contain the Islamist threat. With sustained efforts to target the core and penultimate leadership, it is very likely that the Al Qaeda echelon Osama bin Laden, Dr Ayman Al Zawahiri and even the Taliban leader Mullah Omar will be captured or more likely killed. Nonetheless, Islamist terrorism will outlive Al Qaeda and Islamism as an ideology will persist in the foreseeable future.

The global fight against terrorism will be carried out by the West and Japan—the rich and influential nations with the greatest staying power. With the diffusion of the terrorist threat, the U.S. political, military, economic and diplomatic presence will grow and its influence will expand globally in the months and years ahead.[61] It is a long fight and will have to be fought on all fronts by multiple actors across many countries. To ensure the success of the campaign, the international community must remain focused on targeting Al Qaeda and committed to rebuilding Afghanistan and Pakistan, and now Iraq. Western nations must move beyond rhetoric into concrete action, pour in resources, and build modern model nation-states for the Muslim World in these countries. Protecting Karzai of Afghanistan and Musharraf of Pakistan—the most threatened world leaders—is paramount. Several attempts by Al Qaeda and its associated groups to assassinate these leaders have been frustrated. International assistance to their regimes to politically and economically develop their countries and invest in their publics is key to thwart the Islamists, who are continuously appealing to the politically and economically marginalised.

On the eve of the U.S. intervention in Afghanistan, Osama bin Laden correctly stated that the fight has moved beyond Al Qaeda. Al Qaeda's propaganda war since 9-11, especially after U.S. intervention in Iraq, has escalated several fold. With Al Qaeda and pro–Al Qaeda Web sites proliferating—many of them operationally unconnected but ideologically connected to Al Qaeda—support for Al Qaeda's ideology is slowly growing. Support for Islamism will grow even further if the United States intervenes in Iraq. The world has recently witnessed several isolated terrorist incidents by those influenced by terrorist propaganda. For instance, Hesham Mohamed Hadayet, an Egyptian, walked to the El Al counter at the Los Angeles International Airport and shot two people dead on America's independence day on July 4, 2002.[62] There were arrests worldwide including in the heart of Europe of several politicised and radicalised Muslims providing funds or who were planning and preparing terrorist attacks. Osman Petmezci, a 24-year-old Turkish national, and his American fiancée Astrid Eyzaguirre, 23, were preparing to attack the U.S. Army Europe Headquarters in Heidelberg and were arrested by the German authorities on September 5, 2002.[63] Inside the couple's third-floor apartment, police recovered 130 kilograms of bomb making chemicals, five pipe bombs, a bomb making manual, detonators and a picture of bin Laden. German authorities believe that the "couple was acting alone, despite citing evidence that they admired Osama bin Laden and shared some of [his] convictions, including a hatred for the Jews."[64] There are several similar unreported or under-reported terrorist attacks. For instance, a U.S. helicopter carrying U.S. oil company employees was attacked after taking off from the San'a airport injuring two persons on November 3, 2002. With the steadfast erosion of Al Qaeda personnel and physical infrastructure, Al Qaeda can become a state-of-mind spawning both individual terrorists and successor terrorist organisations. To avoid this real danger, the ideological response to Al Qaeda and Islamism as a doctrine must not be made a secondary task.

If we are to win the campaign, the fight against radical Islam should not be confused with the Muslim world, one-fifth of humanity or 1.44 billion people.[65] It is not a clash of civilisation but a clash among civilisations. It is a fight waged between the progressive Muslims and the radical Muslims. Only a miniscule part of the Muslim public actively supports terrorism.[66] The vast majority of Muslims have suffered as a result of political violence unleashed by a small group of power hungry leaders wearing the garb of religion. If the fight is to be won, efforts must be made to protect the moderate Muslims from virulent ideologies propagated by Mullahs of the Al Qaeda brand of Islam. With the threat of Islamism increasing, the hands of the progressive Muslim leaders both in government and outside government, especially in the non-governmental organisations, must be strengthened. It must involve the best of relations between the Western governmental and non-governmental leaders with their Middle Eastern and Asian counterparts and moreover public diplomacy where governments directly communicate with the public, even of publics across borders.[67] Despite the oil boom, the failure of the Arab leaders to invest in their citizens has increased both the ideological appeal and the welfare programs of terrorist groups. The Arab regimes must take the blame for their failure to build modern education systems, create new jobs, and develop the quality of life of their people. Their fashion of blaming the West for their ills and more importantly their reluctance to counter anti-Western rhetoric makes Western public diplomacy in the Arab World even more necessary. In parallel to Al Jazeera, a CNN, BBC or CBS Arab satellite television station is central to correcting and fashioning the traditional Middle Eastern view of the West. Instead of shying away, the West must engage the Middle East to develop transparency and accountability.[68] Furthermore, joint prophylactic measures—greater investment in the political, socio-economic reform, especially education and welfare—by the West, and working together with the Muslim world is likely to reduce support for terrorism in the long term.[69] Failure to develop a multi-pronged, multi-dimensional, multi-agency and a multinational response to Al Qaeda and its associate groups will lead to a continuity of the threat, and even an escalation.

Dr. Rohan Gunaratna has 20 years of policy, operational, and academic experience in counterterrorism. He is the head of terrorism research at the Institute of Defence and Strategic Studies, Singapore; senior fellow at the Centre for the Study of Terrorism and Political Violence, University of St. Andrews, UK; and honorary fellow at the International Policy Institute for Counter Terrorism Policy, Israel. He directed the team that designed and built the UN Database on Al Qaeda, Taliban and Associates at the UN headquarters. He is the author of six books including *Inside Al Qaeda: Global Network of Terror* (Columbia University Press, New York) and the lead author of *Jane's Counter Terrorism*, a handbook for law enforcement personnel.

Notes

1. I am grateful to Colonel Russell D. Howard and Major Reid L. Sawyer of the United States Military Academy at West Point for their invitation to write this chapter.
2. While guerrilla groups target combatants, terrorist groups target non-combatants.
3. The term was coined by the Counter Terrorism Centre at the Central Intelligence Agency, Langley, Virginia, U.S.A., sometime in the late 1990s. Michael Sheehan, former U.S. Ambassador for Counter Terrorism and currently Deputy Commissioner for Counter Terrorism at the New York Police Department, Senior's Conference, U.S. Military Academy, West Point, June 2003.
4. The meeting was arranged by the former Egyptian Army Captain Ali Mohammad who subsequently became a naturalised American, joined the U.S. military and served as a Supplies Sergeant at Fort Bragg, North Carolina, before joining Al Qaeda and becoming the chief bodyguard of Osama bin Laden and the Principal Instructor of Al Qaeda, both in Afghanistan and Sudan. He is currently in U.S. custody in the mainland United States.
5. However, 10 percent of phone calls from Osama bin Laden's satellite phone went to Iran from 1996 to 1998.
6. Compared to its numerical strength of 4,000 members, estimated at October 2001, the loss of 3,200 members and key supporters is significant. The figure 4,000 members comes from Al Qaeda detainee debriefs, including the FBI interrogation of Mohammad Mansour Jabarah, the 21-year-old Canadian operative of Kuwaiti-Iraqi origin detained in mainland United States since 2002.
7. However, Aum Shinrikyo does not have the same global composition or the global reach of Al Qaeda.
8. For instance, Egyptian Islamic Jihad and the Islamic Group of Egypt has only Egyptians; Armed Islamic Group of Algeria and Salafi Group for Call and Combat has only Algerians; Moro Islamic Liberation Front and the Abu Sayaaf Group has only Moros.
9. For instance, Takfir Wal Hijra, a group active in Europe and North America recruited from North Africa—Egyptians, Algerians, Libyans, Moroccans, and Tunisians—and Jemmah Islamiyah recruited from Southeast Asia and Australia—Indonesians, Malaysians, Thais, Singaporeans, Filipinos, and Australians (both cradle and convert Muslims).
10. Hasan Hattab, the head of the European network of the Armed Islamic Group of Algeria (GIA), broke away from the GIA in 1998 and formed GSPC. Although GSPC is strongest in Europe, a cell in the United States planning to target the MGM hotel and casino in Las Vegas was broken by the FBI in 2002.
11. Interview, Dr Reuven Paz, International Policy Institute for Counter Terrorism, Israel, May 2003.
12. Eliza Manningham-Buller, Terrorism Conference, Royal United Services Institute, London, July 17, 2003
13. Ibid.
14. Osama bin Laden's two-minute audiotape broadcast to mark the first anniversary of the U.S. intervention in Afghanistan, Al Jazeera, Arab Satellite Television Station, Qatar, October 6, 2002.

15. Ayman Al Zawahiri's question and answer with an unidentified reporter, Al Jazeera, October 8, 2002.

16. Debriefing of Umar Al Faruq, held at Baghram Airbase, Afghanistan, on September 9, 2002, enabled the U.S. government to issue an alert immediately before September 11, 2002, the first anniversary of 9-11. Tactical Interrogation Report Umar Al Faruq, CIA, Langley, September 2002.

17. Kashmir, only six hours by road from Afghanistan and the theatre of conflict nearest to Afghanistan, was visited by the author in August 2002. Both reviewing detainee tactical interrogation reports and debriefing of foreign detainees by the author revealed that Al Qaeda is neither abandoning nor deserting Afghanistan or Pakistan but the routine flow of foreigners to fight in Indian Kashmir is continuing.

18. For instance, the 9-11 mastermind Khalid Sheikh Mohammad, Al Qaeda's head of the military committee, tasked Jayashi-e-Mohammad member Ahmed Saeed Omar Sheikh to kill Daniel Pearl, the first U.S. casualty in a terrorist attack since 9-11. Operating through Lashkar-e-Omar, an umbrella group mooted by Al Qaeda, six terrorists opened fire and killed 17 Christians including five children and a policeman and injuring 17 in a church in Bahawalpur, Punjab, on October 28, 2001. Similarly, a grenade attack on a church in the heavily guarded diplomatic enclave in Islamabad killed 5, including a U.S. official's wife and daughter, and injured 41 on March 17, 2002. Al Qaeda also financed a car-bombing to kill President Musharraf, and when it failed used the same car bomb to attack the U.S. consulate. While Pakistanis mounted reconnaissance and organised the explosives and the vehicle, an Arab Al Qaeda member finally arrived and conducted the suicide bombing killing 12 Pakistanis and injuring 51, including one U.S. Marine guard in Karachi on June 14, 2002.

19. Al Qaeda Website al.neda.com claimed that it attacked the "French oil tanker off the coast of Yemen."

20. Terrorist connections of Abubakar Basyir; and further details on terrorist connection and activities of Umar Faruq, Orange Alert Document, September 2002, p. 2.

21. Umar Faruq's Terrorist Activities in Indonesia, Badan Inteligen Nasional (BIN: National Intelligence Agency), Jakarta, June 2002, p.1.

22. al.neda.com claimed that it attacked the "Fialka base in Kuwait."

23. al.neda.com claimed that it attacked the "nightclubs and whorehouses in Indonesia."

24. Analysis of the Latest Bombing Incident in Indonesia and Its Possible Connections with Al-Qaeda and Jemmah Islamiyah, National Intelligence Coordinating Agency, Philippines, October 2002.

25. USAID is the lead disaster relief agency engaged in agriculture, water, and humanitarian programs.

26. The same group had claimed responsibility for killing of Israeli diamond merchant Yitzhak Snir, a man in his 50s, who was slain near Foley's home on August 6, 2001. The group said the attack was in response to Israeli behaviour against Palestinians. Israeli security officials suspected that two previous attacks conducted against Israeli citizens in Jordan were also by the same group. On December 5, 2000, an unidentified gunman shot and slightly wounded Israeli diplomat Shlomo Razabi in the left foot as he was leaving an Amman store. On November 19, 2000, Israeli diplomat Yoram Havivian was slightly wounded in the arm and the leg when a gunman fired on his vehicle.

27. Osama bin Laden's two-minute audiotape broadcast to mark the first anniversary of the U.S. intervention in Afghanistan, Al Jazeera, Arab Satellite Television Station, Qatar, October 6, 2002.

28. Al-Qa'ida Declarations of Continued Attacks, CIA, Langley, October 2002, p. 1.

29. Valeria Korchagina, "Hostage-takers 'Keen on Dying.'" *USA Today*, October 25, 2002, p. 14 A. Article uses the term "rebels."

30. After the first Chechen war (December 1994–November 1996), Russian troops withdrew from Chechnya but returned in 1999 in response to a series of apartment bombings in Moscow that killed 300 Russians.

31. Chechen Tape, Al Jazeera, October 24, 2002.

32. Movsar's aunt Khava Barayev, 19, conducted a suicide attack killing two Russian soldiers at the Russian base in Alkhan-Yurt in June 2000.

33. Poisoned Letter Killed Chechen Commander Khattab, Kavkaz-Tsentr News Agency Web Site in Russian, April 28, 2002.

34. Al Qaeda's former Southeast Asian representative Umar Al Faruq's cell phone number 081-2802-7614 was in the phone memory of Ibn-ul-Khattab as well as the phone book of another Al Qaeda leader, Abu Talha alias Muhammad Abdallah Nasir Ubayd al Dusari, arrested by the Kuwaitis. Tactical Interrogation Report Umar Al Faruq, CIA, Langley, September 2002.

35. George Tenet, CIA director, visited Riyadh a few weeks before the attack and apprised the House of al Saud of the impending threat. Interview, CIA officer, May 2003.

36. Information derived from Mohammed Mansour Jabarah, Federal Bureau of Investigations, U.S. Department of Justice, August 21, 2002, p. 2.

37. Ibid.

38. Ibid.

39. Umar Faruq's Terrorist Activities in Indonesia, BIN, Jakarta, June 2002, p. 2.

40. Ibid., p. 2.

41. Although BIN, headed by A.M. Hendropriyono, targeted Al Qaeda cells, the Indonesian government was reluctant to target JI and its associated Majlis Mujahidin Indonesia (MMI: Mujahidin Council of Indonesia), headed by Abu Bakar Bashir and Lashkar Jundullah, headed by Agus Dwikarna.

42. Debriefing of John Walker Lindh, Virginia, U.S., July 25, 2002.

43. Margo O'Neill, Lateline, Australian Broadcasting Corporation, October 9, 2002. Australian government saw no significant threat to Australia or to its interests.

44. Despite a JI surveillance video of the Australian target having been recovered in the residence of the late Al Qaeda military commander Mohomad Atef alias Abu Haf's in Afghanistan, the Australian government did not take the threat seriously—some officials believed that Al Qaeda/JI had included the Australian High Commission in the target list because it was next to the U.S. Embassy. Even in March 2002, some Australian intelligence officials who participated at a counter-terrorism meeting organised by the Institute for Defence and Strategic Studies in Singapore disbelieved that JI was under Al Qaeda control.

45. Nida'ul Islam (Call to Islam), Islamic Youth Movement magazine, Sydney, February–March 1997.

46. Ibid.

47. "The latest Indonesian crisis: causes and solutions," JI political manifesto, May 1998.

48. Debriefing of JI members, September–October 2002.

49. Interview, Jeff Pentrose, former director, Australian Federal Police Intelligence, October 2002.

50. Ibid.

51. The author reviewed over 200 tapes, including training tapes, recovered by CNN's Nic Robertson from Al Qaeda's registry in Afghanistan, CNN Centre, Atlanta, August–September 2002.

52. The second meeting of the Rabitat-ul Mujahidin held in Kuala Lumpur, Malaysia, presided over by the JI leader Abu Bakar Basyir in mid-2000 included both Islamists and separatist leaders—Agus Dwikarna from Sulawesi, Tenku Idris from Aceh, Ibrahim Maidin from Singapore, Abdul Fatah from Thailand, Nik Adli Abdul Aziz from Malaysia, representatives from Myanmar and Egyptian Islamic Jihad. Interview, Intelligence official, Department of the Prime Minister, Malaysia, November 2002.

53. Tony Davis, "The Complexities of Unrest in Southern Thailand," *Jane's Intelligence Review*, Volume 14 Number 9, September 2002, p. 17

54. Ibid., p. 17.

55. Iqbal, the JI member, detonated a backpack of explosives that he carried into the Paddy's Bar in Bali.

56. Al-Qa'ida Declarations of Continued Attacks, CIA, Langley, October 2002, p. 1.

57. Ayman Al Zawahiri's question and answer with an unidentified reporter, Al Jazeera, October 8, 2002.

58. Interviews, U.S. military and intelligence officials, Washington DC, October 29–November 1, 2002.

59. Brian Michael Jenkins. Countering Al Qaeda: An Appreciation of the Situation and Suggestions for Strategy, RAND, 2002.

60. None of the CIA documents until August 1998 refers to Osama bin Laden's organisation as Al Qaeda. It refers to the group as UBL or OBL network and as Islamic Army. Furthermore, the list of U.S. designated foreign terrorist groups in 1997 does not include "Al Qaeda."

61. In addition to the rise of Islamism, another factor that is driving an increased U.S. presence worldwide is the re-emergence of the Peoples Republic of China and U.S. efforts to contain the next superpower.

62. "Shooting at Los Angeles International Airport Kills Two, Injures Others on July 4," FBI Press Release, Los Angeles Field Office, July 5, 2002.

63. Tony Czuczka, "Germans Had Hints about Suspected Bomb Plot Against U.S.," *Associated Press*, September 8, 2002.

64. Ibid.

65. For statistics, U.S. Centre for World Mission 2002 Report.

66. Husain Haqqani, "The Gospel of Jihad," *Foreign Policy*, September–October, 2002, p. 74.

67. Perception that the Indonesian military was behind the Bali bombing found resonance in Indonesia because U.S. government only engaged the Indonesian government and not the public. While strengthening government-to-government cooperation, it is necessary also to engage the public in a dialogue and keep them informed of the active presence of an Al Qaeda-JI network in Indonesia.

68. For instance, charities should not be permitted to raise funds or transfer funds unless and until the end user has been verified and validated.

69. Marina Ottaway, "Nation Building," *Foreign Policy*, September–October 2002, pp. 16–24.

Audrey Kurth Cronin, 2002

Behind the Curve

Globalization and International Terrorism

The coincidence between the evolving changes of globalization, the inherent weaknesses of the Arab region, and the inadequate American response to both ensures that terrorism will continue to be the most serious threat to U.S. and Western interests in the twenty-first century. There has been little creative thinking, however, about how to confront the growing terrorist backlash that has been unleashed. Terrorism is a complicated, eclectic phenomenon, requiring a sophisticated strategy oriented toward influencing its means and ends over the long term. Few members of the U.S. policymaking and academic communities, however, have the political capital, intellectual background, or inclination to work together to forge an effective, sustained response. Instead, the tendency has been to fall back on established bureaucratic mind-sets and prevailing theoretical paradigms that have little relevance for the changes in international security that became obvious after the terrorist attacks in New York and Washington on September 11, 2001.

The current wave of international terrorism, characterized by unpredictable and unprecedented threats from nonstate actors, not only is a reaction to globalization but is facilitated by it; the U.S. response to this reality has been reactive and anachronistic. The combined focus of the United States on state-centric threats and its attempt to cast twenty-first-century terrorism into familiar strategic terms avoids and often undermines effective responses to this nonstate phenomenon. The increasing threat of globalized terrorism must be met with flexible, multifaceted responses that deliberately and effectively exploit avenues of globalization in return; this, however, is not happening.

As the primary terrorist target, the United Sates should take the lead in fashioning a forward-looking strategy. As the world's predominant military, economic, and political power, it has been able to pursue its interests throughout the globe with unprecedented freedom since the breakup of the Soviet Union more than a decade ago. Even in the wake of the September 11 terrorist attacks on the World Trade Center and the Pentagon, and especially after the U.S. military action in Afghanistan, the threat of terrorism, mostly consisting of underfunded and ad hoc cells motivated by radical fringe ideas, has seemed unimportant by comparison. U.S. strategic culture has a long tradition of downplaying such atypical concerns in favor of a focus on more conventional state-based military power.[1] On the whole, this has been an effective approach: As was dramatically demonstrated in Afghanistan, the U.S. military knows how to destroy state governments and their armed forces, and the American political leadership and public have a natural bias toward using power to achieve the quickest results. Sometimes it is important to show resolve and respond forcefully.

29

The United States has been far less impressive, however, in its use of more subtle tools of domestic and international statecraft, such as intelligence, law enforcement, economic sanctions, educational training, financial controls, public diplomacy, coalition building, international law, and foreign aid. In an ironic twist, it is these tools that have become central to the security of the United States and its allies since September 11. In an era of globalized terrorism, the familiar state-centric threats have not disappeared; instead they have been joined by new (or newly threatening) competing political, ideological, economic, and cultural concerns that are only superficially understood, particularly in the West. An examination of the recent evolution of terrorism and a projection of future developments suggest that, in the age of globalized terrorism, old attitudes are not just anachronistic; they are dangerous.

Terrorism as a phenomenon is not new, but for reasons explained below, the threat it now poses is greater than ever before. The current terrorist backlash is manifested in the extremely violent asymmetrical response directed at the United States and other leading powers by terrorist groups associated with or inspired by al-Qaeda. This backlash has the potential to fundamentally threaten the international system. Thus it is not just an American problem. Unless the United States and its allies formulate a more comprehensive response to terrorism, better balanced across the range of policy instruments, the results will be increasing international instability and long-term failure.

The article proceeds in five main sections. First, it provides a discussion of the definition, history, causes, and types of terrorism, placing the events of September 11, 2001, in their modern context. Second, it briefly describes key trends in modern terrorism, explaining how the phenomenon appears to be evolving. Third, it analyzes the implications of these trends for the stability and security of the international community generally, and the United States and its allies more specifically. Fourth, the article outlines the prospects of these trends. It concludes with a range of policy recommendations suggested by the analysis.

Definition, Origins, Motivations, and Types of Modern Terrorism

The terrorist phenomenon has a long and varied history, punctuated by lively debates over the meaning of the term. By ignoring this history, the United States runs the risk of repeating the plethora of mistakes made by other major powers that faced similar threats in the past. This section begins with an explanation of the definition of terrorism, then proceeds to an examination of terrorism's origins, major motivations, and predominant types.

Definition of Terrorism

Terrorism is notoriously difficult to define, in part because the term has evolved and in part because it is associated with an activity that is designed to be subjective. Generally speaking, the targets of a terrorist episode are not the victims who are killed or maimed in the attack, but rather the governments, publics, or constituents among whom the terrorists hope to engender a reaction—such as fear, repulsion, intimidation, overreaction, or radicalization. Specialists in the area of terrorism studies have devoted hundreds of pages toward trying to develop an unassailable definition of the term, only to realize the fruitlessness of their efforts: Terrorism is intended to be a matter of perception and is thus seen differently by different observers.[2]

Although individuals can disagree over whether particular actions constitute terrorism, there are certain aspects of the concept that are fundamental. First, terrorism always has a political nature. It involves the commission of outrageous acts designed to precipitate political change.[3] At its root, terrorism is about justice, or at least someone's perception of it, whether man-made or divine. Second, although many other uses of violence are inherently political, including conventional war among states, terrorism is distinguished by its nonstate character—even when terrorists receive military, political, economic, and other means of support from state sources. States obviously employ force for political ends: When state force is used internationally, it is considered an act of war; when it is used domestically, it is called various things, including law enforcement, state terror, oppression, or civil war. Although states can terrorize, they cannot by definition be terrorists. Third, terrorism deliberately targets the innocent, which also distinguishes it from state uses of force that inadvertently kill innocent bystanders. In any given example, the latter may or may not be seen as justified; but again, this use of force is different from terrorism. Hence the fact that precision-guided missiles sometimes go astray and kill innocent civilians is a tragic use of force, but it is not terrorism. Finally, state use of force is subject to international norms and conventions that may be invoked or at least consulted; terrorists do not abide by international laws or norms and, to maximize the psychological effect of an attack, their activities have a deliberately unpredictable quality.[4]

Thus, at a minimum, terrorism has the following characteristics: a fundamentally political nature, the surprise use of violence against seemingly random targets, and the targeting of the innocent by nonstate actors.[5] All of these attributes are illustrated by recent examples of terrorism—from the April 2000 kidnapping of tourists by the Abu Sayyaf group of the Philippines to the various incidents allegedly committed by al-Qaeda, including the 1998 bombings of the U.S. embassies in Kenya and Tanzania and the September 11 attacks. For the purposes of this discussion, the shorthand (and admittedly imperfect) definition of terrorism is the threat or use of seemingly random violence against innocents for political ends by a nonstate actor.

Origins of Terrorism

Terrorism is as old as human history. One of the first reliably documented instances of terrorism, however, occurred in the first century B.C.E. The Zealots-Sicarri, Jewish terrorists dedicated to inciting a revolt against Roman rule in Judea, murdered their victims with daggers in broad daylight in the heart of Jerusalem, eventually creating such anxiety among the population that they generated a mass insurrection.[6] Other early terrorists include the Hindu Thugs and the Muslim Assassins. Modern terrorism, however, is generally considered to have originated with the French Revolution.[7]

The term "terror" was first employed in 1795, when it was coined to refer to a policy systemically used to protect the fledgling French republic government against counterrevolutionaries. Robespierre's practice of using revolutionary tribunals as a means of publicizing a prisoner's fate for broader effect within the population (apart from questions of legal guilt or innocence) can be seen as a nascent example of the much more highly developed, blatant manipulation of media attention by terrorist groups in the mid- to late twentieth century.[8] Modern terrorism is a dynamic concept, from the outset dependent to some degree on the political and historical context within which it has been employed.

Decolonization and Antiglobalization: Drivers of Terrorism?

Although individual terrorist groups have unique characteristics and arise in specific local contexts, an examination of broad historical patterns reveals that the international system within which such groups are spawned does influence their nature and motivations. A distinguishing feature of modern terrorism has been the connection between sweeping political or ideological concepts and increasing levels of terrorist activity internationally. The broad political aim has been against (1) empires, (2) colonial powers, and (3) the U.S.-led international system marked by globalization. Thus it is important to understand the general history of modern terrorism and where the current threat fits within an international context.

David Rapoport has described modern terrorism such as that perpetuated by al-Qaeda as part of a religiously inspired "fourth wave." This wave follows three earlier historical phases in which terrorism was tied to the breakup of empires, decolonization, and leftist anti-Westernism.[9] Rapoport argues that terrorism occurs in consecutive if somewhat overlapping waves. The argument here, however, is that modern terrorism has been a power struggle along a continuum: central power versus local power, big power versus small power, modern power versus traditional power. The key variable is a widespread perception of opportunity, combined with a shift in a particular political or ideological paradigm. Thus, even though the newest international terrorist threat, emanating largely from Muslim countries, has more than a modicum of religious inspiration, it is more accurate to see it as part of a larger phenomenon of antiglobalization and tension between the have and have-not nations, as well as between the elite and underprivileged within those nations. In an era where reforms occur at a pace much slower than is desired, terrorists today, like those before them, aim to exploit the frustrations of the common people (especially in the Arab world).

In the nineteenth century, the unleashing of concepts such as universal suffrage and popular empowerment raised the hopes of people throughout the western world, indirectly resulting in the first phase of modern terrorism. Originating in Russia, as Rapoport argues, it was stimulated not by state repression but by the efforts of the czars to placate demands for economic and political reforms, and the inevitable disappointment of popular expectations that were raised as a result. The goal of terrorists was to engage in attacks on symbolic targets to get the attention of the common people and thus provoke a popular response that would ultimately overturn the prevailing political order. This type of modern terrorism was reflected in the activities of groups such as the Russian Narodnaya Volya (People's Will) and later in the development of a series of movements in the United States and Europe, especially in territories of the former Ottoman Empire.

The dissolution of empires and the search for a new distribution of political power provided an opportunity for terrorism in the nineteenth and twentieth centuries. It climaxed in the assassination of Archduke Franz Ferdinand on June 28, 1914, an event that catalyzed the major powers into taking violent action, not because of the significance of the man himself but because of the suspicion of rival state involvement in the sponsorship of the killing. World War I, the convulsive systemic cataclysm that resulted, ended the first era of modern terrorism, according to Rapoport.[10] But terrorism tied to popular movements seeking greater democratic representation and political power from coercive empires has not ceased. Consider, for example, the Balkans after the downfall of the former state of Yugoslavia. The struggle for power among various Balkan ethnic groups can be seen as the final devolution of power from the former Ottoman Empire. This postimperial scramble is also in evidence elsewhere— for example, in Aceh, Chechnya, and Xinjiang, to mention just a few of the trouble spots within vast (former) empires. The presentation of a target of opportunity, such as a liberalizing state or regime, frequently evokes outrageous terrorist acts.

According to Rapoport, a second, related phase of modern terrorism associated with the concept of national self-determination developed its greatest predominance after World War I. It also continues to the present day. These struggles for power are another facet of terrorism against larger political powers and are specifically designed to win political independence or autonomy. The mid–twentieth-century era of rapid decolonization spawned national movements in territories as diverse as Algeria, Israel, South Africa, and Vietnam.[11] An important by-product was ambivalence toward the phenomenon in the international community, with haggling over the definition of terrorism reaching a fever pitch in the United Nations by the 1970s.

The question of political motivation became important in determining international attitudes toward terrorist attacks, as the post–World War II backlash against the colonial powers and the attractiveness of national independence movements led to the creation of a plethora of new states often born from violence. Arguments over the justice of international causes and the designation of terrorist struggles as "wars of national liberation" predominated, with consequentialist philosophies excusing the killing of innocent people if the cause in the long run was "just." Rapoport sees the U.S. intervention in Vietnam, and especially the subsequent American defeat by the Vietcong, as having catalyzed a "third wave" of modern terrorism; however, the relationship between the Vietnam conflict and other decolonization movements might just as easily be considered part of the same phase. In any case, the victory of the Vietcong excited the imaginations of revolutionaries throughout the world and, according to Rapoport, helped lead to a resurgence in terrorist violence. The Soviet Union underwrote the nationalist and leftist terrorist agendas of some groups, depicting the United States as the new colonial power—an easy task following the Vietnam intervention—and furthering an ideological agenda oriented toward achieving a postcapitalist, international communist utopia. Other groups, especially in Western Europe, rejected both the Soviet and capitalist models and looked admiringly toward nationalist revolutionaries in the developing world.[12] Leftist groups no longer predominate, but the enduring search for national self-determination continues, not only in the areas mentioned above but also in other hot spots such as the Basque region, East Timor, Sri Lanka, and Sudan.

Terrorism achieved a firmly international character during the 1970s and 1980s,[13] evolving in part as a result of technological advances and partly in reaction to the dramatic explosion of international media influence. International links were not new, but their centrality was. Individual, scattered national causes began to develop into international organizations with links and activities increasingly across borders and among differing causes. This development was greatly facilitated by the covert sponsorship of states such as Iran, Libya, and North Korea, and of course the Soviet Union, which found the underwriting of terrorist organizations an attractive tool for accomplishing clandestine goals while avoiding potential retaliation for the terrorist attacks.

The 1970s and 1980s represented the height of state-sponsored terrorism. Sometimes the lowest common denominator among the groups was the concept against which they were reacting—for example, "Western imperialism"—rather than the specific goals they sought. The most important innovation, however, was the increasing commonality of international connections among the groups. After the 1972 Munich Olympics massacre of eleven Israeli athletes, for example, the Palestinian Liberation Organization (PLO) and its associated groups captured the imaginations of young radicals around the world. In Lebanon and elsewhere, the PLO also provided training in the preferred techniques of twentieth-century terrorism such as airline hijacking, hostage taking, and bombing.

Since the September 11 attacks, the world has witnessed the maturation of a new phase of terrorist activity, the jihad era, spawned by the Iranian Revolution of 1979 as well as the Soviet defeat in Afghanistan shortly thereafter. The powerful attraction of religious and spiritual movements has overshadowed the nationalist or leftist revolutionary ethos of earlier terrorist phases (though many of those struggles continue), and it has become the central characteristic of a growing international trend. It is perhaps ironic that, as Rapoport observes, the forces of history seem to be driving international terrorism back to a much earlier time, with echoes of the behavior of "sacred" terrorists such as the Zealots-Sicarii clearly apparent in the terrorist activities of organizations such as al-Qaeda and its associated groups. Religious terrorism is not new; rather it is a continuation of an ongoing modern power struggle between those with power and those without it. Internationally, the main targets of these terrorists are the United States and the U.S.-led global system.

Like other eras of modern terrorism, this latest phase has deep roots. And given the historical patterns, it is likely to last at least a generation, if not longer. The jihad era is animated by widespread alienation combined with elements of religious identity and doctrine—a dangerous mix of forces that resonate deep in the human psyche.

What is different about this phase is the urgent requirement for solutions that deal both with the religious fanatics who are the terrorists and the far more politically motivated states, entities, and people who would support them because they feel powerless and left behind in a globalizing world. Thus if there is a trend in terrorism, it is the existence of a two-level challenge: the hyperreligious motivation of small groups of terrorists and the much broader enabling environment of bad governance, nonexistent social services, and poverty that punctuates much of the developing world. Al-Qaeda, a band driven by religious extremism, is able to do so much harm because of the secondary support and sanctuary it receives in vast areas that have not experienced the political and economic benefits of globalization. Therefore, the prescription for dealing with Osama bin Laden and his followers is not just eradicating a relatively small number of terrorists, but also changing the conditions that allow them to acquire so much power. Leaving aside for the moment the enabling environment, it is useful to focus on the chief motivations of the terrorists themselves, especially the contrasting secular and spiritual motivations of terrorism.

Leftist, Rightist, Ethnonationalist/Separatist, and "Sacred" Terrorism

There are four types of terrorist organizations currently operating around the world, categorized mainly by their source of motivation: left-wing terrorists, right-wing terrorists, ethnonationalist/separatist terrorists, and religious or "sacred" terrorists. All four types have enjoyed periods of relative prominence in the modern era, with left-wing terrorism intertwined with the Communist movement,[14] right-wing terrorism drawing its inspiration from Fascism,[15] and the bulk of ethnonationalist/separatist terrorism accompanying the wave of decolonization especially in the immediate post–World War II years. Currently, "sacred" terrorism is becoming more significant.[16] Although groups in all categories continue to exist today, left-wing and right-wing terrorist groups were more numerous in earlier decades. Of course, these categories are not perfect, as many groups have a mix of motivating ideologies—some ethnonationalist groups, for example, have religious characteristics or agendas[17]—but usually one ideology or motivation dominates.

Categories are useful not simply because classifying the groups gives scholars a more orderly field to study (admittedly an advantage), but also because different motivations have sometimes led to differing styles and modes of behavior. Understanding the type of terrorist group involved can provide insight into the likeliest manifestations of its violence and the most typical patterns of its development. At the risk of generalizing, left-wing terrorist organizations, driven by liberal or idealist political concepts, tend to prefer revolutionary, antiauthoritarian, antimaterialistic agendas. (Here it is useful to distinguish between the idealism of individual terrorists and the frequently contradictory motivations of their sponsors.) In line with these preferences, left-wing organizations often engage in brutal criminal-type behavior such as kidnapping, murder, bombing, and arson, often directed at elite targets that symbolize authority. They have difficulty, however, agreeing on their long-term objectives.[18] Most left-wing organizations in twentieth-century Western Europe, for example, were brutal but relatively ephemeral. Of course, right-wing terrorists can be ruthless, but in their most recent manifestations they have tended to be less cohesive and more impetuous in their violence than leftist terrorist groups. Their targets are often chosen according to race but also ethnicity, religion, or immigrant status, and in recent decades at least, have been more opportunistic than calculated.[19] This makes them potentially explosive but difficult to track.[20] Ethnonationalist/separatist terrorists are the most conventional, usually having a clear political or territorial aim that is rational and potentially negotiable, if not always justifiable in any given case. They can be astoundingly violent, over lengthy periods. At the same time, it can be difficult to distinguish between goals based on ethnic identity and those rooted in the control of a piece of land. With their focus on gains to be made in the traditional state-oriented international system, ethnonationalist/separatist terrorists often transition in and out of more traditional paramilitary structures, depending on how the cause is going. In addition, they typically have sources of support among the local populace of the same ethnicity with whom their separatist goals (or appeals to blood links) may resonate. That broader popular support is usually the key to the greater average longevity of ethnonationalist/ separatist groups in the modern era.[21]

All four types of terrorist organizations are capable of egregious acts of barbarism. But religious terrorists may be especially dangerous to international security for at least five reasons.

First, religious terrorists often feel engaged in a Manichaean struggle of good against evil, implying an open-ended set of human targets: Anyone who is not a member of their religion or religious sect may be "evil" and thus fair game. Although indiscriminate attacks are not unique to religious terrorists, the exclusivity of their faith may lead them to dehumanize their victims even more than most terrorist groups do, because they consider nonmembers to be infidels or apostates—as perhaps, for instance, al-Qaeda operatives may have viewed Muslims killed in the World Trade Center.

Second, religious terrorists engage in violent behavior directly or indirectly to please the perceived commands of a deity. This has a number of worrisome implications: The whims of the deity may be less than obvious to those who are not members of the religion, so the actions of violent religious organizations can be especially unpredictable. Moreover, religious terrorists may not be as constrained in their behavior by concerns about the reactions of their human constituents. (Their audience lies elsewhere.)

Third, religious terrorists consider themselves to be unconstrained by secular values or laws. Indeed the very target of the attacks may be the law-based secular society that is embodied in most modern states. The driving motivation, therefore, is to overturn the current post-Westphalian state system—a much more fundamental threat than is, say, ethnonationalist terrorism purporting to carve out a new secular state or autonomous territory.

Fourth, and related, religious terrorists often display a complete sense of alienation from the existing social system. They are not trying to correct the system, making it more just, more perfect, and more egalitarian. Rather they are trying to replace it. In some groups, apocalyptic images of destruction are seen as a necessity—even a purifying regimen—and this makes them uniquely dangerous, as was painfully learned on September 11.[22]

Fifth, religious terrorism is especially worrisome because of its dispersed popular support in civil society. On the one hand, for example, groups such as al-Qaeda are able to find support from some Muslim nongovernmental foundations throughout the world,[23] making it truly a global network. On the other hand, in the process of trying to distinguish between the relatively few providers of serious support from the majority of genuinely philanthropic groups, there is the real risk of igniting the very holy war that the terrorists may be seeking in the first instance.

In sum, there are both enduring and new aspects to modern terrorism. The enduring features center on the common political struggles that have characterized major acts of international terrorism. The newest and perhaps most alarming aspect is the increasingly religious nature of modern terrorist groups. Against this historical background, the unique elements in the patterns of terrorist activity surrounding September 11 appear starkly.

Key Trends in Modern Terrorism

By the late 1990s, four trends in modern terrorism were becoming apparent: an increase in the incidence of religiously motivated attacks, a decrease in the overall number of attacks, an increase in the lethality per attack, and the growing targeting of Americans.

Statistics show that, even before the September 11 attacks, religiously motivated terrorist organizations were becoming more common. The acceleration of this trend has been dramatic: According to the RAND–St. Andrews University Chronology of International Terrorism,[24] in 1968 none of the identified international terrorist organizations could be classified as "religious"; in 1980, in the aftermath of the Iranian Revolution, there were 2 (out of 64), and that number had expanded to 25 (out of 58) by 1995.[25]

Careful analysis of terrorism data compiled by the U.S. Department of State reveals other important trends regarding the frequency and lethality of terrorist attacks. The good news was that there were fewer such attacks in the 1990s than in the 1980s: Internationally, the number of terrorist attacks in the 1990s averaged 382 per year, whereas in the 1980s the number per year averaged 543.[26] But even before September 11, the absolute number of casualties of international terrorism had increased, from a low of 344 in 1991 to a high of 6,693 in 1998.[27] The jump in deaths and injuries can be partly explained by a few high-profile incidents, including the bombing of the U.S. embassies in Nairobi and Dar-es-Salaam in 1998;[28] but it is significant that more people became victims of terrorism as the decade proceeded. More worrisome, the number of people killed per incident rose significantly, from 102 killed in 565 incidents in 1991 to 741 killed in 274 incidents in 1998.[29] Thus, even though the number of terrorist attacks declined in the 1990s, the number of people killed in each one increased.

Another important trend relates to terrorist attacks involving U.S. targets. The number of such attacks increased in the 1990s, from a low of 66 in 1994 to a high of 200 in the year 2000.[30] This is a long-established problem: U.S. nationals consistently have been the most targeted since 1968.[31] But the percentage of international attacks against U.S. targets or U.S. citizens rose dramatically over the 1990s, from about 20 percent in 1993–95 to almost 50 percent in 2000.[32] This is perhaps a consequence of the increased role and profile of the United States in the world, but the degree of increase is nonetheless troubling.

The increasing lethality of terrorist attacks was already being noticed in the late 1990s, with many terrorism experts arguing that the tendency toward more casualties per incident had important implications. First it meant that, as had been feared, religious or "sacred" terrorism was apparently more dangerous than the types of terrorism that had predominated earlier in the twentieth century. The world was facing the resurgence of a far more malignant type of terrorism, whose lethality was borne out in the larger death toll from incidents that increasingly involved a religious motivation.[33] Second, with an apparent premium now apparently placed on causing more casualties per incident, the incentives for terrorist organizations to use chemical, biological, nuclear, or radiological (CBNR) weapons would multiply. The breakup of the Soviet Union and the resulting increased availability of Soviet chemical, biological, and nuclear weapons caused experts to argue that terrorist groups, seeking more dramatic and deadly results, would be more drawn to these weapons.[34] The 1995 sarin gas attack by the Japanese cult Aum Shinrikyo in the Tokyo subway system seemed to confirm that worry. More recently, an examination of evidence taken from Afghanistan and Pakistan reveals al-Qaeda's interest in chemical, biological, and nuclear weapons.[35]

In addition to the evolving motivation and character of terrorist attacks, there has been a notable dispersal in the geography of terrorist acts—a trend that is likely to continue. Although the Middle East continues to be the locus of most terrorist activity, Central and South Asia, the Balkans, and the Transcaucasus have been growing in significance over the past decade. International connections themselves are not new: International terrorist organizations inspired by common revolutionary principles date to the early nineteenth century; clandestine state use of foreign terrorist organizations occurred as early as the 1920s (e.g., the Mussolini government in Italy aided the Croat Ustasha); and complex mazes of funding, arms, and other state support for international terrorist organizations were in place especially in the 1970s and 1980s.[36] During the Cold War, terrorism was seen as a form of surrogate warfare and seemed almost palatable to some, at least compared to the potential prospect of major war or nuclear cataclysm.[37] What has changed is the self-generating nature of international terrorism, with its diverse economic means of support allowing terrorists to carry out attacks sometimes far from the organization's base. As a result, there is an important and growing distinction between where a terrorist organization is spawned and where an attack is launched, making the attacks difficult to trace to their source.

Reflecting all of these trends, al-Qaeda and its associated groups[38] (and individuals) are harbingers of a new type of terrorist organization. Even if al-Qaeda ceases to exist (which is unlikely), the dramatic attacks of September 2001, and their political and economic effects, will continue to inspire similarly motivated groups—particularly if the United States and its allies fail to develop broad-based, effective counterterrorist policies over the long term. Moreover, there is significant evidence that the global links and activities that al-Qaeda and its associated groups perpetuated are not short term or anomalous. Indeed they are changing the nature of the terrorist threat as we move further into the twenty-first century. The resulting intersection between the United States, globalization, and international terrorism will define the major challenges to international security.

The United States, Globalization, and International Terrorism

Whether deliberately intending to or not, the United States is projecting uncoordinated economic, social, and political power even more sweepingly than it is in military terms. Globalization,[39] in forms including Westernization, secularization, democratization, consumerism, and the growth of market capitalism, represents an onslaught to less privileged people in conservative cultures repelled by the fundamental changes that these forces are bringing—or angered by the distortions and uneven distributions of benefits that result.[40] This is especially true of the Arab world. Yet the current U.S. approach to this growing repulsion is colored by a kind of cultural naïveté, an unwillingness to recognize —let alone appreciate or take responsibility for—the influence of U.S. power except in its military dimension. Even doing nothing in the economic, social, and political policy realms is still doing something, because the United States is blamed by disadvantaged and alienated populations for the powerful Western-led forces of globalization that are proceeding apace, despite the absence of a focused, coordinated U.S. policy. And those penetrating mechanisms of globalization, such as the internet, the media, and the increasing flows of goods and peoples, are exploited in return. Both the means and ends of terrorism are being reformulated in the current environment.

The Means

Important changes in terrorist methods are apparent in the use of new technologies, the movement of terrorist groups across international boundaries, and changes in sources of support. Like globalization itself, these phenomena are all intertwined and overlapping but, for ease of argument, they are dealt with consecutively here.

First, the use of information technologies such as the internet, mobile phones, and instant messaging has extended the global reach of many terrorist groups. Increased access to these technologies has so far not resulted in their widely feared use in a major cyberterrorist attack: In Dorothy Denning's words, terrorists "still prefer bombs to bytes."[41] Activists and terrorist groups have increasingly turned to "hacktivism"—attacks on internet sites, including web defacements, hijackings of websites, web sit-ins, denial-of-service attacks, and automated email "bombings"—attacks that may not kill anyone but do attract media attention, provide a means of operating anonymously, and are easy to coordinate internationally.[42] So far, however, these types of attacks are more an expense and a nuisance than an existential threat.

Instead the tools of the global information age have led to enhanced efficiency in many terrorist-related activities, including administrative tasks, coordination of operations, recruitment of potential members, communication among adherents, and attraction of sympathizers.[43] Before the September 11 attacks, for example, members of al-Qaeda communicated through Yahoo email; Mohammed Atta, the presumed leader of the attacks, made his reservations online; and cell members went online to do research on subjects such as the chemical-dispersing powers of crop dusters. Although not as dramatic as shutting down a power grid or taking over an air traffic control system, this practical use of technology has significantly contributed to the effectiveness of terrorist groups and the expansion of their range.[44] Consider, for example, the lethal impact of the synchronized attacks on the U.S. embassies in 1998 and on New York andWashington in 2001, neither of which would have been possible without the revolution in information technology. When he was arrested in 1995, Ramzi Yousef, mastermind of the 1993 World Trade Center attack, was planning the simultaneous destruction of eleven airliners.[45]

The internet has become an important tool for perpetuating terrorist groups, both openly and clandestinely. Many of them employ elaborate list serves, collect money from witting or unwitting donors, and distribute savvy political messages to a broad audience online.[46] Groups as diverse as Aum Shinrikyo, Israel's Kahane Chai, the Popular Front for the Liberation of Palestine, the Kurdistan Workers' Party, and Peru's Shining Path maintain user-friendly official or unofficial websites, and almost all are accessible in English.[47] Clandestine methods include passing encrypted messages, embedding invisible graphic codes using steganography,[48] employing the internet to send death threats, and hiring hackers to collect intelligence such as the names and addresses of law enforcement officers from online databases.[49] All of these measures help to expand and perpetuate trends in terrorism that have already been observed: For example, higher casualties are brought about by simultaneous attacks, a diffusion in terrorist locations is made possible by internet communications, and extremist religious ideologies are spread through websites and videotapes accessible throughout the world.

More ominous, globalization makes CBNR weapons increasingly available to terrorist groups.[50] Information needed to build these weapons has become ubiquitous, especially through the internet. Among the groups interested in acquiring CBNR (besides al-Qaeda) are the PLO, the Red Army Faction, Hezbollah, the Kurdistan Workers' Party, German neo-Nazis, and the Chechens.[51]

Second, globalization has enabled terrorist organizations to reach across international borders, in the same way (and often through the same channels) that commerce and business interests are linked. The dropping of barriers through the North American Free Trade Area and the European Union, for instance, has facilitated the smooth flow of many things, good and bad, among countries. This has allowed terrorist organizations as diverse as Hezbollah, al- Qaeda, and the Egyptian al-Gama'at al-Islamiyya to move about freely and establish cells around the world.[52] Movement across borders can obviously enable terrorists to carry out attacks and potentially evade capture, but it also complicates prosecution if they are apprehended, with a complex maze of extradition laws varying greatly from state to state. The increased permeability of the international system has also enhanced the ability of nonstate terrorist organizations to collect intelligence (not to mention evade it); states are not the only actors interested in collecting, disseminating, and/or acting on such information. In a sense, then, terrorism is in many ways becoming like any other international enterprise—an ominous development indeed.

Third, terrorist organizations are broadening their reach in gathering financial resources to fund their operations. This is not just an al-Qaeda phenomenon, although bin Laden's organization—especially its numerous business interests—figures prominently among the most innovative and wealthy pseudocorporations in the international terrorist network. The list of groups with global financing networks is long and includes most of the groups identified by the U.S. government as foreign terrorist organizations, notably Aum Shinrikyo, Hamas, Hezbollah, and the Tamil Tigers. Sources of financing include legal enterprises such as nonprofit organizations and charities (whose illicit activities may be a small or large proportion of overall finances, known or unknown to donors); legitimate companies that divert profits to illegal activities (such as bin Laden's large network of construction companies); and illegal enterprises such as drug smuggling and production (e.g., the Revolutionary Armed Forces of Colombia—FARC), bank robbery, fraud, extortion, and kidnapping (e.g., the Abu Sayyaf group, Colombia's National Liberation Army, and FARC).[53] Websites are also important vehicles for raising funds. Although no comprehensive data are publicly available on how lucrative this avenue is, the proliferation of terrorist websites with links or addresses for contributions is at least circumstantial evidence of their usefulness.

The fluid movement of terrorists' financial resources demonstrates the growing informal connections that are countering the local fragmentation caused elsewhere by globalization. The transit of bars of gold and bundles of dollars across the border between Afghanistan and Pakistan as U.S. and allied forces were closing in on the Taliban's major strongholds is a perfect example. Collected by shopkeepers and small businessmen, the money was moved by operatives across the border to Karachi, where it was transferred in the millions of dollars through the informal *hawala* or *hundi* banking system to the United Arab Emirates.[54] There it was converted into gold bullion and scattered around the world before any government could intervene. In this way, al-Qaeda preserved and dispersed a proportion of its financial resources.[55] In addition to gold, money was transferred into other commodities—such as diamonds in Sierra Leone and the Democratic Republic of Congo, and tanzanite from Tanzania—all while hiding the assets and often making a profit,[56] and all without interference from the sovereign governments that at the time were at war with al-Qaeda and the Taliban.[57]

As this example illustrates, globalization does not necessarily require the use of high technology: It often takes the form of traditional practices used in innovative ways across increasingly permeable physical and commercial borders. Terrorist groups, whose assets comparatively represent only a small fraction of the amount of money that is moved by organized crime groups and are thus much more difficult to track, use everything from direct currency transport (by couriers) to reliance on traditional banks, Islamic banks, money changers (using accounts at legitimate institutions), and informal exchange (the *hawala* or *hundi* system).

This is by no means a comprehensive presentation of global interpenetration of terrorist means, and some of the connections described above have existed for some time and in other contexts. The broad strategic picture, however, is of an increasing ability of terrorist organizations to exploit the same avenues of communication, coordination, and cooperation as other international actors, including states, multinational corporations, non-governmental organizations, and even individuals. It would be naïve to assume that what is good for international commerce and international communication is not also good for international terrorists[58]—who are increasingly becoming opportunistic entrepreneurs whose "product" (often quite consciously "sold") is violence against innocent targets for a political end.

The Ends

The objectives of international terrorism have also changed as a result of globalization. Foreign intrusions and growing awareness of shrinking global space have created incentives to use the ideal asymmetrical weapon, terrorism, for more ambitious purposes.

The political incentives to attack major targets such as the United States with powerful weapons have greatly increased. The perceived corruption of indigenous customs, religions, languages, economies, and so on, are blamed on an international system often unconsciously molded by American behavior. The accompanying distortions in local communities as a result of exposure to the global marketplace of goods and ideas are increasingly blamed on U.S.-sponsored modernization and those who support it. The advancement of technology, however, is not the driving force behind the terrorist threat to the United States and its allies, despite what some have assumed.[59] Instead, at the heart of this threat are frustrated populations and international movements that are increasingly inclined to lash out against U.S.-led globalization.

As Christopher Coker observes, globalization is reducing tendencies toward instrumental violence (i.e., violence between states and even between communities), but it is enhancing incentives for expressive violence (or violence that is ritualistic, symbolic, and communicative).[60] The new international terrorism is increasingly engendered by a need to assert identity or meaning against forces of homogeneity, especially on the part of cultures that are threatened by, or left behind by, the secular future that Western-led globalization brings.

According to a report recently published by the United Nations Development Programme, the region of greatest deficit in measures of human development—the Arab world—is also the heart of the most threatening religiously inspired terrorism.[61] Much more work needs to be done on the significance of this correlation, but increasingly sources of political discontent are arising from disenfranchised areas in the Arab world that feel left behind by the promise of globalization and its assurances of broader freedom, prosperity, and access to knowledge. The results are dashed expectations, heightened resentment of the perceived U.S.-led hegemonic system, and a shift of focus away from more proximate targets within the region.

Of course, the motivations behind this threat should not be oversimplified: Anti-American terrorism is spurred in part by a desire to change U.S. policy in the Middle East and Persian Gulf regions as well as by growing antipathy in the developing world vis-à-vis the forces of globalization. It is also crucial to distinguish between the motivations of leaders such as Osama bin Laden and their followers. The former seem to be more driven by calculated strategic decisions to shift the locus of attack away from repressive indigenous governments to the more attractive and media-rich target of the United States.

The latter appear to be more driven by religious concepts cleverly distorted to arouse anger and passion in societies full of pent-up frustration. To some degree, terrorism is directed against the United States because of its engagement and policies in various regions.[62] Anti-Americanism is closely related to antiglobalization, because (intentionally or not) the primary driver of the powerful forces resulting in globalization is the United States.

Analyzing terrorism as something separate from globalization is misleading and potentially dangerous. Indeed globalization and terrorism are intricately intertwined forces characterizing international security in the twenty-first century. The main question is whether terrorism will succeed in disrupting the promise of improved livelihoods for millions of people on Earth. Globalization is not an inevitable, linear development, and it can be disrupted by such unconventional means as international terrorism. Conversely, modern international terrorism is especially dangerous because of the power that it potentially derives from globalization—whether through access to CBNR weapons, global media outreach, or a diverse network of financial and information resources.

Prospects for the Future

Long after the focus on Osama bin Laden has receded and U.S. troops have quit their mission in Afghanistan, terrorism will be a serious threat to the world community and especially to the United States. The relative preponderance of U.S. military power virtually guarantees an impulse to respond asymmetrically. The lagging of the Arab region behind the rest of the world is impelling a violent redirection of antiglobalization and antimodernization forces toward available targets, particularly the United States, whose scope and policies are engendering rage. Al-Qaeda will eventually be replaced or redefined, but its successors' reach may continue to grow via the same globalized channels and to direct their attacks against U.S. and Western targets. The current trajectory is discouraging, because as things currently stand, the wellspring of terrorism's means and ends is likely to be renewed: Arab governments will probably not reform peacefully, and existing Western governments and their supporting academic and professional institutions are disinclined to understand or analyze in depth the sources, patterns, and history of terrorism.

Terrorism is a by-product of broader historical shifts in the international distribution of power in all of its forms—political, economic, military, ideological, and cultural. These are the same forms of power that characterize the forces of Western-led globalization. At times of dramatic international change, human beings (especially those not benefiting from the change—or not benefiting as much or as rapidly from the change) grasp for alternative means to control and understand their environments. If current trends continue, widening global disparities, coupled with burgeoning information and connectivity, are likely to accelerate—unless the terrorist backlash, which is increasingly taking its inspiration from misoneistic religious or pseudoreligious concepts, successfully counters these trends. Because of globalization, terrorists have access to more powerful technologies, more targets, more territory, more means of recruitment, and more exploitable sources of rage than ever before. The West's twentieth-century approach to terrorism is highly unlikely to mitigate any of these long-term trends.

From a Manichean perspective, the ad hoc and purportedly benign intentions of the preponderant, secular West do not seem benign at all to those ill served by globalization. To frustrated people in the Arab and Muslim world, adherence to radical religious philosophies and practices may seem a rational response to the perceived assault, especially when no feasible alternative for progress is offered by their own governments. This is not to suggest that terrorists should be excused because of environmental factors or conditions. Instead, Western governments must recognize that the tiny proportion of the population that ends up in terrorist cells cannot exist without the availability of broader sources of active or passive sympathy, resources, and support. Those avenues of sustenance are where the center of gravity for an effective response to the terrorist threat must reside. The response to transnational terrorism must deal with the question of whether the broader enabling environment will increase or decrease over time, and the answer will be strongly influenced by the policy choices that the United States and its allies make in the near future.

Conclusions and Policy Prescriptions

The characteristics and causes of the current threat can only be analyzed within the context of the deadly collision occurring between U.S. power, globalization, and the evolution of international terrorism. The U.S. government is still thinking in outdated terms, little changed since the end of the Cold War. It continues to look at terrorism as a peripheral threat, with the focus remaining on states that in many cases are not the greatest threat. The means and the ends of terrorism are changing in fundamental, important ways; but the means and the ends of the strategy being crafted in response are not.

Terrorism that threatens international stability, and particularly U.S. global leadership, is centered on power-based political causes that are enduring: the weak against the strong, the disenfranchised against the establishment, and the revolutionary against the status quo. Oversimplified generalizations about poverty and terrorism, or any other single variable, are caricatures of a serious argument.[63] The rise in political and material expectations as a result of the information revolution is not necessarily helpful to stability, in the same way that rising expectations led terrorists to take up arms against the czar in Russia a century ago. Indeed the fact that so many people in so many nations are being left behind has given new ammunition to terrorist groups; produced more sympathy for those willing to take on the United States; and spurred Islamic radical movements to recruit, propagandize, and support terrorism throughout many parts of the Muslim world. The al-Qaeda network is an extremist religious terrorist organization, its Taliban puppet regime was filled with religious zealots, and its suicide recruits were convinced that they were waging a just holy war. But the driving forces of twenty-first-century terrorism are power and frustration, not the pursuit of religious principle. To dismiss the broad enabling environment would be to focus more on the symptoms than the causes of modern terrorism.

The prescriptions for countering and preventing terrorism should be twofold: First, the United States and other members of the international community concerned about this threat need to use a balanced assortment of instruments to address the immediate challenges of the terrorists themselves. Terrorism is a complex phenomenon; it must be met with short-term military action, informed by in-depth, long-term, sophisticated analysis. Thus far, the response has been virtually all the former and little of the latter. Second, the United States and its counterterrorist allies must employ a much broader array of longer-term policy tools to reshape the international environment, which enables terrorist networks to breed and become robust. The mechanisms of globalization need to be exploited to thwart the globalization of terrorism.

In the short term, the United States must continue to rely on capable military forces that can sustain punishing air strikes against terrorists and those who harbor them with an even greater capacity for special operations on the ground. This requires not only improved stealthy, long-range power projection capabilities but also agile, highly trained, and lethal ground forces, backed up with greater intelligence, including human intelligence supported by individuals with language skills and cultural training. The use of military force continues to be important as one means of responding to terrorist violence against the West, and there is no question that it effectively preempts and disrupts some international terrorist activity, especially in the short term.[64]

Over time, however, the more effective instruments of policy are likely to remain the nonmilitary ones. Indeed the United States needs to expand and deepen its nonmilitary instruments of power such as intelligence, public diplomacy, cooperation with allies, international legal instruments, and economic assistance and sanctions. George Kennan, in his 1947 description of containment, put forth the same fundamental argument, albeit against an extremely different enemy.[65] The strongest response that the United States can muster to a serious threat has to include political, economic, and military capabilities—in that order; yet, the U.S. government consistently structures its policies and devotes its resources in the reverse sequence.

The economic and political roots of terrorism are complex, increasingly worrisome, and demanding of as much breadth and subtlety in response as they display in their genesis. The United States must therefore be strategic in its response: An effective grand strategy against terrorism involves planning a global campaign with the most effective means available, not just the most measurable, obvious, or gratifying. It must also include plans for shaping the global environment after the so-called war on terrorism has ended—or after the current political momentum has subsided.

The United States, working with other major donor nations, needs to create an effective incentive structure that rewards "good performers"—those countries with good governance, inclusive education programs, and adequate social programs—and works around "bad performers" and intervenes to assist so-called failed states. Also for the longer term, the United States and its allies need to project a vision of sustainable development—of economic growth, equal access to basic social needs such as education and health, and good governance—for the developing world. This is particularly true in mostly Muslim countries whose populations are angry with the United States over a perceived double standard regarding its long-standing support for Israel at the expense of Palestinians, policies against the regime of Saddam Hussein at the expense of some Iraqi people, and a general abundance of American power, including the U.S. military presence throughout the Middle East. Whether these policies are right or wrong is irrelevant here; the point is that just as the definition of terrorism can be subjective and value laden, so too can the response to terrorism take into account perceptions of reality. In an attempt to craft an immediate military response, the U.S. government is failing to put into place an effective long-term grand strategy.

This is not just a problem for the U.S. government. The inability to develop a strategy with a deep-rooted, intellectually grounded understanding of the history, patterns, motivations, and types of terrorism is reflective of the paucity of understanding of the terrorist phenomenon in the academic community. Terrorism is considered too policy-oriented an area of research in political science,[66] and it operates in an uncomfortable intersection between disciplines unaccustomed to working together, including psychology, sociology, theology, economics, anthropology, history, law, political science, and international relations. In political science, terrorism does not fit neatly into either the realist or liberal paradigms, so it has been largely ignored.[67] There are a few outstanding, well-established senior scholars in the terrorism studies community— people such as Martha Crenshaw, David Rapoport, and Paul Wilkinson—but in the United States, most of the publicly available work is being done in policy-oriented research institutes or think tanks that are sometimes limited by the narrow interests and short time frames of the government contracts on which they depend. Some of that research is quite good,[68] but it is not widely known within the academy. The situation for graduate students who wish to study terrorism is worse: A principal interest in terrorism virtually guarantees exclusion from consideration for most academic positions. This would not necessarily be a problem if the bureaucracy were more flexible and creative than the academy is, but as we know from the analysis of the behavior of U.S. agencies shortly before September 11, it is not. In the United States, academe is no more strategic in its understanding of terrorism than is the U.S. government.

The globalization of terrorism is perhaps the leading threat to long-term stability in the twenty-first century. But the benefit of globalization is that the international response to terrorist networks has also begun to be increasingly global, with international cooperation on law enforcement, intelligence, and especially financial controls being areas of notable recent innovation.[69] If globalization is to continue—and there is nothing foreordained that it will—then the tools of globalization, including especially international norms, the rule of law, and international economic power, must be fully employed against the terrorist backlash. There must be a deliberate effort to move beyond the current episodic interest in this phenomenon: Superficial arguments and short attention spans will continue to result in event-driven policies and ultimately more attacks. Terrorism is an unprecedented, powerful nonstate threat to the international system that no single state, regardless of how powerful it may be in traditional terms, can defeat alone, especially in the absence of long-term, serious scholarship engaged in by its most creative minds.

Audrey Kurth Cronin is specialist in international terrorism at the Congressional Research Service at the Library of Congress. The article was written when she was visiting associate professor at the Edmund A. Walsh School of Foreign Service and a research fellow at the Center for Peace and Security Studies, Georgetown University.

Notes

1. The issue of U.S. strategic culture and its importance in the response to international terrorism is explored in more depth in Audrey Kurth Cronin, "Rethinking Sovereignty: American Strategy in the Age of Terror," *Survival*, Vol. 44, No. 2 (Summer 2002), pp. 119–139.
2. On the difficulty of defining terrorism, see, for example, Omar Malik, *Enough of the Definition of Terrorism!* Royal Institute of International Affairs (London: RIIA, 2001); and Alex P. Schmid, *Political Terrorism: A Research Guide* (New Brunswick, N.J.: Transaction Books, 1984). Schmid spends more than 100 pages grappling with the question of a definition, only to conclude that none is universally accepted.
3. Saying that terrorism is a political act is not the same as arguing that the political ends toward which it is directed are necessarily negotiable. If violent acts do not have a political aim, then they are by definition criminal acts.

4. The diabolical nature of terrorism has given resonance to Robert Kaplan's view that the world is a "grim landscape" littered with "evildoers" and requiring Western leaders to adopt a "pagan ethos." But such conclusions deserve more scrutiny than space allows here. See Steven Mufson, "The Way Bush Sees the World," *Washington Post*, Outlook section, February 17, 2002, p. B1.

5. R.G. Frey and Christopher W. Morris, "Violence, Terrorism, and Justice," in Frey and Morris, eds., *Violence, Terrorism, and Justice* (Cambridge: Cambridge University Press, 1991), p. 3.

6. Walter Laqueur, *Terrorism* (London: Weidenfeld and Nicolson, 1977, reprinted in 1978), pp. 7–8; and David C. Rapoport, "Fear and Trembling: Terrorism in Three Religious Traditions," *American Political Science Review*, Vol. 78, No. 3 (September 1984), pp. 658–677.

7. David C. Rapoport, "The Fourth Wave: September 11 in the History of Terrorism," *Current History*, December 2001, pp. 419–424; and David C. Rapoport, "Terrorism," *Encyclopedia of Violence, Peace, and Conflict* (New York: Academic Press, 1999).

8. Ironically, Robespierre's tactics during the Reign of Terror would not be included in this article's definition of terrorism, because it was state terror.

9. Rapoport, "The Fourth Wave."

10. Ibid., pp. 419–420.

11. Ibid., p. 420.

12. Adrian Gulke, *The Age of Terrorism and the International Political System* (London: I.B. Tauris, 1995), pp. 56–63.

13. This is not to imply that terrorism lacked international links before the 1970s. There were important international ties between anarchist groups of the late nineteenth century, for example. See David C. Rapoport, "The Four Waves of Modern Terrorism," in Audrey Kurth Cronin and James Ludes, eds., *The Campaign against International Terrorism* (Washington, D.C.: Georgetown University Press, forthcoming).

14. Groups such as the Second of June Movement, the Baader-Meinhof Gang, the Red Brigades, the Weathermen, and the Symbionese Liberation Army belong in this category.

15. Among right-wing groups would be other neo-Nazi organizations (in the United States and Europe) and some members of American militia movements such as the Christian Patriots and the Ku Klux Klan.

16. The list here would be extremely long, including groups as different as the Tamil Tigers of Sri Lanka, the Basque separatist party, the PLO, and the Irish Republican Army (IRA) and its various splinter groups.

17. Bruce Hoffman notes that secular terrorist groups that have a strong religious element include the Provisional IRA, Armenian factions, and perhaps the PLO; however, the political/separatist aspect is the predominant characteristic of these groups. Hoffman, "Terrorist Targeting: Tactics, Trends, and Potentialities," *Technology and Terrorism* (London: Frank Cass, 1993), p. 25.

18. An interesting example is France's Action Directe, which revised its raison d'être several times, often altering it to reflect domestic issues in France—anarchism and Maoism, dissatisfaction with NATO and the Americanization of Europe, and general anticapitalism. See Michael Dartnell, "France's Action Directe: Terrorists in Search of a Revolution," *Terrorism and Political Violence*, Vol. 2, No. 4 (Winter 1990), pp. 457–488.

19. For example, in the 1990s Germany and several other European countries experienced a rash of random arson attacks against guest houses and offices that provided services to immigrants, many of whom were Middle Eastern in origin. Other examples include the violence associated with groups such as Europe's "football hooligans." A possible American example of the opportunistic nature of right-wing terrorism may be the anthrax letter campaign conducted in October 2001. See Susan Schmidt, "Anthrax Letter Suspect Profiled: FBI Says Author Likely Is Male Loner; Ties to Bin Laden Are Doubted," *Washington Post*, November 11, 2001, p. A1; and Steve Fainaru, "Officials Continue to Doubt Hijackers' Link to Anthrax: Fla. Doctor Says He Treated One for Skin Form of Disease," *Washington Post*, March 24, 2002, p. A23.

20. It is interesting to note that, according to Christopher C. Harmon, in Germany, 1991 was the first year that the number of indigenous rightist radicals exceeded that of leftists. Harmon, *Terrorism Today* (London: Frank Cass, 2000), p. 3.

21. For example, in discussing the longevity of terrorist groups, Martha Crenshaw notes only three significant terrorist groups with ethnonationalist ideologies that ceased to exist within ten years of their formation (one of these, EOKA, disbanded because its goal—the liberation of Cyprus—was attained). By contrast, a majority of the terrorist groups she lists as having existed for ten years or longer have recognizable ethnonationalist ideologies, including the IRA (in its many forms), Sikh separatist groups, Euskadi Ta Askatasuna, the various Palestinian nationalist groups, and the Corsican National Liberation Front. See Crenshaw, "How Terrorism Declines," *Terrorism and Political Violence*, Vol. 3, No. 1 (Spring 1991), pp. 69–87.

22. On the characteristics of modern religious terrorist groups, see Bruce Hoffman, *Inside Terrorism* (New York: Columbia University Press, 1998), especially pp. 94–95; and Bruce Hoffman, "Terrorism Trends and Prospects," in Ian O. Lesser, Bruce Hoffman, John Arguilla, Michelle Zanini, and David Ronfeldt, eds., *Countering the New Terrorism* (Santa Monica, Calif.: RAND, 1999), especially pp. 19–20. On the peculiar twists of one apocalyptic vision, see Robert Jay Lifton, *Destroying the World to Save It: Aum Shinrikyo, Apocalyptic Violence, and the New Global Terrorism* (New York: Henry Holt, 1999).

23. There is a long list of people and organizations sanctioned under Executive Order 13224, signed on September 23, 2001. Designated charitable organizations include the Benevolence International Foundation and the Global Relief Foundation. The list is available at http://www.treas.gov/offices/enforcement/ofac/sanctions/t11ter.pdf (accessed November 26, 2002).

24. The RAND–St. Andrews University Chronology of International Terrorism is a databank of terrorist incidents that begins in 1968 and has been maintained since 1972 at St. Andrews University, Scotland, and the RAND Corporation, Santa Monica, California.

25. Hoffman, *Inside Terrorism*, pp. 90–91; and Nadine Gurr and Benjamin Cole, *The New Face of Terrorism: Threats from Weapons of Mass Destruction* (London: I.B. Tauris, 2000), pp. 28–29.

26. Statistics compiled from data in U.S. Department of State, *Patterns of Global Terrorism*, published annually by the Office of the Coordinator for Counterterrorism, U.S. Department of State.

27. Ibid. For a graphical depiction of this information, created on the basis of annual data from *Patterns of Global Terrorism*, see Cronin, "Rethinking Sovereignty," p. 126.

28. In the 1998 embassy bombings alone, for example, 224 people were killed (with 12 Americans among them), and 4,574 were injured (including 15 Americans). U.S. Department of State, *Patterns of Global Terrorism, 1998*.

29. Ibid. For a graphical depiction of deaths per incident, created on the basis of annual data from *Patterns of Global Terrorism*, see Cronin, "Rethinking Sovereignty," p. 128.

30. Ibid.

31. Hoffman, "Terrorist Targeting," p. 24.

32. U.S. Department of State, *Patterns of Global Terrorism*, various years.

33. Examples include Bruce Hoffman, *"Holy Terror": The Implications of Terrorism Motivated by a Religious Imperative*, RAND Paper P-7834 (Santa Monica, Calif.: RAND, 1993); and Mark Juergensmeyer, "Terror Mandated by God," *Terrorism and Political Violence*, Vol. 9, No. 2 (Summer 1997), pp. 16–23.

34. See, for example, Steven Simon and Daniel Benjamin, "America and the New Terrorism," *Survival*, Vol. 42, No. 1 (Spring 2000), pp. 59–75, as well as the responses in the subsequent issue, "America and the New Terrorism: An Exchange," *Survival*, Vol. 42, No. 2 (Summer 2000), pp. 156–172; and Hoffman, "Terrorism Trends and Prospects," pp. 7–38.

35. See Peter Finn and Sarah Delaney, "Al-Qaeda's Tracks Deepen in Europe," *Washington Post*, October 22, 2001, p. A1; Kamran Khan and Molly Moore, "2 Nuclear Experts Briefed Bin Laden, Pakistanis Say," *Washington Post*, December, 12, 2001, p. A1; James Risen and Judith Miller, "A Nation Challenged: Chemical Weapons—Al Qaeda Sites Point to Tests of Chemicals," *New York Times*, November 11, 2001, p. B1; Douglas Frantz and David Rohde, "A Nation Challenged: Biological Terror—2 Pakistanis Linked to Papers on Anthrax Weapons," *New York Times*, November 28, 2001; and David Rohde, "A Nation Challenged: The Evidence—Germ Weapons Plans Found at a Scientist's House in Kabul," *New York Times*, December 1, 2001.

36. Laqueur, *Terrorism*, pp. 112–116.

37. Ibid., pp. 115–116.

38. Groups with known or alleged connections to al-Qaeda include Jemaah Islamiyah (Indonesia, Malaysia, and Singapore), the Abu Sayyaf group (Philippines), al-Gama'a al-Islamiyya (Egypt), Harakat ul-Mujahidin (Pakistan), the Islamic Movement of Uzbekistan (Central Asia), Jaish-e-Mohammed (India and Pakistan), and al-Jihad (Egypt).

39. For the purposes of this article, globalization is a gradually expanding process of interpenetration in the economic, political, social, and security realms, uncontrolled by (or apart from) traditional notions of state sovereignty. Victor D. Cha, "Globalization and the Study of International Security," *Journal of Peace Research*, Vol. 37, No. 3 (March 2000), pp. 391–393.

40. With respect to the Islamic world, there are numerous books and articles that point to the phenomenon of antipathy with the Western world, either because of broad cultural incompatibility or a specific conflict between Western consumerism and religious fundamentalism. Among the earliest and most notable are Samuel P. Huntington, "The Clash of Civilizations?" *Foreign Affairs*, Vol. 72, No. 3 (Summer 1993); Benjamin R. Barber, *Jihad vs. McWorld: Terrorism's Challenge to Democracy* (New York: Random House, 1995); and Samuel P. Huntington, *The Clash of Civilizations and the Remaking of World Order* (New York: Simon and Schuster, 1996).

41. For more on cyberterrorism, see Dorothy Denning, "Activism, Hacktivism, and Cyberterrorism: The Internet as a Tool for Influencing Foreign Policy," paper presented at Internet and International Systems: Information Technology and American Foreign Policy Decision-making Workshop at Georgetown University, http://www.nautilus.org/info-policy/workshop/papers/denning.html (accessed January 5, 2003); Dorothy Denning, "Cyberterrorism," testimony before the U.S. House Committee on Armed Services, Special Oversight Panel on Terrorism, 107th Cong., 1st sess., May 23, 2001, available on the Terrorism Research Center website, http://www.cs.georgetown.edu/?denning/infosec/cyberterror.html (accessed January 5, 2003); Jerold Post, Kevin Ruby, and Eric Shaw, "From Car Bombs to Logic Bombs: The Growing Threat of Information Terrorism," *Terrorism and Political Violence*, Vol. 12, No. 2 (Summer 2000), pp. 97–122; and Tom Regan, "When Terrorists Turn to the Internet," *Christian Science Monitor*, July 1, 1999, http://www.csmonitor.com (accessed January 5, 2003).

42. Ibid. Dorothy Denning cites numerous examples, among them: In 1989, hackers released a computer worm into the NASA Space Physics Analysis Network in an attempt to stop a shuttle launch; during Palestinian riots in October 2000, pro-Israeli hackers defaced the Hezbollah website; and in 1999, following the mistaken U.S. bombing of the Chinese embassy in Belgrade during the war in Kosovo, Chinese hackers attacked the websites of the U.S. Department of the Interior, showing images of the three journalists killed during the bombing.

43. Paul R. Pillar, *Terrorism and U.S. Foreign Policy* (Washington, D.C.: Brookings, 2001), p. 47.

44. Ibid.

45. Simon Reeve, *The New Jackals: Ramzi Yousef, Osama bin Laden, and the Future of Terrorism* (Boston: Northeastern University Press, 1999), p. 260.

46. Dorothy Denning, "Cyberwarriors: Activists and Terrorists Turn to Cyberspace," *Harvard International Review*, Vol. 23, No. 2 (Summer 2001), pp. 70–75. See also Brian J. Miller, "Terror.org: An Assessment of Terrorist Internet Sites," Georgetown University, December 6, 2000.

47. Miller, "Terror.org," pp. 9, 12.

48. Steganography is the embedding of messages usually in pictures, where the messages are disguised so that they cannot be seen with the naked eye. See Denning, "Cyberwarriors."

49. I am indebted to Dorothy Denning for all of this information. The Provisional IRA hired contract hackers to find the addresses of British intelligence and law enforcement officers. See Denning, "Cyberterrorism"; and Denning, "Cyberwarriors."

50. There are many recent sources on CBNR. Among the best are Jonathan B. Tucker, ed., *Toxic Terror: Assessing Terrorist Use of Chemical and Biological Weapons* (Cambridge, Mass.: MIT Press, 2000); Joshua Lederberg, *Biological Weapons: Limiting the Threat* (Cambridge, Mass.: MIT Press, 1999); Richard A. Falkenrath, Robert D. Newman, and Bradley A. Thayer, *America's Achilles' Heel: Nuclear, Biological, and Chemical Terrorism and Covert Attack* (Cambridge, Mass.: MIT Press, 1998); Gurr and Cole, *The New Face of Terrorism*; Jessica

Stern, *The Ultimate Terrorists* (Cambridge, Mass.: Harvard University Press, 1999); and Brad Roberts, ed., *Terrorism with Chemical and Biological Weapons: Calibrating Risks and Responses* (Alexandria, Va.: Chemical and Biological Arms Control Institute, 1997).

51. See Falkenrath, Newman, and Thayer, *America's Achilles' Heel*, pp. 31–46.

52. A clear example of this phenomenon was the uncovering in December 2001 of a multinational plot in Singapore by the international terrorist group Jemaah Islamiyah to blow up several Western targets, including the U.S. embassy. A videotape of the intended targets (including a description of the plans in Arabic) was discovered in Afghanistan after al-Qaeda members fled. Thus there are clear connections between these organizations, as well as evidence of cooperation and coordination of attacks. See, for example, Dan Murphy, "'Activated' Asian Terror Web Busted," *Christian Science Monitor*, January 23, 2002, http://www.csmonitor.com (accessed January 23, 2002); and Rajiv Chandrasekaran, "Al Qaeda's Southeast Asian Reach," *Washington Post*, February 3, 2002, p. A1.

53. Rensselaer Lee and Raphael Perl, "Terrorism, the Future, and U.S. Foreign Policy," issue brief for Congress, received through the Congressional Research Service website, order code IB95112, Congressional Research Service, Library of Congress, July 10, 2002, p. CRS-6.

54. Roger G. Weiner, "The Financing of International Terrorism," Terrorism and Violence Crime Section, Criminal Division, U.S. Department of Justice, October 2001, p. 3. According to Weiner, the *hawala* (or *hundi*) system "relies entirely on trust that currency left with a particular service provider or merchant will be paid from bank accounts he controls overseas to the recipient specified by the party originating the transfer." Ibid. See also Douglas Frantz, "Ancient Secret System Moves Money Globally," *New York Times*, October 3, 2001, http://www.nytimes.com (accessed October 3, 2001).

55. International efforts to freeze bank accounts and block transactions between suspected terrorists have hindered, at least to some degree, al-Qaeda's ability to finance attacks; however, a proportion remains unaccounted for. "Cash Moves a Sign Al-Qaeda Is Regrouping," *Straits Times*, March 18, 2002, http://www.straitstimes.asia1.com.sg (accessed March 18, 2002).

56. U.S. Department of State, *Patterns of Global Terrorism, 2001*. According to the U.S. Department of State, Hezbollah also may have transferred resources by selling millions of dollars' worth of Congolese diamonds to finance operations in the Middle East.

57. Douglas Farah, "Al Qaeda's Road Paved with Gold," *Washington Post*, February 17, 2002, pp. A1, A32.

58. Pillar, *Terrorism and U.S. Foreign Policy*, p. 48.

59. Many in the United States focus on the technologies of terrorism, with a much less developed interest in the motivations of terrorists. Brian M. Jenkins, "Understanding the Link between Motives and Methods," in Roberts, *Terrorism with Chemical and Biological Weapons*, pp. 43–51. An example of a study that focuses on weapons and not motives is Sidney D. Drell, Abraham D. Sofaer, and George W. Wilson, eds., *The New Terror: Facing the Threat of Biological and Chemical Weapons* (Stanford, Calif.: Hoover Institution, 1999).

60. Christopher Coker, *Globalisation and Insecurity in the Twenty-first Century: NATO and the Management of Risk*, Adelphi Paper 345 (London: International Institute for Strategic Studies, June 2002), p. 40.

61. The indicators studied included respect for human rights and human freedoms, the empowerment of women, and broad access to and utilization of knowledge. See United Nations Development Programme, Arab Fund for Economic and Social Development, *Arab Human Development Report, 2002: Creating Opportunities for Future Generations* (New York: United Nations Development Programme, 2002).

62. Martha Crenshaw, "Why America? The Globalization of Civil War," *Current History*, December 2001, pp. 425–432.

63. A number of recent arguments have been put forth about the relationship between poverty and terrorism. See, for example, Anatol Lieven, "The Roots of Terrorism, and a Strategy against It," Prospect (London), October 2001, http://www.ceip.org/files/Publications/lieventerrorism.asp?from=pubdate (accessed November 17, 2002); and Daniel Pipes, "God and Mammon: Does Poverty Cause Militant Islam?" *National Interest*, No. 66 (Winter 2001/02), pp. 14–21. This is an extremely complex question, however, and much work remains to be done. On the

origins of the new religious terrorism, see Hoffman, *Inside Terrorism*; and Mark Juergensmeyer, *Terror in the Mind of God: The Global Rise of Religious Violence* (Berkeley: University of California Press, 2000). Important earlier studies on the sources of terrorism include Martha Crenshaw, "The Causes of Terrorism," *Comparative Politics*, July 1981, pp. 379–399; Martha Crenshaw, *Terrorism in Context* (University Park: Pennsylvania State University Press, 1995); and Walter Reich, ed., *Origins of Terrorism: Psychologies, Ideologies, Theologies, States of Mind*, 2d ed. (Washington, D.C.: Woodrow Wilson Center for International Scholars, 1998).

64. For more discussion on the traditional elements of U.S. grand strategy, especially military strategy, see Barry R. Posen, "The Struggle against Terrorism: Grand Strategy, Strategy, and Tactics," *International Security*, Vol. 26, No. 3 (Winter 2001/02), pp. 39–55.

65. George F. Kennan, "The Sources of Soviet Conduct," *Foreign Affairs*, Vol. 25, No. 4 (July 1947), pp. 575–576.

66. See the extremely insightful article by Bruce W. Jentleson, "The Need for Praxis: Bringing Policy Relevance Back In," *International Security*, Vol. 26, No. 4 (Spring 2002), pp. 169–183.

67. I am indebted to Fiona Adamson for this observation.

68. Important terrorism scholars in the think tank community include Walter Laqueur (Center for Strategic and International Studies), Brian Jenkins (RAND), Bruce Hoffman (RAND) and, from the intelligence community, Paul Pillar. This list is illustrative, not comprehensive.

69. On these issues, see Cronin and Ludes, T*he Campaign against International Terrorism.*

I am grateful for helpful comments and criticisms on previous drafts from Robert Art, Patrick Cronin, Timothy Hoyt, James Ludes, and an anonymous reviewer. I have been greatly influenced by conversations and other communications with Martha Crenshaw, to whom I owe a huge debt. None of these people necessarily agrees with everything here. Also beneficial was a research grant from the School of Foreign Service at Georgetown University. My thanks to research assistants Christopher Connell, William Josiger, and Sara Skahill and to the members of my graduate courses on political violence and terrorism. Portions of this article will be published as "Transnational Terrorism and Security: The Terrorist Threat to Globalization," in Michael E. Brown, ed., *Grave New World: Global Dangers in the Twenty-First Century* (Washington, D.C.: Georgetown University Press, forthcoming).

Patrick D. Buckley and Michael J. Meese,* 2003

The Financial Front in the Global War on Terrorism

We will direct every resource at our command to win the war against terrorists: every means of diplomacy, every tool of intelligence, every instrument of law enforcement, every financial influence. We will starve the terrorists of funding, turn them against each other, rout them out of their safe hiding places, and bring them to justice.

—President George W. Bush
September 24, 2001

Since the terrorist attacks of September 11, 2001, the United States has aggressively executed the global war on terrorism on many different fronts. The approval of Executive Order 13224 on September 24, 2001, marked a bold initial step toward targeting terrorists' financial networks. The success of terrorist organizations is dependent upon these financial networks because though terrorist attacks are not necessarily expensive, the support of international terrorist networks, training camps, command and control, and infrastructure requires either a large reserve of available finances or the ability to raise significant funding. Estimates of al-Qaeda's current funding vary widely, but it is believed that prior to the Taliban's removal from power, al-Qaeda's annual expenses were at least $36 million on top of an initial fixed cost of approximately $50 million for equipment and infrastructure.[1]

However, while it is expensive, terrorism is not a profitable economic enterprise. Unlike organized crime, human trafficking, the narcotics trade, or other illegal activities, terrorism requires an independent source of financing to begin and continue its operations. Terrorist organizations also require a method of distributing these funds around the world in order to conduct their operations on a global scale.

Because terrorist organizations must raise, move, and use money, aggressively pursuing terrorists on a financial front can and should be an integral component of any counterterrorism strategy. There are three different but interrelated dimensions of this front that either target terrorists' financial networks or capitalize on terrorists' dependency on finances. Focusing on these aspects of terrorists' finances can contribute to the disruption of terrorists' financial support as well as aid in the identification and, ultimately, the destruction of terrorist organizations.

First, the government can freeze and block financial assets by labeling individuals or organizations as terrorists or as being associated with terrorism. These actions degrade

* The authors teach in the Department of Social Sciences, U.S. Military Academy, West Point, New York. The authors gratefully acknowledge support from the U.S. Army War College Strategic Studies Institute to develop and present this research. The opinions expressed herein reflect the view of the authors and not necessarily those of the United States Military Academy, the Army, or any other government organization.

terrorists' access to funds and increase the costs of raising, transferring, and using funds. This may reduce the resources that terrorists can use to execute attacks and, hence, the geographic scope and lethality of their attacks.

Second, tracking the movement of funds among individuals in terrorist groups and their supporters provides verifiable indications of associations, relationships, and networks. Understanding these financial linkages provides an extremely useful, tangible complement to the connections that are developed from human, signal, open source, and other forms of intelligence. Through a coordinated system of collection, reporting, and analysis, this intelligence can assist authorities in identifying and locating terrorist organizations and their financial support networks.

Third, many of the acts in which terrorist networks engage to raise and move funds are *per se* illegal and would be illegal even if the individuals involved were not associated with terrorism. Terrorists and their financial supporters frequently commit illegal fund raising, money laundering, tax evasion, fraud, and international currency violations. Thus, prosecuting individuals for financial crimes can be effective in coordinating the efforts of law enforcement authorities, can facilitate international investigations, and ultimately may lead to the imprisonment of terrorists.

With this framework we examine some of the actions taken and lessons learned by the multiple agencies, corporations, and individuals that have all played critical roles on the financial front in the global war on terrorism. This analysis reveals insights into the uses and implications of these tactics and how they can effectively fit into an overall campaign to combat terrorism. More importantly, the lessons demonstrate how these tactics are interrelated and will be most effective if law enforcement, financial, intelligence, and military personnel are able to use selective actions against specific terrorist targets.

Freezing and Blocking Financial Assets

The freezing and blocking of financial assets have been the most publicized government actions attacking terrorist financing since September 11. Executive Order 13224 gives the secretary of the treasury the authority to freeze the financial assets of terrorists, terrorist organizations, and those associated with terrorist groups and to impose controls on transactions with these entities. Such sanctions are executed and administered by the Treasury Department's Office of Foreign Assets Control (OFAC) with additional enforcement by the department's Financial Crimes Enforcement Network (FinCEN). OFAC maintains and publishes the list of Special Designated Nationals and Blocked Person (SDNs) in the Federal Register, and U.S. businesses, including banks and securities brokers, are prohibited from executing financial transactions with these persons and groups, or their aliases.

These sanctions are intended to deny terrorists and their associates access to international financial systems and to significantly increase the cost of raising, transferring, and using funds. Freezing assets cuts off the terrorists' money supply, and blocking transactions prevents terrorists from moving the money around. The combination of these two effects simultaneously accomplishes two key strategic objectives. First, decreasing terrorists' resources and disrupting their ability to raise funds reduces their operational capabilities in terms of the sophistication, degree of synchronization, and lethality of their attacks. Second, denying terrorists the ability to transfer funds internationally isolates them and reduces the geographical scope of their activities and operations. These two outcomes support the overall objective of the national counter-terrorism strategy, which is to contain terrorism within the domain of national law enforcement.

Before September 11, the secretary of the treasury had the authority to impose these sanctions, but actions were mostly taken against hostile nations and narcotics traffickers. Executive Order 13224 significantly expanded the authority of the secretary of the treasury to designate for blocking actions not just terrorists and terrorist organizations but also individuals and organizations *associated with* terrorists. Additionally, the order broadened the scope of the sanctions' coverage from terrorism in the Middle Eastern to global terrorism. Because these blocking actions are based upon foreign policy, they are not subject to the same evidentiary standards as criminal proceedings. Moreover, evidence to support an order to block transactions and freeze assets may come from classified sources that do not have to be revealed to anyone other than a reviewing court.[2]

Financial institutions are required to maintain updated SDN lists and to report both the holding of frozen assets and any attempts to conduct transactions to or from an account of a designated individual or group, regardless of whether the designated individual holds the account within the United States. Businesses report matches to the SDN list and any suspected money laundering activity to FinCEN via Suspicious Activities Reports (SARs) in accordance with the Bank Security Act. To comply with these regulations, most banks have developed sophisticated account databases for verifying the legitimacy of transactions. To improve the fidelity in scrutinizing transactions, the 2001 USA PATRIOT Act[3] requires minimum identity verification standards for account holders. However, these standards have proven to be especially problematic for securities brokers, who often conduct business through mail and by phone. The rules have become so troublesome that a recent Securities Industry Association Anti-Money Laundering Compliance Conference focused on clarifying the complicated and sometimes opaque legal requirements of the PATRIOT Act and methods of ensuring compliance.[4]

By September 2002, 236 individuals and groups had been designated for blocking actions, including 112 individuals and 74 front organizations and charities, and $34 million in assets had been frozen in the United States with another $78 million in assets frozen overseas.[5] In most cases, these are multilateral sanctions that involve close cooperation with other governments. In fact, INTERPOL serves as the international clearinghouse for foreign law enforcement agencies for the lists of sanctioned individuals and organizations.[6]

The government has especially highlighted how effective these sanctions have been in disrupting the fund-raising of terrorists' front organizations and charities. Officials have dismantled the al-Barakaat worldwide financial network, which channeled several million dollars yearly to al-Qaeda, and the Holy Land Foundation for Relief and Development, which claimed to be largest U.S.-based Islamic charity and provided millions of dollars to the Hamas terrorist organization. OFAC has also blocked the assets of the Global Relief Foundation (GRF) and the Benevolence International Foundation, two other charities with U.S. branches and alleged ties to terrorist organizations.[7] The GRF claims that it is a legitimate charity that is suffering from the poisonous effects of these financial sanctions. It has filed lawsuits against the government as well as defamation suits against the *New York Times*, *Boston Globe*, and the Associated Press.[8]

In addition to attacking terrorists' finances in the formal financial sector, the government has placed increased scrutiny on the surreptitious movement of funds through the underground banking system. Informal Value Transfer Systems, known as *hawalas* in the

Muslim world, are infamous methods of transferring or laundering money internationally. Because *hawalas* rarely maintain detailed records or require individual identification, they allow terrorists to covertly raise funds and to move these funds around the world without a trace. With the passing of the USA PATRIOT Act, *hawalas* operating in the United States are required to register as "money service businesses," which subjects them to money laundering regulations, including the requirement that they file SARs and Currency Transaction Reports for transactions involving more than $10,000. More than 10,000 money service businesses are now registered with the Treasury Department, which means the government now has some visibility into a previously unregulated financial arena.[9] Additionally, the USA PATRIOT Act criminalizes the transfer of funds that the business owner knows are the proceeds of a crime or are intended to be used in unlawful activity.

Admittedly, however, there may be some limits to the effectiveness of these sanctions. Conduits for money transferring may be created through countries with limited bank supervision, ineffective enforcement of money laundering laws, or governments that tend to "look the other way." Though more than 165 countries have issued blocking orders against terrorists' assets,[10] the Council on Foreign Relations and other foreign policy analysts have severely criticized the degree of scrutiny exercised in the enforcement of these actions in some nations, particularly Saudi Arabia.[11] In fact, the council estimates that only a small fraction of al-Qaeda's available assets have been frozen.[12] However, the Bush administration has downplayed this criticism by noting that more than eighty countries have implemented or are in the process of implementing new laws to combat terrorist financing.[13]

Ultimately, determining the effectiveness of blocking actions in raising terrorists' transaction costs and disrupting terrorists' financial networks will be extremely difficult. Certainly, it has become more difficult for terrorists to raise and move money, but it is unclear how rapidly organizations discount the blocked assets and pursue other financial channels. It is likely that evidence of how effective these blocking actions are will come through testimony from terrorists and anecdotes of increased frugality in operations[14] or, at best, through decreases in the frequency, lethality, and global range of terrorist attacks.

The Intelligence Aspects of Terrorists' Finances— Following the Money

The second dimension of the financial front of the global war on terrorism involves the invaluable intelligence investigators can gain from "following the money." Because financial transactions are normally well-documented, identifying the financial structure of terrorist groups and tracking the movement of funds can provide a hard evidence trail of associations, relationships, and networks. This evidence can ultimately allow authorities in law enforcement, intelligence, the military, and other agencies to identify, locate, and apprehend terrorists. The financial linkages derived from business records provide a tremendous, verifiable complement to the relationships developed from human, signal, and open source intelligence and evidence gained from seized personal records and computer files. The front businesses and charities that raise and launder funds for terrorists are especially susceptible to this line of investigation because they are financial organizations.

The Treasury and Justice Departments attribute many successes in the investigation and dismantling of terrorist organizations to financial intelligence. Shortly after the September 11 attacks, FinCEN and the Federal Bureau of Investigation (FBI) identified the

24 bank accounts (all of which were normal checking accounts) that the hijackers held at four different, well-known banks and linked them to their overseas financial support network.[15] Additionally, the Treasury Department credits over 2,400 arrests in 95 countries and the prevention of terrorist attacks in Singapore, Morocco, and Germany in part to intelligence derived from terrorists' financial trails.[16] The capture of financial coordinators such as Mustafa Ahmed Al-Hawsawi, who was apprehended in the raid that also nabbed al-Qaeda operations chief Khalid Sheikh Mohammed, has made officials especially optimistic about windfalls of financial intelligence. Al-Hawsawi provided the financial support for the September 11 hijackers, and the FBI initially identified him by tracing money transfers from Dubai to Florida, New York, and Germany. In another example, the Treasury Department reported that documents found in the Afghan offices of the Wafa Humanitarian Organization, a Pakistan-based al-Qaeda front organization, intimately linked the charity with terrorist assassination plots and the distribution of chemical and biological warfare manuals.[17]

The development of coordinated systems and procedures to effectively analyze and share data between both domestic and foreign agencies is imperative for deriving intelligence value from financial information. Shortly after September 11, the Department of Justice established the interagency Terrorism Financial Review Group (TFRG) under the FBI as a centralized, comprehensive investigator of terrorist financial matters. The FBI subsequently expanded and restructured the TFRG into the Terrorist Financing Operations Section (TFOS), which has the broad purpose of identifying, investigating, prosecuting, and dismantling all terrorist-related financial and fundraising activities.[18] TFOS's centralized terrorist financial database is critical to its investigations. The database compiles information from subpoenaed account records, Suspicious Activities Reports (of which there were over 265,000 filed in the 12 months after September 11, 2001),[19] Currency Transactions Reports, FBI field office records of foreign bank accounts and wire transfers, and intelligence collected by other agencies.[20] The Herculean task of mining this data allows authorities to follow known leads and to search for signals, patterns, and profiles of financial activities that may identify new leads on active terrorist operations and potential "sleeper" cells.

Besides the FBI, other agencies involved in investigating terrorist finances include OFAC, FinCEN, the U.S. Customs Service's Operation Green Quest, and, at the international level, the Financial Action Task Force. All of these agencies have publicly acclaimed the importance and benefits of financial investigations for developing evidence, linkages, and new leads to terrorists. Interagency cooperation generates an especially dramatic synergy that renders seemingly benign financial records separately obtained by different agencies into a critically informative map of terrorist organizations. For example, alias information from intelligence gained in Afghanistan may lead to OFAC blocking actions resulting in a bank filing an SAR, an investigation of transactions with that account, and ultimately, links to a multitude of terrorists, their supporters, and their locations. If properly managed and exploited, these techniques can exponentially generate new leads and confirm or deny previous reports.

Several measures in the USA PATRIOT Act facilitate the thorough and timely interagency information sharing required for more effective investigations and data-mining. The act permits financial institutions, their regulatory agencies, and law enforcement authorities to share information about individuals suspected of engaging in terrorist acts or money laundering. Additionally, the act reduces the complexity of the signature authority requirements for National Security Letters, which are administrative subpoenas issued in

Figure 1

Intelligence Analysis Problem

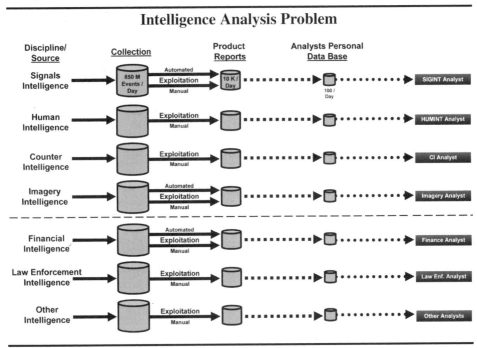

counter-terrorism and counter-intelligence investigations. These changes allow more timely and efficient gathering of records and information from financial institutions, credit bureaus, telephone companies, and Internet service providers.[21]

Interagency cooperation and legislative measures that facilitate information sharing are extremely important first steps in increasing the usefulness of all intelligence data. However, these measures generally represent lateral links between otherwise fairly stove-piped organizations. Military, financial, and law enforcement intelligence collection, reporting, and analysis are all conducted by the respective organizations with limited coordinating oversight, as depicted in Figure 1.[22] While intelligence data certainly can be pushed and pulled between agencies, the challenges of this structure are a lack of a centralized direction for intelligence collection and limitations on conducting meta-analysis of information across the different intelligence systems. The absence of such coordination may reduce the usefulness of financial intelligence because it would be difficult to correlate financial intelligence with all other information. Some critics argue that while financial evidence alone is beneficial for proving a case after the fact, it seldom leads to preventing attacks[23] and that searching financial data for suspicious transaction patterns is analogous to looking for a needle in a haystack.

But, a centralized, coordinating entity might better exploit available financial information through improved linkages with other sources of intelligence, affording information dominance and improving our overall picture of terrorists' networks. The creation of the Department of Homeland Security and efforts to consolidate information by the TFOS are significant advances, at least on the domestic side, toward a coordinated information dom-

Figure 2

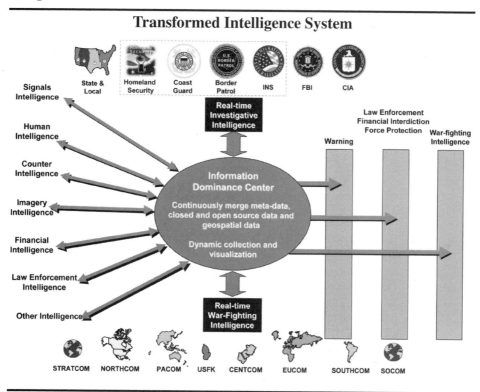

Transformed Intelligence System

inance center (as indicated by Figure 2). However, intelligence collection and analysis by internationally focused agencies are not habitually integrated into these processes. Generally, such coordination occurs through *ad hoc* coordinating groups, as described in the next section of this paper, which typically operate under regional military commanders. The ultimate goal of this financial intelligence integration is to enhance the warning of terrorist attacks, to increase law enforcement interdiction, and to improve war-fighting intelligence.

The Law Enforcement Aspects of Terrorists' Finances

Providing material support to terrorists is illegal, and this type of activity also serves as a predicate action for committing other crimes, such as fraudulent fund raising, money laundering, tax evasion, and fraud. Judicious enforcement of criminal statutes that are typically associated with white-collar and organized crime can be an especially effective tactic against terrorists and their financial supporters in two ways.

First, evidence of illegal financial activity provides a nexus between finance and law enforcement authorities and can facilitate international investigations. Even if some governments or businesses fail to recognize that a group is involved in terrorism, financial crimes provide *prima facie* evidence of wrongdoing that can solidify resolve to investigate or otherwise attack those groups. An example of this is the case of a Hezbollah cell discovered in North Carolina during what was initially a cigarette-smuggling and racke-teering investigation that led to the indictment of more than 20 terrorist supporters.[24]

Second, just as Al Capone was eventually jailed for tax evasion, prosecuting terror-ists and their supporters for their financial crimes may be the most effective way to im-prison them. Financial crimes have audit trails that can be substantively proved in court, and prosecutions can sometimes take place without compromising sensitive intelligence that would otherwise have to be revealed to obtain a conviction on specific acts related to terrorism. To date, federal prosecutors have filed criminal complaints and indictments against individuals related to terrorism for many different financial crimes including rack-eteering, bank fraud, credit card fraud, money laundering, and embezzlement and many other non-financial crimes such as perjury and identification fraud.

One way to illustrate the impact of using criminal investigation and prosecution in the war on terrorism is to analyze one of the most important and successful post–September 11 prosecutions, that of terrorist financial coordinator Enaam Arnaout. The investigation, indictment, and prosecution of Arnaout also highlights the integration of the previous tactics—blocking assets and following financial transactions—which was crucial to devel-oping the information necessary for identifying Arnaout as a target for an international fi-nancial investigation. Additionally, the Arnaout case illustrates the kind of international cooperation that is required to combat terrorism, in this instance between the United States and the Bosnian governments.

The case against Enaam Arnaout started when officials began carefully examining the actions of charitable organizations around the world as potential conduits for terrorist funding and as "covers" for individuals. A detailed *New York Times* article explained that Bosnia was a logical support area for terrorism:

> Much of the worldwide investigation into suspicious charities focuses on Bosnia, a bat-tle-scarred country where dozens of Islamic groups set up shop from 1992 to 1995 dur-ing ethnic warfare with Serbs and Croats. The groups provided aid to Bosnian Muslims and to Arabs who came to fight with them. Hundreds of charity officials stayed… West-ern officials said that some charities had another mission: serving as gateways for ex-tremists to infiltrate Europe and receive money. "Charities are the best cover," an American official said. "They do good works with one hand and provide money and cover for terrorists with the other hand."[25]

OFAC collected information about the finances of one such charity—the Benevolence In-ternational Foundation (BIF)—and determined that some of its activities could reasonably be interpreted as support of terrorism. Consequently, OFAC moved to freeze and block BIF's assets. In an attempt to have these sanctions lifted, Enaam Arnaout, the executive di-rector of BIF, made several sworn statements denying any involvement with terrorism.

Simultaneously, authorities in Bosnia and the United States pursued Arnaout's finan-cial transactions and those of several other Bosnian charities. Officials identified transac-tions that included cash withdrawals of more than $500,000 by Arnaout in the year 2000 alone. One official in the Bosnian government explained, "There is a huge chance… that money was used for terrorist operations."[26] Examination of Citibank records revealed 19 transfers totaling $685,560 sent from BIF to terrorist groups in Chechnya in the first four months of April 2000. Following the financial documentation helped law enforcement and intelligence officials understand BIF's global reach, exposed its support of terrorist activities, and provided additional details about the links and relationships between different terrorist organizations and their supporters.

Eventually, U.S. officials moved beyond blocking assets and gathering intelligence, and identified Enaam Arnaout as the target of a criminal investigation. As Arnaout's indictment eventually explained, the FBI had developed several sources, including confidential informants, who provided information about Arnaout's involvement in terrorist activities and links to Usama Bin Laden.[27] This information was shared with Bosnian authorities, who were able to conduct no-notice searches of eight locations affiliated with BIF in Bosnia. In these locations, authorities recovered computers and other material that unquestionably documented detailed relationships between Usama Bin Laden and Enaam Arnaout.

In Bosnia and in other major regions, the U.S. government has established a Joint Interagency Coordination Group (JIACG) with each regional combatant commander to assist in breaking down the stovepipe nature of the different agencies involved in intelligence collection and analysis. As a publication of the Joint Forces Command explains, "The JIACG is as a multi-functional, advisory element that represents the civilian departments and agencies and facilitates information sharing across the interagency community. It provides regular, timely, and collaborative day-to-day working relationships between civilian and military operational planners."[28] Whether a JIACG that operates under the auspices of the military commander is the best solution for coordinating intelligence efforts is open for discussion. But the Arnaout case indicates that some kind of interagency coordination is absolutely essential for success in the war on terrorism.

Interestingly, Arnaout's initial indictment was based on false statements he made in his request that the United States release BIF's assets. In refusing bail for Arnaout, Magistrate Ian H. Levin declared, "The reality is that this is not a simple perjury case. It is a perjury charge in the context of a terrorism financing investigation."[29] This indictment led to Arnaout's pleading guilty to racketeering in February 2003 and his subsequent cooperation with authorities. The Arnaout case, the case against the North Carolina Hezbollah cell, and the many other financial crimes indictments against terrorist supporters all emphasize the fact that terrorist fund-raising involves criminal acts beyond terrorism. Actively seeking out offenders of these crimes can significantly disrupt terrorist organizations, and prosecuting offenders for financial crimes may prove to be easier and less compromising than prosecutions that are directly related to terrorism.

Conclusions

The ongoing war against terrorism has demonstrated the critical importance of the three main approaches to fighting on the financial front in the global war on terrorism: freezing and blocking assets; following financial transactions to gain intelligence; and prosecuting terrorists and their supporters for financial crimes. Actions taken along these dimensions and the synergistic effects of using them in concert with each other have been extremely useful in disrupting terrorists' financial networks, helping to identify their global networks, and ultimately, leading to their apprehension. Given this framework for understanding the financial front, several important points warrant mentioning.

First, because the vast majority of terrorists' assets are located outside the United States, actions on the financial front must be conducted and facilitated at an international level to be most effective. This implies a need for intense international cooperation by developed countries in the establishment of effective financial monitoring capabilities in poorer nations. One of the obvious advantages for investigators in the Arnaout case was that the major investigative actions occurred in Bosnia, a country in which the United States had been operating for seven years and where a U.S. commander was in charge of the 36-nation peacekeeping force. The commander, General John Sylvester, praised the actions by the Bosnian Coordination Team and claimed that efforts in Bosnia served as good examples of multiethnic cooperation in fighting terrorism.[30] U.S. officials were full participants in the Bosnian counter-terrorism team. This unique situation not only facilitated cooperation with the Bosnian government, but it also helped integrate the multiple U.S. agencies involved in intelligence, military, and law enforcement operations.

The second important point about the financial war on terrorism is that actions taken in one of the three dimensions can actually degrade the effects of other efforts. For example, once an individual's financial assets have been blocked, that individual is effectively "tipped-off" that he is a terrorist suspect, and he may stop any activities that would be incriminating and would provide useful intelligence. Thus, while cooperation among agencies facilitates the effectiveness of individual actions, the involvement of multiple independent agencies makes the selection and implementation of a unified strategy problematic. Officials at the highest levels must understand that operational decision making for complex issues, such as when an investigation should transition from monitoring individuals and collecting information to apprehending and prosecuting them, is subject to different agencies' specific goals.

Finally, some of these recommended actions may have deleterious effects on society. They may place burdens on legitimate businesses and could infringe upon privacy rights and other civil liberties. Not only must the government exercise due diligence in prosecuting the war on terrorism, it should also provide as much transparency as security allows when assessing and making decisions regarding these other aspects of the war.

As time progresses, we will learn in greater detail how actions taken on the financial front are useful in dismantling terrorist organizations and whether they are aiding the prevention of terrorist attacks. There should be a continued focus on determining what legislative, organizational, and diplomatic actions can be taken to improve the effectiveness of different approaches. While the nature of terrorism has changed dramatically in the past few decades and may continue to evolve, one constant will remain: terrorist organizations will always require money. As such, targeting terrorists' financial networks and capitalizing on their dependency on finances will be an integral part of the strategy for combating terrorism.

Patrick D. Buckley is an assistant professor of economics at the United States Military Academy at West Point. He earned his doctorate in labor and public economics from the Massachusetts Institute of Technology.

Michael Meese is currently deputy head and an academy professor at the United States Military Academy at West Point. His research areas include defense economics and national security decision making. He has researched and written on the U.S. Army and the All Volunteer Force, and on the transformation of the South African National Defense Force.

Notes

1. Gunaratna, Rohan, *Inside Al Qaeda—Global Network of Terror*, New York: Columbia University Press, 2002, p. 61.
2. Zagaris, Bruce, "U.S. Court of Appeals Upholds Freeze of Global Relief Foundation," *International Enforcement Law Reporter*, Vol. 19, No. 3.
3. The official name for the act is the Uniting and Strengthening America by Providing Appropriate Tools Required to Intercept and Obstruct Terrorism of 2001, which was immediately known as the USA PATRIOT Act.
4. Securities Industry Association, "Anti-Money Laundering Compliance Conference," *Conference Report, 27 March 2003*. In addition to this printed report, information from the conference is available on line at: http://www.sia.com/antimoney03/.
5. U.S. Department of the Treasury, *Contributions of the Department of the Treasury to the Financial War on Terrorism—Fact Sheet*, September, 2002, p. 8.
6. U.S. Department of the Treasury, p. 22.
7. U.S. Department of the Treasury, pp. 13–14.
8. Jacoby, Mary, "Government Zips Its Lips on Frozen Funds," *St. Petersburg Times* (Florida), January 13, 2002.
9. U.S. Department of the Treasury, p. 16.
10. U.S. Department of the Treasury, p. 20.
11. Council on Foreign Relations, *Terrorist Financing—Report of an Independent Task Force*, 2002, pp. 8–9.
12. Council on Foreign Relations, pp. 15–16. This assessment is supported by others including Gunaratna, pp. 65–66.
13. U.S. Department of the Treasury, p. 20.
14. Gunaratna, pp. 64–65, gives several examples of thriftiness regarding the financing of terrorists operations.
15. U.S. Department of the Treasury, p. 20.
16. U.S. Department of the Treasury, p. 21.
17. U.S. Department of the Treasury, p. 14.
18. Lormel, Dennis, "Statement for the Record on USA PATRIOT ACT/Terrorism Financing Operations Sections Before the Senate Judiciary Committee, Subcommittee on Technology, Terrorism, and Government Information," October 9, 2002.
19. "The SAR Activity Review," February, 2003, p. 5.
20. Lormel.
21. Lormel.
22. These figures are adapted from slides used in a briefing by Admiral Arthur K. Cebrowski, Director of Defense Office of Force Transformation. Admiral Cebrowski emphasized the DoD aspect of intelligence fusion, and we have adapted his concept to include domestic agencies. His original slides were accessed on line at: http://www.oft.osd.mil/library/library_files/briefing_181_Transforming_Defense_13may03.ppt.
23. Malkin, Lawrence, and Yuval Elizur, "Terrorism's Money Trail," *World Policy Journal*, Vol. 19, 2002, p. 62.
24. Roig-Franzia, Manuel, "N.C. Man Convicted Of Aiding Hezbollah: Cigarette Smuggling Said to Fund Terror," *Washington Post*, June 22, 2002.
25. Frantz, Douglas, "Prosecutors See Possible Link between U.S.-Based Charity and Al-Qaeda," *New York Times*, June 14, 2002.
26. Whitmore, Brian, "Bosnian Charities Tied To Terror," *Boston Globe*, July 2, 2002.
27. The reports of the confidential source are detailed in *United States of America v. Benevolence International Foundation, Inc., and Enaam M. Arnaout*, case number 02CR04014, Affidavit by Special Agent Robert Walker, April 29, 2002.
28. United States Joint Forces Command, "Joint Interagency Coordination Group (JIACG)," Fact Sheet, accessed online at http://www.jfcom.mil/about/fact_jiacg.htm.
29. Frantz, *op. cit.*
30. "BiH Is Good Example of the War on Terrorism," *Bosnia Daily* (newspaper), May 9, 2002.

Robert Mandel, 2003

Fighting Fire with Fire
Privatizing Counterterrorism

Since the attack on the United States on September 11, 2001, interest has grown in exploring and implementing counterterrorism measures. Transnational terrorist groups, composed of forces spanning national boundaries seeking to achieve disruptive political ends through violence and threats of violence, are on the rise, and many see their future as bright.[1] President George W. Bush's remarks following the attack underscore the renewed American resolve to deal with this security threat: "We will not rest until terrorist groups of global reach have been found, have been stopped, and have been defeated."[2] To accomplish these goals, most conventional approaches have focused on various types of government action to reduce vulnerability. In the process, one avenue has been largely overlooked—the use of non-state groups to combat terrorism.

This analysis briefly explores this unorthodox strategy to add to—not replace—the counterterrorist arsenal traditionally available to national governments, especially the United States. What is presented here assumes that relevant policy makers have already decided that force is essential to combat this threat, in stark contrast to addressing terrorism through "softer" measures such as alleviating the sources of discontent, facilitating access for those disgruntled about the political process, or enacting new national or international laws. Thus noticeably absent is any discussion of the legitimacy—the legality or morality—of this approach to counterterrorism.

The Need for Unorthodox Counterterrorism Strategies

A primary reason to look outside the traditional responses to terrorism has been the decidedly checkered history of recent government counterterrorist measures. There are two central components to this uneven record: (1) deficiencies in our ability to collect information about these alienated groups, useful to formulate appropriate responses to past terrorist actions, disrupt ongoing terrorist initiatives, and prevent future terrorist attacks; and (2) deficiencies in our ability to implement effective coercive military measures against these groups so as to eliminate directly the sources of immediate danger. Greater success in the first area is clearly a prerequisite to greater success in the second, but—despite throwing lots of government money and personnel in this direction and the recent success in Afghanistan against al Qaeda—the United States and its allies have been largely stymied in correcting both inadequacies.

Looking first at the ability to gather information about this threat, from an intelligence standpoint transnational terrorist groups pose perhaps the most elusive target imaginable, evidenced by concerns expressed right after the September 11, 2001, attack:

> If the perpetrators are in fact Islamic extremists, by the very nature of their organization, there's a real law enforcement security penetration problem. In all likelihood they grew up together, they are related somehow, members of the same tribe and they have a common fervor and hate for Western society. It is not just a matter of saying let's put five agents undercover and penetrate the group.[3]

Because "it takes a long time to build a team of experts who understand the language, culture, politics, society, and economic circumstances surrounding terrorist groups," and because "neither bin Laden nor any other terrorist is likely to confide a full operational plan to a single individual, no matter how carefully placed as a source," terrorist "spying requires great skill and discipline, something that cannot be achieved quickly or by throwing money at it."[4] Many analysts recognize that "the challenge that security forces and militaries around the world have faced in countering terrorism is how to obtain information about an enigmatic enemy who fights unconventionally and operates in a highly amenable environment where he typically is indistinguishable from the civilian populace."[5] These groups are often geographically dispersed, ideologically committed, constantly changing membership, flexible in strategy, and most importantly next-to-impossible to penetrate using moles, bribes, or coercion. Due to these traits, most major foreign terrorist attacks have caught victims by surprise. "'Know your enemy' is one of the most accepted maxims in warfare"; yet even the United States government, even with all of its efforts since September 11, 2001, admits that the "knowledge of the inner workings of some terrorist organizations remains incomplete";[6] in truth the American government now has "only a rough idea of where terrorist training camps, quasi regular units, or clandestine units are hiding."[7]

Turning to the ability to implement effective coercive military measures against this threat, most state responses to terrorism have been largely unsuccessful. Although the United States has responded with military force to only a tiny minority of anti-American terrorist incidents,[8] Israel has used anti-terrorist coercive measures—particularly assassination—much more frequently, but with decidedly mixed results.[9] Often the force employed hits the wrong target, and even when the correct target is struck frequently martyrs are created who spawn even more widespread terrorist activity. The conundrum surrounding what to strike is compounded by the conundrum surrounding what to protect, as the United States (as well as other advanced industrial societies) has a huge number of "high-value potential targets."[10] Moreover, the capacity of terrorists to act "has been greatly enhanced by globalization, organizational networking, and information-based technology"; they employ "stealth and deception to attack in unconventional and asymmetrical ways" while receiving aid and sanctuary from states, private organizations, and individuals.[11]

In his commencement address to the graduating class at the United States Military Academy in 2002, President George W. Bush explained that the September 11, 2001, attack represented "a new kind of war fought by a new kind of enemy," and that these new threats require "new thinking" beyond the traditional premises of deterrence, containment, and international sanctions.[12] In making these remarks, he points to the inadequacy of just relying on standard government defense operating procedures. Even state military forces themselves realize limitations in their ability to combat terrorism: "most military forces are generally uncomfortable with, and inadequately prepared for, counterterrorist operations," as "military forces in such unfamiliar settings must learn to acquire intelligence by methods markedly different from those to which they are accustomed."[13]

The Context of Global Anarchy

Today's anarchic international setting provides further justification for looking for new ways to combat terrorism. National governments have not been able to prevent an ever increasing quantity of deadly transfers[14] from flowing largely unfettered from country to country: across porous national boundaries we witness the unprecedented spread of covert arms, illegal migrants, and illicit narcotics. While Western states have attempted repeatedly to sanction such flows, the results have most frequently been resentment and misunderstanding. The West operates as if a mix of military coercion, economic dependence, legal prohibition, and moral outrage will suffice to quell unruly cross-national behavior, a premise that appears particularly flawed when applied to terrorism.

Within this chaotic structure, non-state groups like terrorists appear particularly empowered to subvert Western desires. For those that feel unable to be upwardly mobile in the global hierarchy, violating global norms may be a primary means for escaping from a stifling and humiliating status quo, a system whose premises they feel powerless to influence.[15] The combination of the promotion of free expression and the absence of coherent norms can increase the potential perceived legitimacy of terrorist claims, making it likely that many will choose to collude with them for private gain or ignore their disruptive behavior as long as it does not affect them directly. Those like terrorists who do not want to play by the rules know that in today's international system it is extremely difficult for any major state power to exert effective long-run pressure on them to change their behavior, and indeed a significant component of their status appears to derive from their ability to thwart in a flagrant way the major powers' rules of the game and to get away with this without suffering devastating consequences. Thus these unruly actors can exploit this major power limitation to their advantage in a way that makes their defiant power ever more visible.

Moreover, Western democracies have found themselves consistently handicapped by their own civility in confronting foreign terrorists. While most terrorist groups utilize any means at their disposal to wreak havoc, with the greatest notoriety and arguably effectiveness associating with tactics that send shock waves around the world, advanced industrial societies usually feel compelled to follow the restrained and civilized rules of modern warfare lest they be accused of stooping to the same level of barbarism as their adversaries. So can terrorism be stopped by the civil, orderly, restrained state methods acceptable within Western democracies? One must respond with a dose of healthy skepticism, as in order to combat effectively ruthless groups like terrorists, adopting bloody-minded warrior principles oneself may be essential.[16] Just as it rarely pays to be saintly in a bad neighborhood, it is rarely effective to rely on moral civility in a battle against desperate violent terrorists.

The Use of Transnational Criminal Organizations

Criminal organizations, coordinated more than ever across national boundaries, seek illegal economic gain through a variety of coercive and salacious business activities. Local, national, and transnational criminal syndicates not only ignore and violate state laws but also find it even easier for these organizations to ignore and violate the more poorly defined and less tightly enforced international laws in the open global environment. Transnational criminal organizations flourish in situations characterized by "weak structures and dubious legitimacy," as "they take advantage of the chaos that exists" and seek to perpetuate "the crisis of governance and decline of civil society that have become familiar features of the post–Cold War world."[17] If tensions emerge when a criminal organization from one country begins to encroach on the turf of another country's organization, the specter of ever larger profits has generally led to a quickly agreed upon coordinated transnational arrangement providing both with more than they had before. Because "there is no economic incentive for transnational organized crime to diminish," it is "growing rapidly and represents a global phenomenon that is penetrating political institutions, undermining legitimate economic growth, threatening democracy and the rule of law, and contributing to the post-Soviet problem of the eruption of small, regionally contained, ethnic violence."[18]

The power of today's transnational criminal organizations, dominated globally by the Italian mafia, Russian mobs, Japanese yakuza, Chinese triads, and Colombian cartels, has thus been growing by leaps and bounds: "in strategy, sophistication, and reach the criminal organizations of the late twentieth century function like transnational corporations and make the gangs of the past look like mom-and-pop operations."[19] The world's first independent mafia state emerged in 1993 when a powerful mafia family living in Sicily and Venezuela bought the sovereign Caribbean island of Aruba using a fortune amassed through the North American heroin trade.[20]

In attempting to remedy the critical information deficiency faced by counterterrorism, it is important to remember that national governments have been using for some time private non-state groups to collect intelligence, with many such groups providing such services as risk-analysis, counter-espionage, counter-intelligence, information security, and physical security advice.[21] Moreover, virtually all government intelligence operations already utilize as sources a variety of unsavory private groups who have direct knowledge about terrorist issues, consistent with the mandate of the American Terrorist Threat Integration Center to enhance the assimilation of comprehensive all-source analysis on terrorism.

Transnational criminal organizations seem particularly well suited to gather intelligence on global terrorism. First, their global interconnections give them special access to keep track of what crosses national boundaries below the radar of state government monitoring. Second, these criminal groups are free to use any methods necessary to get the information they need, a particularly important issue given the clear historical pattern that successfully gathering accurate intelligence on terrorists "has of necessity involved nasty and brutish means" often involving "widespread human-rights abuses, including torture."[22] Third, members of transnational criminal organizations are often deeply embedded in and familiar with local cultures from which terrorists emerge, as in many cases they have been recruited locally. In many ways, penetration of terrorist networks should be much easier when using inconspicuous mafia members rather than government intelligence operatives.

On the surface, there appears to be an insuperable obstacle here because of the difficulty of distinguishing clearly criminals from terrorists:

> The blurred distinction between the criminal and the political is evident in any number of revolutionary groups—Peru's Shining Path, which sells coca leaves to purchase plastique explosives; Sri Lanka's Tamil Tigers, who use kidnapping for ransom to finance their fourteen-year "people's war"; the Montana Freemen, who fill their coffers with proceeds from counterfeit financial instruments and forged checks. Over time, these groups' political agendas merge with their criminal ones, and it becomes difficult to see which agenda is the underlying one. Conversely, many organized criminal groups today employ the methods of traditional terrorism to maintain, protect, and expand their markets.[23]

Moreover, "whether it is the FARC's involvement in the cocaine trade in Colombia, al-Qaida's profiting from the poppy fields in Afghanistan, or Abu Sayyaf's kidnapping for profit in the Philippines, terrorists are increasingly using criminal activities to support and fund their terror."[24] In reality, however, there are constraints working against terrorist-criminal cooperation because of the differences in motives: "criminal groups traffic in illicit goods and services to maximize [economic] profits, whereas terrorists traffic in violence to maximize [political] power."[25] Furthermore, what definitional overlap and operational interdependence exist can in many ways help criminals gain the confidence of terrorists and unique access to information on their plans: for example, drug cartels and clandestine arms dealers would seem to be an excellent source of intelligence information on terrorist threats.

Transnational criminal organizations can help not only in gathering intelligence on terrorism but also in disrupting the flow of financial resources and weapons to terrorists. A significant proportion of the sizable funding terrorists receive comes from transnational criminal organizations.[26] Terrorist funds flow across national boundaries using secret and sordid sources and channels that routinely elude government scrutiny and interdiction:

> They pay their way with funds raised through front businesses, drug trafficking, credit card fraud, extortion, and money from covert supporters. They use ostensibly charitable organizations and non-governmental organizations (NGOs) for funding and recruitment. Money for their operations is transferred surreptitiously through numerous banks, money exchanges, and alternate remittance systems (often known as "hawalas")—some legitimate and unwitting, others not.... Laundered through the international financial system, this money then provides a huge source of virtually untraceable funds to corrupt officials, bypass established financial controls, and further other illegal activities, including arms trafficking and migrant smuggling. These activities ensure a steady supply of weapons and cash and ease the movement of operatives for terrorist organizations worldwide.[27]

The international black market in arms heavily involves transnational criminal organizations. Because transnational criminal organizations both help terrorists raise the money for buying weapons and provide covert arms to terrorists, these criminal groups are in a prime position to monitor and interfere with these activities. State use of transnational criminal organizations in battling terrorism opens up some intriguing possibilities: for example, should there ever be a desire to sever the nexus between crime and terror, it is even conceivably possible to supply weapons with concealed mechanisms designed to thwart concrete acts and develop a split and mistrust between criminals and terrorists.

The Use of Private Military Forces

Globally we are witnessing "the growing privatization of security and violence" in which there is "a growing tendency of individuals, groups, and organizations to rely on private security forces rather than on the state's police and paramilitary formations."[28] Accompanying the uncontrolled proliferation of conventional arms is an explosion in the growth of private military companies, loosely organized mercenary units, vigilante squads, militias, self-defense forces, and survivalist enclaves. These groups have differing agendas, but they are united in their belief that they need to provide their own security—and security for those around them—in a highly threatening environment because national governments are unable or unwilling to do so. For the first time since the emergence of the nation-state, more military weapons are in the hands of private citizens than in the hands of national governments: while national armies have shrunk by about 20 percent, private groups providing security have expanded to a degree that their members outnumber that of most national armies.[29] Over the past ten years private companies have assumed a central role in exporting security, strategy, and training for foreign military units. Worldwide revenues for the private security industry were estimated at $55.6 billion in 1990, have an estimated annual growth rate of 8%, and are projected to hit $202 billion in 2010.[30] In the United States alone, there are at least 20 major private military companies, with the largest grossing $25 million a year in overseas business.[31]

In attempting to remedy the coercive force deficiency faced by counterterrorism, it is important to remember that there is a long history of national governments using private military forces to oppose terrorist threats. More recently, even non-state groups have begun to see advantages here: "multinational corporations, nongovernmental aid organizations, and others exposed to criminal and politically motivated terrorism are increasingly reliant on the services of security firms, which now must be considered antiterrorism actors in their own right, alongside states and international organizations."[32] Such reliance on privatized security has been attractive for centuries for both economic and political reasons. Economically, private armies often ended up saving rulers money, and some argue that even today that privatization of state security functions—including "private 'mercenary' services bought by nation-states"—is the most efficient response to international threats.[33] Politically, utilizing private militaries traditionally allows for the escape route of "plausible deniability" (a concept first mentioned in the seventeenth century), allowing governments employing mercenaries in missions abroad both in the past and the present to disavow any knowledge of actions taken, incur little actual risk, and ultimately wash their hands of any responsibility if things go wrong.[34]

Private sources of military force, whether they are highly unstructured and informal like modern mercenary groups or highly formal and structured like today's major private military companies (such as Virginia-based Military Professional Resources Incorporated), appear to have some special advantages in combating transnational terrorism. Mercenaries could feel free to engage in a wide variety of extra-legal types of force including covert assassination, kidnapping, or sabotage. Speed and flexibility are trademarks of private military action, as there is no need to go through layers of bureaucracy to get approval for a mission or go through months of preparation to ensure there are absolutely no casualties among those undertaking the assignment (unlike in using transnational criminals to gather intelligence, here there is a real specter of loss of life among the non-state groups employed by states). While the mass public and international onlookers care to a certain extent about the deaths of civilians and government soldiers, an average consumer would probably be relatively indifferent to the deaths of unknown mercenaries, and to a certain extent feel free of moral responsibility (arguing to themselves, "we would not have done it this way"). Perceived costs could thus potentially be much lower here, while not sacrificing effectiveness, than with government military action.

Already the war against terrorism has proven to be a boon to private armies, as the Pentagon has one-third fewer soldiers than a decade ago but a growing number of entanglements in unlikely places:

> When the Pentagon talks about training the new Afghan National Army, it doesn't mean with its own soldiers. The Green Berets and other elite U.S. troops are needed elsewhere. Instead, the Defense Department is drawing up plans to use its commandos to jump-start the Afghan force, then hire private military contractors to finish the job.
>
> It would be the most vital role yet taken on by a somewhat clandestine industry accustomed to operating on the fringe of U.S. foreign policy by training foreign armies. As the United States pushes its antiterrorism campaign beyond Afghanistan, the role of these private companies promises to grow right along with it.
>
> "The war on terrorism is the full employment act for these guys," said D. B. Des Roches, spokesman for the Pentagon's Defense Security Cooperation Agency.[35]

As the United States pursues its war on terrorism in more countries without dramatically expanding the number of uniformed American military personnel, private military companies "appear certain to be hired to carry out even more training and other missions."[36]

Indeed, well beyond training functions, private militaries have been "instrumental in providing both operational and logistical support in the war on terrorism in Afghanistan."[37] In the direct aftermath of the September 11, 2001, terrorist attack on the United States, President George W. Bush placed a sizable "wanted dead or alive" reward on key international terrorists specifically to encourage mercenaries and private bounty hunters to enter Afghanistan to hunt them down to assist governments in achieving global security. The role of private military companies later received a significant, if little noted, boost in November 2002 when the Virginia-based contractor DynCorp received a new assignment from the State Department's Diplomatic Security Service to help protect Afghan president Hamid Karzai.[38] When the Defense or State Department hires such private military firms, their work is audited and sometimes supervised by American military personnel, a process the State Department claims helps to prevent abuse.[39] Thus military training, defensive protection, and offensive coercive action are all potentially fruitful counterterrorist avenues for government use of mercenaries and private military companies in the future.

Conditional Utility

The American government is committed to use every means at its disposal to combat terrorism, and so it would be motivated to consider utilizing private help when it felt the benefits deriving from this assistance would outweigh the costs; any solution to the global insecurity deriving from terrorism must balance the possible dangers against the potential for effectiveness. While security policy makers, Congressional representatives, international onlookers, and domestic citizens might initially react to this idea with apprehension, the intense fear of terrorist attack—combined with passion for filling crucial gaps in intelligence and coercive action—would gradually increase the level of acceptance. The United States and other advanced industrial societies have already outsourced key security functions on numerous occasions with great success and little external outcry.

Obviously, however, one cannot use non-state groups indiscriminately as counterterrorist instruments. When is this unorthodox approach most useful? Potentially conflicting interests provide a useful starting point: transnational criminals and private soldiers both generally support maintenance of the status quo, for by keeping a low profile and blending in with society they can attain the profitable image of respectable "business-as-usual" legitimacy in their day-to-day operations; terrorist groups, in contrast, generally try to overturn the status quo and utilize disruptive high-profile shock tactics to weaken and destabilize existing state regimes. This difference opens the door to capitalizing selectively on these opposing orientations and to pitting the two types of non-state groups against each other.

Transnational criminal organizations appear to be most needed and effective in counterterrorist information collection when (1) government intelligence (both human and electronic) has come up empty, yet the threat of terrorist attack seems high; when (2) a state government subject to terrorist threat has leverage over or a special relationship with one or more transnational criminal organizations; when (3) the use of barbaric techniques seems essential to gain needed information from a terrorist group; when (4) a transnational criminal organization has had major operations in the vicinity of a terrorist group for a sufficient amount of time to allow for deep familiarity with the local culture; when (5) a transnational criminal organization is in a particularly advantageous position to monitor ominous covert flows across national boundaries; or when (6) a terrorist group is highly dependent on one or more transnational criminal organizations for money or arms to fuel its continued operations. The greater the number of these conditions fulfilled, the greater the potential for successful utilization of transnational criminal organizations to combat terrorism.

Similarly, private military forces appear to be most needed and effective in coercive counterterrorist action when (1) traditional government military forces have been unsuccessful in coercive measures taken against a demonstrated terrorist group threat; when (2) a state government subject to terrorist threat has a special ability to monitor and manage one or more private military forces; when (3) a state government is concerned about and sensitive to casualties among its own official armed forces but yet feels it needs to employ intense coercion exceeding normal bounds against one or more terrorist groups; when (4) speed and secrecy are essential to cope with limited turmoil, rather than the application of highly visible overwhelming force to manage large-scale disorder; when (5) a private military force possesses a reputation for counterterrorist success and for efficiently providing "more bang for the buck" than government troops; or when (6) a private military force has special strategic advantages—including knowledge of the surrounding culture, familiarity with the leader or membership, or possession of unique military disruption capabilities—against a particular terrorist group. As before, using private military forces to combat terrorism would be more successful when several of these conditions are satisfied.

Thus careful evaluation of the particular circumstances at hand should prudently guide appropriate government authorities to commission transnational criminal organizations or private military forces to undertake particular counterterrorism tasks. The conditions outlined suggest rather narrow application of these unorthodox security instruments based on the situational advantages private assistance can occasionally provide. Ultimately, a prime benefit of this approach is the ability to augment national government capabilities by undertaking quick, covert, and unhesitating action in an area of intense terrorist activity, embodying a much lower probability of identifying those involved as agents of counterterrorism than with government intelligence operatives or special forces.

Limitations and Drawbacks

Several critical dangers and backfire effects may occur if counterterrorism incorporates the use of transnational criminal organizations for intelligence gathering or private armies for military action. The resulting distribution of security benefits could be very unevenly distributed within and across societies. Even if these non-state groups were uniformly effective, utilizing them in this way could embolden unsavory criminals and mercenaries in the scope of their own disruptive activities: the net result could be that states might see a reduction in terrorist activities but at the same time witness an increase in other kinds of severely destabilizing behavior from other unruly non-state groups. Government regime credibility in the eyes of both skeptical, repulsed external allies and shocked, surprised internal citizens could precipitously plummet. Democratic checks on unrestrained government adventurism (using non-state groups) in masterminding preemptive counterterrorist actions may erode. Rather than promoting a general sense of safety and protection, widespread awareness that states employ these unorthodox private instruments could increase uneasiness and fear among onlookers, with widespread apprehension that—through outsourcing key security functions—national governments are gradually abdicating their responsibility to maintain societal order. Under the wrong circumstances, privatizing counterterrorism could potentially cause the United States to face a threat as severe as, if not more so than transnational terrorism in terms of the overall impact on international stability and freedom. Nonetheless, because of the rising influence of transnational private groups in global society, in the near future the security choice for states may end up revolving more around how to use criminals and mercenaries than around whether to use them.

Looking specifically at the first option, the use of transnational criminal organizations for intelligence gathering raises some very serious concerns. Would drug cartels, gun-running, and money laundering flourish as never before? Can transnational criminal organizations be trusted in the long-term not to sell collected secret information to the highest bidder? Would criminals ever shoulder the same kinds of responsibilities and restrictions as do government agencies regarding sharing this data with others, given that the competitive economic marketplace pressures (keeping one's competitors from gaining access to secrets so as to maximize profits) differ sharply from political security pressures (keeping one's enemies from gaining access to secrets so as to maximize strategic advantage)? Would criminal groups end up exploiting poor countries on behalf of rich states? Would government officials dealing with members of transnational criminal organizations succumb to temptation and either be corrupted by this sordid interaction or be dragged down in a degrading public relations nightmare (as occurred during the 1980s when in

Panama Manuel Noriega was simultaneously involved in drug trafficking, money laundering, and acting as an informant for the Central Intelligence Agency)?

Turning to the use of private armies for military action, similar kinds of worries emerge. Given the past use of ruthless violence by some state-sponsored private military forces (such as Executive Outcomes in Sierra Leone), what would ensure any sense of prudent restraint protecting innocent onlookers if private armies worked for states against terrorists? Is it conceivable that such private forces might be even quicker to contemplate use of weapons of mass destruction? Could success in this enterprise eventually lead to the spread of assault weapons and rampaging private armies (as in the Philippines), moving the world toward a "might-makes-right" social order where violent coercion is the tool of choice? Could the current American anti-terrorist zeal return the United States to the dire dilemmas of the 1980s when the country found itself in bed with Central American death squads (in El Salvador, Guatemala, Nicaragua, and Honduras)? Would not any government attempt to utilize plausible deniability about the use of such private force fail in today's cynical and highly interpenetrated global security environment?

Perhaps the most fundamental concern about utilizing transnational criminals or private armies to combat terrorism is the issue of loyalty and accountability. There is clearly a deep-seated and widespread moral revulsion regarding the placement of public safety in the hands of those working simply for profit: more generally, contemplating the privatization of counterterrorism highlights a clash among some basic liberal internationalist values surrounding the competing goals of political security and economic profit,[40] specifically over whether intelligence collection and coercive force should be market commodities or prerogatives of the state. How can we trust non-state groups to keep their commitments, reflect the public interest, and stay on task? Although a basic premise behind the use of these groups as instruments of counterterrorism is that they respond extremely well to monetary incentives since their motives focus more on greed than on political ideology, is this enough to promote full compliance? How do we create effective incentives and disincentives promoting accuracy, honesty, and all out effort among groups presumably not used to these high standards? Without an inherent sense of "right-and-wrong" among these non-state groups matching that of the state sponsor, how can national governments successfully recruit and indoctrinate members of transnational criminal organizations and private military forces? Who will be using whom in this attempt at public-private counterterrorist cooperation?

Conclusion

In raising a somewhat novel approach to combat terrorism, there is always the possibility that those most tied to conventional responses will find what is presented here unconvincing or even ludicrous. Obviously the case for privatizing counterterrorism is very preliminary, and many unexplored questions and unresolved issues emerge. Nonetheless, the hope here is to stimulate further more detailed exploration of this alternative security strategy. Even if the analysis presented here is right that transnational criminal organizations and private military forces could sometimes be effective counterterrorist tools, considerable frank discussion about costs and benefits needs to occur among security policy makers and members of the public in the United States and abroad before such possibilities could be seriously considered for implementation.

This analysis strongly advocates the conditional application of transnational criminal organizations and private military forces as essential elements of counterterrorism. Up until this point, states have clearly underutilized—for a variety of political reasons—these non-state groups' assets in the security-oriented fight against transnational terror. It is certainly time to take a fresh look at their utility. In the end, the principal advantage of using private groups to stop terrorists is that the pursuer can match the ruthlessness, resolve, flexibility, speed, and guile of the pursued. It seems high time that states exploit the competing interests among unencumbered non-state groups not guided by national government interests rather than simply lump them all together indiscriminately as enemies of the state.

Regardless of the current commitment of money and personnel by the United States and its determination to use them, it will probably continue to be outflanked by terrorists in the long run if it does not consider some options that have a better chance of matching the assets of these dangerous groups. The American government clearly cannot handle alone the battle against terrorism: just as it now enlists other state partners in this endeavor, it should be open to taking advantage of the significant capabilities of private non-state groups, even those traditionally seen as unruly themselves. Despite all the deficiencies and uncertainties surrounding privatizing counterterrorism, we had better move in that direction; for if not, even with strength, courage, and resolve we cannot achieve lasting victory.

Robert Mandel has served as the chair of the International Affairs Department at Lewis and Clark College in Portland, Oregon. His research interests include conflict and security, global resource issues, transnational studies, and international relations theory. He has published articles about security threats and is a regular contributor to *Armed Forces and Society*.

Notes

1. Walter Laqueur, "Postmodern Terrorism," *Foreign Affairs*, 75 (September/October 1996): 28.
2. *National Strategy for Combating Terrorism* (Washington, DC: U.S. Department of State Bureau of Public Affairs, February 2003), p. 1.
3. Robert Heibel, "Intelligence and Counterterrorism" (CNN Interview, September 12, 2001) www.cnn.com/2001/COMMUNITY/09/12/heibel/
4. John Deutch and Jeffrey H. Smith, "Smarter Intelligence" *Foreign Policy*, #128 (January/February 2002): 66.
5. Bruce Hoffman, "A Nasty Business," in Russell D. Howard and Reid L. Sawyer, eds., *Terrorism and Counterterrorism: Understanding the New Security Environment, Readings and Interpretations* (Guilford, CT: McGraw-Hill/Dushkin, 2003): 301.
6. *National Strategy for Combating Terrorism*, p. 16.
7. Barry R. Posen, "The Struggle Against Terrorism: Grand Strategy, Strategy, and Tactics," in Howard and Sawyer, *Terrorism and Counterterrorism*: 397.
8. Michele L. Malvesti, "Explaining the United States' Decision to Strike Back at Terrorists," in Howard and Sawyer, *Terrorism and Counterterrorism*: 404.
9. Gus Martin, *Understanding Terrorism* (Thousand Oaks, CA: Sage Publications, 2003): 350-351.
10. Richard K. Betts, "The Soft Underbelly of American Primacy: Tactical Advantages of Terror," in Howard and Sawyer, *Terrorism and Counterterrorism*: 345.
11. Richard H. Shultz and Andreas Vogt, "The Real Intelligence Failure on 9/11 and the Case for a Doctrine of Striking First," in Howard and Sawyer, *Terrorism and Counterterrorism*: 385.

12. http://www.whitehouse.gov/news/releases/2002/06/20020601-3.html

13. Hoffman, p. 301

14. Much of this section is taken from Robert Mandel, *Deadly Transfers and the Global Playground* (Westport, CT: Praeger Publishers, 1999).

15. Zeev Maoz, *Paradoxes of War* (Boston: Unwin Hyman, 1990), 327.

16. Several anecdotes in Robert D. Kaplan, *Eastward to Tartary* (New York: Random House, 2000) illustrate this central point.

17. Phil Williams, "Transnational Criminal Organizations and International Security," *Survival*, 36 (Spring 1994): 109.

18. Louise L. Shelley, "Transnational Organized Crime: An Imminent Threat to the Nation-State?," *Journal of International Affairs*, 48 (Winter 1995): 488–489.

19. Senator John Kerry, *The New War: The Web of Crime that Threatens America's Security* (New York: Simon & Schuster, 1997): 19–21.

20. Claire Sterling, *Thieves' World* (New York: Simon & Schuster, 1994), 21.

21. Captain C. J. van Bergen Thirion, "The Privatisation of Security: A Blessing or a Menace," 1998 http://www.mil.za/CSANDF/CJSupp/TrainingFormation/DefenceCollege/Researchpapers1998/privatisation_of_security.htm

22. Hoffman, pp. 302–303.

23. Kerry, pp. 111–112.

24. *National Strategy for Combating Terrorism*, p. 8.

25. James H. Anderson, "International Terrorism and Crime: Trends and Linkages" http://www.jmu.edu/orgs/wrni/it.htm

26. Martin, 399–400.

27. *National Strategy for Combating Terrorism* (Washington, DC, February 2003), pp. 7, 22.

28. Robert Mandel, *Armies without States: The Privatization of Security* (Boulder, CO: Lynne Rienner, 2002); and Michael T. Klare, "The Global Trade in Light Weapons and the International System in the Post–Cold War Era," in Jeffrey Boutwell, Michael T. Klare, and Laura W. Reed, eds., *Lethal Commerce* (Cambridge, MA: Committee on International Security Studies of the American Academy of Arts and Sciences, 1995): p. 40.

29. John B. Alexander, *Future War* (New York: Thomas Dunne Books, 1999): p. xv.

30. Herbert M. Howe, *Ambiguous Order: Military Forces in African States* (Boulder, CO: Lynne Rienner, 2001), p. 188; and Kevin A. O'Brien, "PMCs, Myths and Mercenaries: The Debate on Private Military Companies," *Royal United Service Institute Journal* (February 2000).

31. Justin Brown, "The Rise of the Private-Sector Military," *Christian Science Monitor* (July 5, 2000): p. 3.

32. Ian O. Lesser, "Countering the New Terrorism: Implications for Strategy," in Ian O. Lesser, Bruce Hoffman, John Arquilla, David F. Ronfeldt, Michele Zanini, and Brian Michael Jenkins, eds., *Countering the New Terrorism* (Santa Monica, CA: Rand Corporation, 1999): 106.

33. Jurgen Brauer, "An Economic Perspective on Mercenaries, Military Companies, and the Privatization of Force," *Cambridge Review of International Affairs* 13 (Autumn-Winter 1999): 130–146.

34. Mandel, *Armies without States*, 30–31; and Janice E. Thomson, *Mercenaries, Pirates, and Sovereigns: State-Building and Extraterritorial Violence in Early Modern Europe* (Princeton, NJ: Princeton University Press, 1994): p. 21.

35. Esther Schrader, "U.S. Companies Hired to Train Foreign Armies" (*Los Angeles Times*, April 14, 2002) http://www.globalpolicy.org/security/peacekpg/training/pmc.htm

36. Deborah Avant, "Privatizing Military Training" *Foreign Policy in Focus*, vol. 7 (May 2002) http://www.fpif.org/briefs/vol7/v7n06miltrain_body.html

37. Mafruza Khan, "Business on the Battlefield: The Role of Private Military Companies" (December 2002) http://www.ctj.org/itep/crp/dec02.htm.

38. David Isenberg, "Security for Sale in Afghanistan" (*Asia Times Online*, January 4, 2003) http://www.atimes.com/atimes/Central_Asia/EA04Ag01.html

39. Schrader.

40. Mandel, *Deadly Transfers and the Global Playground*, p. 91; and Thomson, p. 2.

James S. Robbins, 2003

Defeating Networked Terrorism

Since September 11, 2001, the United States and its coalition partners have waged a relentless war on the al Qaeda terrorist network, its supporters and patrons. This war has been prosecuted through traditional counter-terrorism, unconventional warfare, and major theater combat. For the most part, the anti-terror Coalition has been successful. Yet this raises the question of what constitutes victory in the war on terrorism, and how do we know if we are moving toward it?

There are basically two ways to measure progress in any war—the extent to which one is achieving one's objectives, and the extent to which the enemy is failing to meet theirs. In the case of the war on terrorism, these two metrics are closely related. The National Strategy for Combating Terrorism defines victory as ending the ability of the global terrorist network to pursue attacks on the United States, its interests and allies. Strategic progress is measured not by ending all terrorism everywhere, which is an impossible task; but rather by destroying the ability of terrorists to maintain international linkages and project power globally.

The National Strategy defines the terrorist threat as "a flexible, transnational network structure, enabled by modern technology and characterized by loose interconnectivity both within and between groups."[1] (Figure 1) Terror groups operate on three levels, locally, regionally, and globally. The linkages between these various levels, enabled by technology and fueled by ideology, distinguish the contemporary terrorist threat from those the United States faced in previous decades. Like wars that target state systems and their regimes, in this conflict the network structure itself, rather than individual leaders or personalities, is the principal target.

The global network has been able to magnify the pre-existing terrorist threat by coordinating and focusing its various functions: funding, personnel (recruitment, training and retention), planning (at strategic, operational and tactical levels), communications, intelligence and counterintelligence, and the critical functions of inspiration and legitimation. The network thus serves as a global terrorist force multiplier by increasing the web of linkages across all of these functional areas. Disrupting or destroying the network short-circuits this global synergy and returns the terrorist threat to levels that are more manageable. The overall strategic objective of the war is to sunder these linkages, to deny terrorists the ability to prosecute their struggle globally, and to push terrorism down to the local level where it will be both less threatening, and more easily dealt with (Figure 2). As stated in the National Strategy, the objective is "to compress the scope and capability of terrorist organizations, isolate them regionally, and destroy them within state borders."[2]

The al Qaeda terrorist network, comprised of its core group led by Osama bin Laden, affiliated terrorist organizations (such as the Egyptian Islamic Jihad, and the Abu Sayyaf

Figure 1

Transnational Terrorist Networks

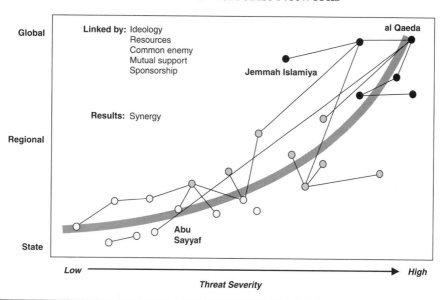

group in the Philippines), and various sympathizers, flourished in the pre-9/11 environment in which the threat it posed was either misunderstood or disregarded. The network was well adapted to the rule sets prevalent at the time. It was able to grow by exploiting seams in its adversaries' social, political and legal structures, which enabled a series of low-level attacks against American and other Western interests without courting a serious threat to the network's existence. Al Qaeda's strategy, described in detail in Osama bin Laden's December 1996 Declaration of War, envisioned a long-term guerrilla struggle against a militarily superior but morally deficient foe, which would grow in intensity and ultimately wear down the will of the "Crusaders" to resist the unrelenting Mujahedin onslaught. This would lead to the withdrawal of the United States from the Middle East, the overthrow of the corrupt regimes in the region, the consolidation of a new Caliphate, the destruction of the state of Israel, and eventual punishment of the United States for its legacy of crimes against the Muslim people.[3]

Bin Ladin's strategy, as well as the organization with which he intended to execute it, was based on a series of premises that were proven to be erroneous, for example that the United States could not respond effectively to large-scale terrorist attacks, or that Afghanistan was an impregnable safe haven.[4] In the initial phase of the response to 9/11, from September to December 2001, al Qaeda's original strategic concept was heavily strained, if not completely destroyed. Since then the al Qaeda network has been forced to adapt and evolve to cope with new rule sets imposed by the United States. Al Qaeda has been described as a "complex adaptive system," but the network has not demonstrated an ability to adapt robustly. Al Qaeda has been unable to maintain the level of effectiveness it possessed before 9/11, and thus can be said to be more maladaptive than adaptive. This being said, it is difficult to assess the degree to which the global terrorist network has been disrupted. Terrorist

Figure 2

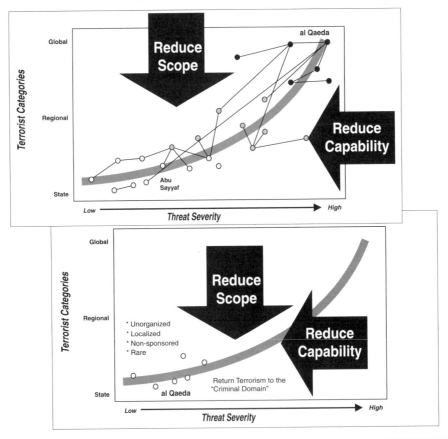

Operationalizing the Strategy

groups are secretive by nature, and al Qaeda has been particularly low profile since the fall of Afghanistan. Yet one can establish metrics by examining key aspects of the network structure, things the network needs to survive, as well as indicants that the network has lost or is losing functionality.

1. Initiative

The Coalition has seized and maintains the initiative, while the terror network has become ad hoc and defensive. The members of the terrorist network are being mercilessly hunted with an intensity far exceeding anything they ever experienced or expected. Because of this, the primary focus of the members of al Qaeda is survival. This is a qualitatively different focus because the terrorists must maintain a constant state of vigilance. Being on the run imposes substantial opportunity costs on the organization and makes it extremely difficult for them to coordinate offensive operations in the manner to which they were accustomed. They can take action after a fashion, of course, but with nowhere near the effectiveness they used to. Planning, command and control, and adaptive decisionmaking proceed at a much slower tempo. This point is fundamental to the concept of disruption—terrorists cannot spend significant amounts of time planning and executing offensive actions when they are being forced to concentrate on arranging complex defensive operations simply to survive. Maintaining this level of intensity both increases the probability of mistakes on their part, and magnifies the consequences of error.

2. Safe Havens

Central to the defensive posture of the network is its loss of its principal safe haven in Afghanistan. Even though networks are not completely dependent on location to exist, their members must be physically located somewhere. When they can cluster freely, the number of connections in the network multiply, as does its effectiveness. Bin Laden described Afghanistan as the "mountain fastness" of his revolutionary movement, an impregnable bastion within which he could plan offensive operations, train his followers in terrorist tradecraft, and openly exhort the masses to join his movement against the Crusaders and Zionists.[5] The Taliban government was both sympathetic to bin Laden's cause, and drew substantial financial support from him. Neighboring Pakistan propped up the Taliban regime, and in return bin Laden's training camps provided foot soldiers for the anti-Indian insurgency in Kashmir. Denying this sanctuary and its established structures struck at the heart of the network. With the Taliban overthrown, Afghanistan occupied and Pakistan part of the Coalition, this safe haven has been reduced to a dwindling number of safe houses in less secure frontier areas.

The argument has been made that this state of affairs is actually an advantage—that al Qaeda can "maintain a transnational and clandestine organizational scheme with minimal dedicated physical infrastructure." Being "more virtual" it is "harder to identify and neutralize."[6] While this may be true of individuals within the organization, the overriding point is that without its base of operations in Afghanistan, al Qaeda has lost the focal point of its network with all its attendant benefits. Furthermore, since bin Laden's strategic goals cannot be realized unless ground is seized and held, it places the network that much further from its objectives.

3. International Cooperation

For al Qaeda to grow and flourish, it must attract new members to its network. The Coalition has deterred international cooperation with al Qaeda by raising the price to those who might be so inclined. When President Bush defined the enemies of the United States as global terrorists, and included those who harbored and supported terrorism, the message to both terror groups and state actors was to put distance between themselves and al Qaeda. Any group publicly siding with bin Laden would be fair game for immediate, unlimited Coalition action. Consequently, implications of ties to al Qaeda are met with immediate denials. Hizbollah, for example, strongly rejected any linkages to bin Laden when it was accused of complicity.[7] Iran expelled former Afghan Mujahedin Gubaldin Hekmatyar, in exile in Teheran, after he made pro-jihadist statements. He, too, denies ties to al Qaeda, even though he has declared war on the United States.[8] Iran has also reportedly concluded an extradition agreement with Saudi Arabia following the May 12, 2003, bombings in

Riyadh, perhaps to facilitate the transfer of terrorists who have sought haven.[9] Osama bin Laden expected anti-American groups to rally around him after 9/11, but al Qaeda has not announced the accession of any affiliate groups since.

4. State Sponsorship

To an extent as yet underestimated, the al Qaeda terrorist network had a working relationship with established states. Afghanistan has already been noted as a facilitator, though the Taliban never enjoyed the full rights of statehood in the international system. However, while it is still debatable to what degree Saddam Hussein supported the global terrorist network, it is becoming increasingly clear that Iraq provided terror groups with some forms of logistical, intelligence, transportation, training, weapons, and other support. Emerging evidence points to the conclusion that al Qaeda had a cooperative relationship—that is, a strategic alliance—with Iraq.

The motive for the alliance was a common hatred for the United States and Israel. Saddam Hussein was the only state leader to praise the attacks of September 11. It has been argued that bin Laden, an Islamicist fanatic, and Saddam, a Baathist modernizer, could never align or cooperate. However, ideology is seldom a determinant of wartime alliance structures, and for both Iraq and al Qaeda the 1990s were wartime. This combination is as reasonable as the strategic alliance between the United States and the Soviet Union against Nazi Germany, or Syrian and American troops fighting side by side during Operation Desert Storm.[10]

Saddam Hussein showed no reluctance to support terrorism per se. The fact that he gave money to the families of Palestinian suicide terrorists and had a close working relationship with the PLO was well known, and something he admitted. He also harbored Abu Nidal and other members of his international terror organization in Baghdad, that is until Abu Nidal died under suspicious circumstances in Baghdad in the fall of 2002.[11] Abd-al-Rahman Isa, Abu Nidal's second in command based in Amman, Jordan, was kidnapped September 11, 2002, and has not been heard from since.[12] Coalition forces did apprehend Khala Khadr al-Salahat in Baghdad, the man who reputedly made the bomb that brought down Pan Am Flight 103 over Lockerbie, Scotland.[13] The Iraqi regime maintained a terrorist training camp at Salam Pak near Baghdad where terrorists were instructed in methods to take over commercial aircraft using weapons no more sophisticated than knives.

Several important ties to al Qaeda have surfaced. Iraq made direct payments to the Abu Sayyaf group. Hamsiraji Sali, an Abu Sayyaf leader on the U.S. most-wanted terrorist list, that his gang received about one million pesos (around $20,000) each year from Iraq, for chemicals to make bombs.[14] The link was substantiated immediately after a bombing in Zamboanga City in October 2002 (in which three people were killed, including an American Green Beret), when Abu Sayyaf leaders called up the deputy secretary of the Iraqi embassy in Manila, Husham Hussain. Six days later, the cell phone used to call Hussain was employed as the timer on a bomb set to go off near the Philippine military's Southern Command headquarters. Fortunately, the bomb failed to detonate, and the phone yielded various contact numbers, including Hussain's and Sali's. This evidence, coupled with other intelligence the Philippine government would not release, led to Hussain's expulsion in February 2003. In March, ten Iraqi nationals, some with direct links to al Qaeda, were rounded up in the Philippines and deported as undesirable aliens. In addition, two more consulate officials were expelled for spying.[15] Other links include the case of Abu-Zubayr, an officer in Saddam's secret police who was also the ringleader of the al Qaeda cell in Morocco seeking to attack U.S. ships as they passed through the Strait of Gibraltar.[16] Abu-Zubayr had also met with 9/11 financial chief Ramzi Bin-al-Shibh in Spain on September 5, 2001, six days before the attacks in the United States.[17] Al Qaeda refugees from Afghanistan took refuge in northern Iraq until being driven out by Coalition forces, and Abu Musab Al-Zarqawi, an al Qaeda terrorist active in Europe and North Africa, fled from Baghdad during Operation Iraqi Freedom, and has been sent back to coordinate al Qaeda activities there.[18] Since the occupation of Baghdad, some Iraqi intelligence documents have been found that support direct links between bin Laden and Saddam Hussein.[19]

Saddam Hussein had means, motive, and opportunity to be involved with global terrorism. While much still remains to be revealed, the overthrow of his regime removed, to a greater or lesser extent, one of the props of bin Laden's network.

5. Finances

The financial picture is difficult to piece together for a variety of reasons. Al Qaeda's finances have been put under pressure through direct confiscation and efforts to end fund transfers to front groups from legitimate sources. Yet, al Qaeda has had many other sources of income, from bin Laden's personal fortune to illegal diamond smuggling to extortion. There are no firm numbers on exactly how much money is in the network, or how much it needs to survive. It is true that terror operations are relatively inexpensive to mount, but substantial sums must be needed for overhead—payoffs, bribes, day-to-day security, and personnel costs. The al Qaeda network moved assets in ways that made them invisible to most technical means of detection, for example relying on middlemen to shift funds physically from place to place, doing so in non-monetary form such as diamonds and gold, and keeping few records as to who had what. This security measure also introduces substantial risks into the terrorist finance system. Pushing money into the underground economy makes it subject to internal looting. Organized crime groups, which frequently serve as middlemen, routinely skim funds, and the transfer cost for unauditable money can amount to as much as 80 percent.[20] Because al Qaeda is on the run, it has fewer means of enforcing its will against those who misbehave. This aspect of system breakdown is difficult to detect, but for example, recently $2.5 million went missing from an al Qaeda bank account in Pakistan after the account holder was killed, which led to some finger-pointing but no resolution.

When al Qaeda attempted to audit the network, the results showed how difficult imposing control could be even before 9/11. Auditors undertook investigations of financial or other irregularities, for example in one case a terrorist working out of London was accused of extravagant spending on office equipment and furnishings. However, conducting this type of investigation is extremely difficult in the terrorist milieu. One of the investigators, a *Sharia* judge named Abu al-Hasan, complained of various impediments to completing his assignment:

- Terrorists are hard to find; they move around, use multiple identities, give false addresses and phone numbers as a matter of course, so it's hard to locate an individual even if he isn't trying to hide from the investigator;

- Terror networks are highly dispersed and the need for the investigator to travel long distances also contributes to these difficulties, especially when multiple parties are involved;
- Secure long-distance communication is time consuming and expensive;
- Terrorists, because of cell structures necessary for security, do not all know each other, and Hasan did not know *any* of them, so it was difficult to understand the relationships to build a case;
- Witnesses kept introducing details unrelated to the core investigation;
- The accused tend to lay accusations at the accusers—in one case the person being investigated kept maintaining he was in fact the plaintiff, and was oblivious to the charges against him;
- The accused tend to be very slow in responding or completely non-responsive to calls for evidence, and it is very difficult to assemble a complete case.

Thus the very fact that more of al Qaeda's financial activity has been driven deeper underground imposes punishing costs on the organization, more so than could ever be achieved by confiscations.

6. Personnel

Al Qaeda has experienced significant personnel losses since September 11, 2001. Up to two thirds of its key operatives have been captured or killed.[21] Some of the most noteworthy have been Mohammed Atef, one of bin Laden's closest advisors and operations planners, killed in Afghanstan, and Hazma al-Qatari, also killed, who handled finances. Ali Qaed Senyan al-Harthi, who was involved in the U.S.S. *Cole* bombing was slain in Yemen. Yussuf al-Ayyeri, a theoretician and planner, was killed in a shootout in Saudi Arabia in June, 2003. Among those captured are Khalid Sheik Mohammed, Ramzi Binalshibh (a key 9/11 planner), Abu Zubaydah (operations planner), Abd al Rahim al-Nashiri (mastermind of the U.S.S. *Cole* bombing), Riduan bin Isomuddin, known as Hambali, head of the al Qaeda affiliate Jemmah Islamiya group, and other leaders who cannot easily be replaced. The effects of the losses of key leaders in an organization the size of al Qaeda are highly damaging. Not only do they remove these critical nodes from the network, but also they become sources for important intelligence leading to others still at large. The losses among the lower level organizers and foot soldiers number in the thousands.

7. Leadership

It is extremely difficult for analysts to know the inner workings of the al Qaeda leadership. We are not even certain about the fate of Osama bin Laden. Nevertheless, there is some evidence of factionalization within the organization. The notion that terrorists are naturally cohesive is highly questionable. Even those groups led by charismatic leaders such as Osama bin Laden will show strains based on personality conflicts and competition for power within the organization. It is common for extremist groups to self-destruct over internal squabbles, and people driven by strong ideological convictions are likely to have intense disputes with their coreligionists.[22] The same anti-social personality factors that draw people to the extremist lifestyle make it difficult for them not to exhibit those same traits within the organization, especially when placed under pressure. A September 2003 CIA

Table 1

Assessing the Disruption of the Al Qaeda Network

Network Aspect	Pre-9/11	Post-9/11
Initiative	Al Qaeda on the Offensive	Al Qaeda on the Defensive
Safe Havens	Afghanistan, with numerous gray areas and safe houses in other countries	Afghan/Pakistan frontier, shrinking number of safe houses
Network Building	Able to attract overt and/or covert support of other terrorist groups of state sympathizers	Al Qaeda a "third rail," no group will openly declare allegiance
State Sponsorship	Major patron Afghanistan, alliance of convenience with Iraq	No evident state sponsorship
Finances	Apparently well financed by bin Laden's personal fortune, local means of fundraising, and Saudi and other monies	Apparently in financial straits; high potential for internal looting of untraceable funds
Personnel	Secure, established means of recruiting, training, and utilizing personnel	Highly insecure and shrinking ability to maintain personnel; many losses to death or capture
Leadership	Strong, directed leadership under charismatic leader and core group	Uncertain and diffuse leadership, potential internal factionalization, many losses of leadership cadres
Tactics	Focused, centrally planned, dramatic attacks on important targets	Less focused, less planned attacks on softer targets, diminished impact, harsh response by Coalition forces leading to unacceptable cost/benefit calculus
Strategic Focus	Step by step execution of 1996 strategy as laid out in Declaration of War	Strategic drift; disconnect between actions and rhetoric

report notes that "the central leadership of Al Qaeda is at growing risk of breaking apart as our blows against the group create a level of disarray and confusion throughout the organization that we have not seen since the collapse of the Taliban in late 2001."[23]

It is noteworthy that the al Qaeda network could not forge a complete alliance with the Egyptian Islamic Jihad when the two organizations merged in 1998. Its leader, Ayman al-Zawahiri, Osama bin Laden's right-hand man and the intellectual pillar of the al Qaeda movement, fled Egypt in the 1980s and joined bin Laden in Afghanistan sometime in the 1990s. From there he oversaw his terrorist operation, masterminding the 1997 Luxor Massacre, which fomented a brutal crackdown inside Egypt. Those terrorists who had remained in Egypt switched tactics from armed struggle to political activity, chiefly because of the effectiveness of Egyptian counterterrorism. Zawahiri, safe in Afghanistan, called this tantamount to surrender.[24]

The 1998 *fatwa* establishing the "World Front for Jihad against Jews and Crusaders" formally unified the Egyptian Islamic Jihad (among others) with al Qaeda. However, the alliance did not sit well with everyone. Few of Zawahiri's followers back in Egypt approved, and even those who endorsed the union did not trust Osama bin Laden. Most of the objections centered on the core al Qaeda strategy; the dissenters did not think it was wise to challenge a country as powerful as the United States. Others simply believed bin Laden was trouble. A tense meeting followed in Afghanistan, in which Zawahiri attempted to coerce agreement by threatening to resign as leader of the group. He told his followers that this was a deal they could not pass up. He noted that bin Laden had broken promises before, but he sensed that Osama was now a changed man. "My honest opinion is that this is a great opportunity for us," he stated.[25]

After the 1998 African embassy bombings, the United States and its European allies rolled up many terrorist sub-networks then operating in European cities. A large number of terrorists were arrested in Albania and deported to Cairo for trial. Muntasir al-Zayyat, a lawyer for the terrorists, prudently distanced his clients from Zawahiri's persistent calls for violence at home and abroad. Zawahiri denounced Zayyat, who issued a letter stating that his credibility was being questioned by fools.[26] Ultimately, Zayyat was able successfully to defend many of his clients, while Zawahiri and his brother Mohammed "the Engineer" were sentenced to death in absentia. What this demonstrates is that among groups most likely to align, with leaders in full agreement, and pre-9/11 conditions, it was difficult to maintain unity.

Since 9/11, there have been numerous communiqués that indicate that the leadership of al Qaeda is in disorder. The messages are uncoordinated, sometimes contradictory, varying in tone and style. Many are released in bin Laden's name, others only refer to him, and some, significantly, do not. In the summer of 2002 a statement was issued that Osama bin Laden's eldest son Sad had taken over day-to-day operations of al Qaeda while his father was recovering from illness. Sad is in his twenties, a skilled computer user who allegedly controls the bin Laden audio and videotape archives. Mohammed bin Laden, seen by many as the favored son to succeed his father, was reportedly killed months prior, paving the way for Sad's ascent to power.[27] This was followed quickly by another statement that Osama was feeling much better and was back in charge.[28] The abortive move reportedly raised the hackles of other more seasoned al Qaeda leaders, particularly Zawahiri. He himself was reported dead by the Russian press in early October 2002, and rushed out a few statements and an interview to show he was still alive and fighting the infidels.[29]

This is the necessary background to understand Osama bin Laden's will, dated December 14, 2001, reportedly in the possession of the London-based magazine *Majallah*.[30] In it, he denounces the Taliban for betraying him when the battle against the Allies went worse than expected. "The situation was overturned as we saw the coward Crusaders and the humiliated Jews remain steadfast in the fighting while the soldiers of our nation lift a white flag and surrender to their enemies like women—may God give us strength—only the very few from the [Taliban] remained steadfast." He instructs his sons to have nothing to do with them, al Qaeda, or with the World Front for Fighting Jews and Crusaders—the organization which he co-founded with Zawahiri. He further instructs that attacks should be halted "until you purge your ranks of the cowards and stooges." Around the time the contents of the will were made known, Ramzi Bin al-Shib, who claimed on al-Jazeera to have masterminded the 9/11 attacks and presented himself as the senior al Qaeda military commander, was arrested, based on a tip.

The Kuwaiti terrorists who were killed attacking U.S. Marines before the invasion of Iraq wrote a statement in praise of Kuwait-born Abu Gaith, the al Qaeda spokesman. They named him as their inspiration four times, but did not mention bin Laden at all. Shortly thereafter a new spokesman appeared, Abd al Rakhman al-Rashid, saying Osama is alive and well, and has put on weight. Abu Gaith then went silent for months, and was last reported under arrest in Iran.[31] Taliban leader Mullah Omar issued a statement October 7, 2002, in which he claimed that the Afghans are God's chosen people and vowed that jihad would continue. He too did not mention Osama or al Qaeda.[32] Yet, the October 12, 2002, bin Laden statement mentioned above praises both the Taliban and al Qaeda, contradicting the contents of the alleged will. In the spring of 2003 a new spokesman, Thabit bin Qays, announced that al Qaeda had undergone a radical change in structure as a security measure. He said that leadership duties were given to "a new team," though from the context it appears he was referring to operations planners for attacks on the United States. However, he did not mention bin Laden at all.[33]

If Osama bin Laden is still alive, as al Qaeda operatives have consistently claimed, his purported statements show a level of disorganization. If he is dead, this type of activity reflects attempts by individuals and factions within the organization to attain leadership positions. It is not self-evident that al Qaeda has a succession plan, or that this plan would be honored by others in the group. A contender such as Sad has legitimacy based on the name and bloodline. Others such as Zawahiri have age, experience, and personal support networks. Abu Gaith, if reports are true, may have thought he could move up the ranks by his own initiative but was purged. None will make a decisive move until he is certain it will succeed. In the meantime, they may be waging a positional war through statements issued under the revered leader's name.

8. Tactics

The ante-bellum view of terrorism was that terror attacks seek body counts, and the more killed the more successful the attack. The global terror network, however, has grand strategic goals that necessitate a more sophisticated operational approach. The 9/11 attacks, for example, were intended not just to kill, but to provoke, and to demonstrate that the United States could be wounded. For the terrorists to successfully execute their strategy, their attacks cannot simply be random bombings, even if they succeed. The attacks must fit within a larger plan.

Most of the planned post-9/11 attacks have not been carried out, which is itself a direct indicant of terror network disruption. The network is dysfunctional in direct proportion to the number of attacks that are pre-empted, broken up, or simply not attempted. This is difficult to measure, but there were for example three waves of spectacular attacks planned for September 2001, of which 9/11 was the first. As of this writing (September 2003), no large scale, centrally directed attacks have been carried out within the United States, which is a solid measure of network disruption, and of the effectiveness of U.S. domestic anti- and counter-terrorist measures.

Many attacks have been carried out overseas, and this is important for al Qaeda in order to show that they are still capable of fighting, to demonstrate relevance, and to inspire current and potential future followers. Yet the network has demonstrated no capability to translate sporadic low-level violence into operational or strategic gains. The attacks are less sophisticated, less dramatic, and less effective. Tactical targeting decisions have apparently been left in the hands of pre-existing local affiliate terrorist and guerrilla groups. Targets tend to be softer, and have only nominal connection to the strategic goals of the organization.

The 2003 bombings in Morocco for example, while an example of successful attacks, have done little to promote and further the terrorist strategy. Osama bin Laden (or someone purporting to be him) stated that Morocco was "ready for liberation," but the attacks, against Western, non-military targets, seemed more an act of frustration than calculation. While the terrorists showed aptitude at the tactical level (the attacks were, after all, successfully carried out), it is unclear how Morocco was to be destabilized by them. Furthermore, because there was no capacity for follow-on attacks, the campaign was a singular event lacking depth, mass, or momentum.

The Morocco attack also demonstrated the inability of al Qaeda to protect the extended arms of its network, in this case the affiliate group Assirate al Moustakim. The fourteen suicide bombers were of course never expected to survive, and it is noteworthy that authorities had not had them under surveillance, and they had not previously been to al Qaeda training camps. This shows some capability to recruit and train post-9/11. Yet, Mohammed Omari, the tactical coordinator of the attacks who was also supposed to die, chose to abort his mission with two others and was captured. The national coordinator for al Qaeda in Morocco, who was based in Fez, was rounded up but died under interrogation. However, he did reveal his go-between outside the country, who was linked to Abu Musab Zarqawi, the head of an al Qaeda affiliate known as al Tawhid, who funded the operation. Zarqawi had been hiding in Iraq, and was last reported under arrest in Iran. Thus this one operation—targeting several restaurants, a hotel, and a Jewish graveyard[34]—cost al Qaeda its entire Morocco operational structure.[35] This is not the kind of punishment the network can afford to absorb for the minimal gains they achieved. Further, it validates the U.S. strategy of pushing terrorist activities to local levels where the network can more easily be broken.

9. Strategic Focus

Finally, the global terrorist network is not achieving the sustained gains the strategy requires. Al Qaeda is no closer to unifying the Muslim *ummah* than it was before 9/11. Because of this the strategy itself has come into question, and the organization has shown some signs of strategic drift.

In December 2001 Osama bin Laden stressed that the United States must be the primary target of terrorist attacks, and that the U.S. economy is the center of gravity. In the October 12, 2002, al Qaeda statement on the anniversary of our attacks on Afghanistan, "Osama" ordered that efforts should be concentrated on the United States and Israel, and not on other countries—while also congratulating the Yemeni bombers of the French oil tanker.[36] A few days later a rambling statement was issued under his name in which he said either the Yemen bombing was al Qaeda's responsibility, or it wasn't; he was not telling, and it was bad for the United States either way. "We leave [the enemy] to drown in all the assumptions and possibilities," he wrote.[37] In later statements attributed to bin Laden, he urges his cohorts to strike at "the head of the snake" and pledges to personally lead an attack "in the belly of the eagle."[38] Yet, recent attacks have been scattered, and have not conformed to the strategy. Al Qaeda has for example targeted Spain (for supporting the Iraq war) and Belgium (for placing al Qaeda members on trial), and threatened Norway (perhaps for expelling Mullah Krekar). These targets seem more an expression of anger and frustration than a calculated strategic move. Such attacks will only serve to solidify the global coalition against terror, when al Qaeda should be attempting to drive wedges between the United States and its supporters.

Abu-Muhammad al-Ablaj, who oversees al Qaeda training, has stated that everything is going according to plan. "Let me emphasize here that there are no differences, disputes, or anything of the sort," he said. "The organization is under the command of leader Abu-Abdallah (bin Laden)." He added that attacks on the United States are planned, but would come at a time and place of the network's choosing. "I swear to you, my brother, that the strike is coming.... You don't use the winning card at anytime. The strike must be well prepared. This means that it must be timed to occur when the giant starts staggering in his blood. At that time, he is ready for the fatal strike."[39] Communiqués from the fall of 2003 suggest that the central front for al Qaeda's struggle has shifted to Iraq, and some sympathetic commentators have suggested that the Coalition has in fact fallen into an Al Qaeda trap.[40]

Ironically, al Qaeda is on the verge of witnessing the accomplishment of one of its most critical strategic goals, namely the departure of United States forces from Saudi Arabia. The deployment of U.S. troops to the "land of the two holy places" was what motivated bin Laden to start the war in the first place. Al Qaeda may draw some satisfaction from this development, even if they had nothing to do with causing it. However, they are further than ever from seeing the United States leave the region. With Coalition forces active in Afghanistan, Saddam Hussein overthrown and Iraq liberated, a firm U.S. presence in Kuwait, Qatar, and Bahrain, and basing agreements in Uzbekistan and Kyrgyzstan, the United States is more a presence in the region than ever. If anything the execution of bin Laden's strategy has led to the opposite outcome; he has guaranteed American presence—military, diplomatic, and economic—for decades to come.

Conclusion

The threat from the al Qaeda terrorist network is real, and continuing. However, al Qaeda has not demonstrated the ability to adapt fully to the circumstances of the global war on terrorism post-9/11. Bin Laden's initial strategic plan failed, and the terrorist network has not been able to mount the kind of sustained counter-offensive necessary to achieve any of its stated objectives. As such, the Coalition has moved demonstrably towards victory as defined by the National Strategy for Combating Terrorism. However, it is imperative to note that this situation could change dramatically if the Coalition, and the United States in particular, diminishes its efforts against the terrorists and allows the network to reconstitute. Disruption is not the same as destruction. Al Qaeda will seek to regain the initiative at first opportunity, and whether or not the terrorists can regain a strategic footing, they are still capable of attempting dramatic vengeance strikes on the U.S. homeland. The war is being won, but it is far from over.

Portions of this article were previously published by the author in *National Review Online*.

James Robbins is a professor of international relations at the National Defense University. Previously employed for the U.S. Marine Corps Command and Staff College in Quantico, VA, he served as associate professor of international relations and course director for Military Operations Other Than War (MOOTW). His research interests include Russia and the former Soviet Union, political theory, and classics.

Notes

1. *The National Strategy for Combating Terrorism*, Washington DC: The White House, February, 2003, p. 8.
2. Ibid, p. 12.
3. See the "Declaration of War Against the Americans Occupying the Land of the Two Holy Places (Expel the Infidels from the Arab Peninsula): A Message from Osama bin Ladin to his Muslim Brethren All Over the World Generally and in the Arab Peninsula Specifically," December 1996.
4. The failure of the al Qaeda strategy is addressed in detail in James S. Robbins, "Bin Laden's War," in Howard and Sawyer (eds), *Terrorism and Counterterrorism*, Guilford, CT: McGraw-Hill/Dushkin (2003).
5. The al Qaeda 1996 Declaration of War, *op. cit.*
6. Jonathan Stevenson, "Al-Qa'ida May Be Weaker, but Also Harder to Eliminate," *The Times* of London, May 17, 2003.
7. Interview with Hizballah's Deputy Secretary General Shaykh Na'im al-Qasim, by Qasim Qasir, "Hizballah's Deputy Secretary General Shaykh Na'im Al-Qasim: We Overtook Stage of U.S. Pressure But Dangers Have Not Ended," *Beirut Al-Mustaqbal*, September 11, 2003.
8. "Hekmatyar Denies Links with Taliban, al-Qa'ida," Voice of the Islamic Republic of Iran External Service, February 22, 2003.
9. See Peter Finn and Susan Schmidt, "Al Qaeda Plans a Front in Iraq," *Washington Post*, September 7, 2003, p. A1. The facts surrounding the alleged extradition agreement are in some dispute. See Abd-al-Muhsin al-Murshid, "Informed Sources: Iran Has Not Extradited to Saudi Arabia Any of al-Qa'ida's Important Members, but Handed Over 13 Persons of No Security Importance, Among Them 11 Children and Women," *Al-Sharq al-Awsat*, September 9, 2003, p. 4.
10. Note that it is hard to distinguish Syria from Iraq ideologically, and Baathist solidarity was certainly not a motivating factor in the relationship between the two countries.
11. Con Coughlin, "Saddam Killed Abu Nidal Over Al-Qa'ida Row," *The Sunday Telegraph* (London), August 25, 2002.
12. "Who Kidnapped Abd-al-Rahman Isa, Abu-Nidal's Confidante, Abu-Nidal Organization's Second-in-Command, Last to Meet Abu-Nidal Before Killed," *Al-Majallah*, October 20, 2002, pp. 62–3.
13. News Release, Headquarters United States Central Command, April 19, 2003.
14. Julie S. Alipala, Rosa-May V. de Guzman, and TJ Burgonio, "Iraqis Aiding Us, Abu Leader Admits," *Philippine Daily Inquirer*, March 2, 2003.
15. Hong Kong AFP, March 24, 2003.
16. Pedro Arnuero, "Bin-Ladin's Aide in Morocco Was an Iraqi Intelligence Services Official," *Madrid La Razon*, October 1, 2002.
17. Pedro Arnuero "Al-Qa'idah Held 'Summit' in Spain Six Days Before 11 September," *Madrid La Razon*, June 26, 2002.
18. Peter Finn and Susan Schmidt, "Al Qaeda Plans a Front in Iraq," *op. cit.*
19. See Inigo Gilmore, "The Proof that Saddam Worked With bin Laden," *The Sunday Telegraph* (London), April 27, 2003.
20. John Ellis, June 5, 2003, at "Senior Conference 40: Combating Terrorism: Challenges and Opportunities in the Use of Power," United States Military Academy, West Point, NY.
21. Gerry J. Gilmore, "Bush: Global Terrorists Are Meeting the Fate They Chose for Themselves," *American Forces Press Service*, August 14, 2003.
22. For example, note the number of Palestinian terrorist organizations with nearly identical agendas and a fierce antipathy toward each other. Furthermore the hatred of Osama bin Laden for Ur-terrorist Yassir Arafat is well known.
23. Quoted by Deputy Secretary of Defense Paul Wolfowitz, Prepared Testimony before the Senate Armed Services Committee, Washington, D.C., Tuesday, September 9, 2003.
24. Muhammad al-Shafi'i, "Al-Zawahiri's Secret Papers; Al-Zawahiri Talks About the Blessed Fruits After Bombing of U.S. Embassies," *Al-Sharq al-Awsat*, December 17, 2002, p. 5.

25. Muhammad al-Shafi'i, "'Contracting Company' Is Coded Reference to Al-Qa'ida and 'Contractor' Means Bin Ladin and 'Emirate' the Jihad Organization; Letters Exchanged Between Al-Zawahiri and Leaders in Yemen Reveal Struggle Inside Jihad Because of Differences Over Joining Bin Ladin's Front; Jihad Leader Criticizes Initiative To Stop Violence in Egypt Severely, Regards Its Surrender, and Speaks About Betrayal in his Letters," *Al-Sharq al-Awsat*, December 13, 2002, p. 3.
26. "Al-Zayyat: Al-Zawahiri Is Going Through a Difficult Time," interview with fundamentalist lawyer Muntasir al-Zayyat, *Al-Sharq al-Awsat*, December 15, 2002.
27. "Reports of Sa'd Bin Ladin Leading Al-Qa'ida Organization," *Al-Sharq al-Awsat*, July 29, 2002, p. 1.
28. Mahmud Khalil, "Al-Qa'ida Sources: Bin Ladin Will Be Heard and Seen After Operation in August," *Al-Sharq al-Awsat*, July 30, 2002, p. 1.
29. *ITAR-TASS*, October 3, 2002; Al-Jazirah Satellite Channel Television, October 8, 2002.
30. "Al-Majallah Obtains Bin Ladin's Will: It Bears His Signature in His Own Hand and Is Dated Ramadan 1422 Hegira, Corresponding to 14 December 2001. To His Friends: If It Was Not for Treachery, the Situation Would Not Be What It Is Now; To His Wives: Do Not Marry After Me and Devote Yourselves to the Children; To His Sons: Stay Away From Al-Qa'ida and the Front," *Al-Majallah*, October 27, 2002, pp. 22–26.
31. Abd-al-Rahman al-Rashid, "Al-Qa'ida Spokesman Abu-Ghayth Arrested in Iran," *Al-Sharq al-Awsat*, May 30, 2003.
32. "Mullah Omar Calls for Jihad Against U.S., Kabul Regime," *Islam Online*, October 8, 2002.
33. *Al Majalla*, May 11, 2003, p. 17.
34. The reader may well ponder the dysfunctionality, not to mention irony, of using suicide bombers to attack graveyards.
35. "Eight Terrorists Belong to the Tangier and Fes Cells Involved. Jihad Through Attacks, Smuggling and Murder," *Casablanca Al Bayane*, June 19, 2003; Peter Finn, "In Moroccan Slum, Zealotry Took Root: Bombers Linked to Al Qaeda Worked Under Radar of Authorities," *Washington Post*, June 3, 2003, page A1.
36. "Statement from Shaykh Usama Bin Ladin, May God Protect Him, and Al-Qa'ida Organization," *Al-Qal'ah*, October 14, 2002.
37. "Al-Qa'ida Statement Congratulates Yemenis on the Bombing of the French Tanker off Yemen's Coast," *Al-Quds al-Arabi*, October 16, 2002.
38. "Exposing the New Crusader War," Text of New Audio Message attributed to Usama Bin Ladin, *Waaqiah*, February 14, 2003.
39. *Al-Majallah*, June 22, 2003, pp. 10–11.
40. Abd-al-Bari Atwan, "Bush, Al-Qa'ida Nightmare," *Al-Quds al-Arabi*, September 12, 2003, p. 1; Peter Finn and Susan Schmidt, "Al Qaeda Plans a Front in Iraq," *op. cit.*

Michael R. Eastman and Robert B. Brown, 2003

Security Strategy in the Gray Zone

Alternatives for Preventing WMD Handoff to Non-State Actors

Over the past several years, national awareness of and sensitivity to the dangers posed by the shadowy networks of international terror have increased significantly. When combined with the potentially catastrophic consequences of future terrorist attacks conducted not with passenger planes but weapons of mass destruction, the need for comprehensive security strategies that address this threat has never been more pressing. Serious academic and policy work in this area has produced a fair amount of consensus on the merits of deterrence as a strategy to prevent a WMD attack from a rational adversary, as well as the need to resort to preemption when dealing with both irrational opponents and non-state actors with few if any values to hold hostage. However, neither of these security strategies is necessarily appropriate for what we believe to be an understudied aspect of the threat: How to prevent the proliferation of weapons of mass destruction from states to non-state actors. This article assesses three potential strategies directed at the link between a proliferating state and the terrorist end user. Upon examination of the assumptions, strengths and weaknesses of each, we conclude that preventing potentially hostile states from acquiring mature WMD production capabilities is the best of three bad options for safeguarding the public well-being and national interests of the United States.

President Bush, in the 2002 *National Security Strategy*, highlights the threat posed by weapons of mass destruction (WMD) in the hands of radical groups as "the gravest danger our Nation faces…"[1] This emphasis is similarly reflected in the companion document, the *National Strategy to Combat Weapons of Mass Destruction*.[2] However, both strategic blueprints suffer from a common shortcoming. They do not directly confront the critical link between states that might have the capability, intent, and incentive to hand off WMD and terrorists groups with the global reach to employ them against the United States. Despite acknowledging that current approaches to counter-proliferation have not proven foolproof, attention in these strategic blueprints quickly shifts to two propositions that enjoy general

The views expressed in this paper are those of the authors and do not necessarily reflect the official policy or position of the United States Military Academy, the Department of the Army, the Department of Defense, or the U.S. government.

consensus. The first is that America's long-standing reliance on deterrence, based on our substantial nuclear arsenal, continues to present sufficient threats to discourage a WMD strike by a rational state actor. The second is that non-state actors, and religiously motivated terrorist groups in particular, are increasingly undeterrable and must instead be dealt with preemptively.[3]

While we do not disagree with either of these propositions, it is not immediately apparent that either is necessarily appropriate when applied toward the issue of WMD transfer from states to non-state actors. WMD counterproliferation lingers in what we have termed the gray zone between states and non-state actors, where the requirements for both deterrence and preemption confront significant, and often unexplored, difficulties.

This paper is organized in three stages. We first examine the unique challenges posed by WMD handoff between hostile states and non-state actors. Particular emphasis is placed on disrupting the connections between potential state proliferators of WMD and non-state end users. This is based on our belief that, absent the independent ability of terrorist groups to manufacture effective nuclear, biological, chemical or radiological weapons capable of inflicting mass casualties, it is the link between producer and consumer that has not received sufficient attention. After bounding the problem and defining key terms, we then examine three distinct strategic options available to the U.S. national leadership as it evaluates ways to best secure vital American interests at home and abroad. Although current administration policy combines elements of deterrence, preemption and prevention, we choose to examine the theoretical foundations and practical limitations of each strategic option in isolation, hoping to clearly identify the strengths and weaknesses of each. Finally, we compare WMD counterproliferation strategies built on these respective options and highlight key operational requirements and difficulties.

There are fundamental differences between deterrence, preemption and prevention. By identifying the strengths and weaknesses of each we can determine the alternative that is most likely to stop terrorist groups from acquiring WMD. Our conclusion is that a preventive strategy, despite the clear negative consequences it implies for international cooperation and American military overextension, is the only option that promises to halt the transfer of WMD from hostile proliferators to terrorist organizations at a level of risk tolerable to this country.

WMD Handoff—Issues and Challenges

The emergence of Al Qaeda as a major terrorist threat marks a turning point in Western societies' struggles against terrorism. Prior to September 11, most observers discounted the likelihood that terrorists would employ weapons of mass destruction for a variety of reasons: difficulty of acquisition, likelihood of detection and apprehension, and the desire to make a political statement rather than inflict maximum casualties.[4] However, terrorist acts throughout the last decade have shown a troubling trend toward greater violence and destruction, often for its own sake, rather than to achieve a political end. As Al Qaeda's suicide hijackers clearly demonstrated, terrorists and other non-state actors will resort to any means available to inflict harm on the United States and its interests. Therefore, it is no longer reasonable to assume that terrorists will not resort to weapons of mass destruction if the opportunity presents itself. Given this new environment, the United States cannot discount the possibility that terrorists will use weapons of mass destruction.

Serious discussion of the issue, however, first requires setting limits on the threat. Much of the confusion associated with the discussion of counterproliferation strategies results from the application of the term WMD to a wide assortment of loosely related items, from nuclear weapons on one extreme to hijacked commercial airliners on the other. While perhaps useful from a political standpoint, undisciplined usage clouds an already complex issue. While we reluctantly adopt the term WMD for this paper, it is used in a narrowly defined sense to refer to a class of weapons that meets several criteria. First, weapons of mass destruction must actually be independently capable of inflicting significant numbers of casualties under reasonable conditions. An attack on the scale of the World Trade Center is a useful measure as a lower bound. This requirement recognizes that most any well-planned attack can inflict large numbers of deaths in a short period of time, but only under rather unlikely circumstances. Employment of a true weapon of mass destruction directly results in thousands of casualties, ruling out nearly all chemical attacks and the vast majority of biological strikes as well.

Second, the time between a WMD attack and the infliction of casualties is extremely short. There is a necessary distinction between campaigns of terror and the true weapon of mass destruction. This physical quality is most easily satisfied with the detonation of nuclear and radiological weapons. Biological weapons that are highly contagious and rapidly spread would clear this hurdle, as would lethal chemicals capable of efficient, widespread dissemination. However, lesser attacks that could be reasonably contained, such as the anthrax letters of a year ago, would not be considered using this definition.

Finally, genuine weapons of mass destruction create damage of an almost unknowable and uncontrollable quantity. For nuclear and radiological weapons, it is the lasting effects of radioactive contamination that distinguish such bombs from a like quantity of conventional explosives. The threat from weaponized smallpox or a similarly virulent biological agent rests not only in the immediate casualties it would inflict, but the sheer uncertainty implied by its release into a population. How, if at all, can the spread of a contagion be restricted to the target state? It is this final characteristic that makes this class of weapons unconventional in the most basic sense.

Taken together, these qualifiers rule out a large number of weapons normally considered under the rubric of WMD, to include those weapons non-state actors are perhaps most capable of acquiring or producing independently. Terrorists are certainly capable of acquiring or developing chemical and biological agents to inflict widespread damage. In two well-known cases, the Rajneesh cult used *Salmonella* bacteria in Oregon in 1984 and Aum Shinrikyo used sarin nerve agent in Japan in 1995. Although both of these incidents were limited in their scope and resulted in only a handful of deaths, these attacks demonstrated that well-organized and well-financed terror groups have the capability to develop or acquire biological and chemical weapons. We also know that Al Qaeda had crude labs in Afghanistan that experimented with anthrax and chemical agents. But the failure of even the sophisticated and well-funded Al Qaeda to develop weaponized biological and chemical agents capable of being delivered in large quantities is instructive. Despite a strong desire to acquire them, safe haven from which they could operate at will, substantial financial backing, and an extremely sophisticated organization, Al Qaeda was unable to develop such agents on their own. Therefore, we make the distinction between unconventional weapons in the general sense and weapons that have been refined so that they truly have the ability to inflict mass destruction. Fortunately, weapons that are truly capable of inflicting mass destruction remain beyond the grasp of most states, much less terrorist non-state actors.[5] It is therefore on the proliferating states themselves that we focus our attention.

Deterrence—A Classic Response

The manipulation of incentives remains a cornerstone of our security policy, and one that has been successful across many issues of critical importance. In the area of nuclear strategy, for example, the threat of annihilation by secure second strike produced a wary stability between the United States and the Soviet Union for the duration of the Cold War. Applied to WMD handoff, a deterrent strategy is built around a promise of overwhelming retaliation against any adversary who transfers such weapons to non-state actors. Faced with a credible threat of overwhelming punishment, it is hoped that potential proliferators will conclude that it is not in their best interests to transfer WMD to non-state users. The costs simply exceed the benefits. What follows is an overview of the theoretical foundations of a deterrent strategy, along with a brief sketch of how it might be applied to WMD handoff.

The work of Thomas Schelling remains the basis for much of our understanding of deterrence, particularly as it applies to nuclear weapons.[6] In general terms, a deterrent strategy works by threatening the use of force to persuade an adversary not to act in certain ways.[7] An opponent must weigh the possible gains to be had by acting against the costs that the threat, if delivered, would impose. Because such a strategy leaves the initiative to the opponent, proving success is often elusive. However, deterrence is presumed to work when an adversary does not behave in ways that are proscribed. We simply assume that his behavior was modified by the imposition of the threat. Whether or not the Soviets ever truly intended to launch a nuclear attack on this country, for example, we conclude that our ability to strike back was sufficient disincentive to prevent them from acting.

When deterrence fails, lack of success is usually attributed to a lack of credibility on the part of the threatening state. The adversary has either judged the threatened punishment as insufficiently costly, unlikely to be imposed, or some combination of the two.[8] In short, deterrent strategies hinge on credibility as determined from the perspective of the target state. The initiator must seem to possess both the capability and the intent to inflict the threatened punishment, and the adversary must conclude that the risks of acting outweigh the benefits.

Deterrence remains a useful component of our national security strategy. For example, it is generally assumed that any nuclear attack on this country or its allies by a state would meet with an overwhelming response in kind, and this creates enormous disincentives for an enemy contemplating a WMD attack.[9] The issue, however, is whether or not this same strategy will deter states from proliferating weapons to terrorist groups that do not fear retribution. A number of prominent scholars have argued that deterrence does work and assume that the nuclear deterrent threat extends to the case of WMD proliferation. Ken Waltz, for example, believes that the mere suspicion of an Iraqi WMD transfer to a terrorist group would, in the aftermath of an attack, be sufficient to incur a retaliatory nuclear strike from the United States.[10] In similar fashion, John Mearsheimer and Stephen Walt contend that "Saddam could never be sure that we would not incinerate him anyway if we merely suspected that he had made it possible for anyone to strike the United States with nuclear weapons."[11] They then conclude that the risks of an American response are sufficient to convince states not to proliferate.

There are a number of questionable assumptions in this position. First, there is some ambiguity concerning whether or not a nuclear retaliatory strike would be visited upon any state responsible for providing weapons to a non-state actor. Nor is it clear that every WMD attack merits nuclear retaliation. Nonetheless, in the aftermath of a WMD strike on the United States, the desire for punishment would be quite strong. Non-state actors lack tangible assets that might be struck in such a response. The only viable candidates for retaliation after a non-state WMD attack are the countries responsible for providing the weapons and technology needed to carry out the attack. Just as in the current *War on Terrorism*, deterrence holds state sponsors accountable for the actions of any terrorist groups they have empowered through proliferation. It is therefore the risk tolerance of the proliferating state that lies at the core of a deterrent strategy.

Without ruling out conventional responses altogether, the threat of total regime destruction through a nuclear response does pose the greatest conceivable disincentive for a state contemplating WMD handoff. If this level of punishment fails to deter the targeted behavior, then it seems reasonable to assume that lesser included conventional responses would be equally ineffective. Furthermore, because a deterrent strategy presumes that the adversary has a mature WMD program, American threats of conventional punishment are less than credible, if not self-deterred altogether, by our potential fear of escalation. Adversaries need look no further than our recent dealings with North Korea to draw this conclusion, accurate or not. This combination of factors supports the position that our nuclear deterrent would be extended to include WMD transfer.

Relying on a deterrent strategy for WMD handoff produces a straightforward declaratory policy. The United States promises regime destruction for any state that transfers weapons of mass destruction to non-state actors. Successful application of this strategy hinges on two basic conditions. First, the United States must have the ability to monitor WMD transactions and demonstrate to potential adversaries that any attempt to sell or hand off WMD will not go undetected. If a proliferating state thinks it will not get caught, then concerns about potential punishment can be brushed off. Second, efforts should be taken to make the threatened response credible. Proliferators must believe that there is a reasonable chance that the United States has both the capability and the will to impose the promised penalties. If both conditions are met, then a deterrent strategy stands a reasonable chance of success.

Preemption—Just-in-Time Disruption

The 2002 National Security Strategy acknowledges that no state "need suffer an attack before they can lawfully take action to defend themselves against forces that present an imminent threat of attack."[12] Unlike deterrence, a preemptive strategy relies not on the threat of force, but its actual use against an enemy that has demonstrated the intent and the capability to carry out an attack. It is a strategy of striking first, where the initiative is taken by the intended victim. In a general sense, preemptive strategies are "designed to forestall the mobilization and deployment of the adversary's existing military forces."[13] More specifically, rather than relying on the risk tolerance of the aggressor, preemption removes an opponent's ability to strike just before he attacks.

Against terrorists, for example, there is a strong case to be made that preemption is the only appropriate strategy. Non-state actors pose unique challenges for deterrence. They possess no territory or population that may be targeted. They own nothing of sufficient value that may be held hostage. As noted historian John Gaddis and others have argued quite convincingly, there is no effective way to deter someone willing to commit suicide to achieve their aims.[14] Using a similar rationale, the Bush administration has clearly incorporated elements of preemption into the National Security Strategy, vowing to strike first against terrorist organizations rather than retaliate against them in the aftermath of an attack.[15] However, much like deterrence, there is no reason to assume that preemption is an effective way to approach the specific threat of WMD proliferation without first examining the strategy's theoretical and operational requirements.

In the context of WMD handoff, preemption is narrowly bounded to address only the physical transfer of weapons, technology, and expertise from states to non-state actors. It implies no first strike against states that merely develop WMD programs; in fact, a preemptive approach to counterproliferation accepts that states will acquire weapons of mass destruction and requires that the United States maintain a robust nuclear deterrent as a disincentive for their use. What preemption in the gray zone does promise, however, is the use of force justified by the imminent act of proliferation. It is a strategy based on disrupting WMD transactions at the point of exchange, of removing the capability of non-state actors to strike by preventing them from acquiring the means themselves.[16]

Launching a preemptive attack against a likely proliferator requires gathering evidence of two theoretical prerequisites: capability and intent. Potential target states must possess the ability to produce and distribute weapons and/or enabling materials to non-state actors. These may range from transportable nuclear devices and fissile material on one extreme to small vials of biological cultures on the other.[17] Second, the United States must discern the proliferator's intent to conduct the prohibited transfer. As previously stated, malicious intent on the part of the terrorist organization is presumed. However, this is secondary to this approach as striking terrorists already in possession of WMD is both stated policy and an obvious indication that the counterproliferation has already failed. In order to justify preemption, however, the intent of the proliferation to carry out a transfer to a non-state actor must also be determined prior to the act itself.

A preemptive strategy to counter WMD handoff focuses on the potential contacts and transfer options available to states willing to provide weapons and the terrorist organizations trying to acquire them. On the supply side of this relationship, preemption requires intense monitoring of all states that have acquired or are in the process of developing WMD production capabilities. While the bulk of this intelligence effort could be directed at states hostile to the United States, even allies would be subject to intense monitoring in the area of dual-use technologies, unguarded military facilities, and even the flow of trained researchers and weapons experts. Production and movement of weapons and enabling components by land, sea and air would be tracked.

Similar energy would be directed toward terrorist organizations themselves. In addition to ongoing intelligence work aimed at locating and dismantling the command nodes of these shadowy networks, emphasis would be placed on identifying and monitoring individuals in close contact with potential proliferators. Evidence of such ties is a necessary step toward proving the intent to hand off weapons on the part of the state actor. The intent to proliferate would be further reinforced by indications that prohibited weapons or materials were being covertly moved toward a range of viable transfer nodes, ranging from commercial shipping ports to private airfields.

Although it poses significant operational challenges, a preemptive counterproliferation strategy is theoretically viable. Given the generally accepted belief that terrorists would not acquire WMD without the intent to use them, evidence of dealings between states that possess such weapons and terrorist organizations could justify a preemptive strike. Assuming the United States can muster the immense intelligence and analysis assets needed to monitor potential proliferation across the spectrum of transfer modes available to states, and couple it with a military strike complex capable of rapidly interdicting WMD handoff immediately before it occurs, preemption remains a viable policy option.

Prevention—You Can't Transfer What You Don't Have

In contrast to preemption, a preventive strategy seeks to remove the chance that a potentially hostile state may transfer WMD by stripping it of a mature weapons development capability altogether. The concept of prevention is hardly a newcomer to international politics or military affairs. As a motivation for war, states have launched preventive strikes "in an attempt to block or retard the rise of a challenger while that opportunity is still available."[18] Such wars generally assume a hostile intent on the part of an adversary who is in the process of increasing its military capabilities. In practice, they are undertaken to address a threat while the balance of power favors the initiating state, or at the very least at a time and place of the preventer's choosing. Applied more narrowly to the case of WMD counterproliferation, prevention requires that the United States simply presume that mature WMD programs in certain states pose an intolerable proliferation risk. Whether this is due to hostile intent or lack of positive control within the target state is theoretically immaterial. Rather than ceding initiative to a proliferation threat or awaiting definitive evidence of a desire to transfer WMD to a non-state actor, the United States would initiate a range of preventive actions, up to and including the use of force, to stop the acquisition of a mature WMD program.

The causal logic underpinning a preventive strategy is undeniably straightforward. States that are not permitted to develop WMD do not pose a proliferation risk. Take away the weapons themselves, and neither friends with loose arsenals nor enemies with hostile intentions pose a proliferation risk. As Lawrence Freedman has recently written, "prevention provides a means of confronting factors that are likely to contribute to the development of a threat before it has a chance to become imminent."[19] Rather than attempting to discern the intention to proliferate, prevention requires the United States to seek evidence of the intent to develop WMD capabilities. This knowledge alone then justifies a range of passive and active preventive measures designed to counter the acquisition of mature WMD production capabilities.

While significant, the operational prerequisites for a preventive strategy are also less demanding than the two previous options. First, our more restrictive definition of WMD precludes a wide range of weapons currently implied by the term as it is commonly used. It is evident that certain chemical and biological weapons, such as sarin and *E. coli*, can be manufactured by relatively unsophisticated actors. However, weapons meeting more stringent requirements require the collocation of significant assets, assets only available to state actors.[20] It is these that a preventive strategy would target. Furthermore, even though the assets required to monitor potential WMD development around the globe are significant, they are less extensive than those needed to track the transfer of weapons and their component parts through the myriad of private and commercial venues open to a determined proliferator. In fact, the intelligence framework for a strategy of prevention closely resembles the assets currently dedicated to monitoring potential adversaries.

Current passive mechanisms of prevention fall under the rubric of existing non-proliferation regimes such as the Non-Proliferation Treaty and the Nunn-Lugar Cooperative Threat Reduction Program.[21] These programs have met with limited success minimizing the number of nuclear-capable states through both diplomatic pressure to discourage non-nuclear nations from developing WMD capability, and economic assistance to help nuclear-capable nations secure their existing stocks of weapons, raw materials, and technology. However, existing regimes cannot be considered comprehensive tools for a prevention strategy, as they require full cooperation of the states of concern; they have no active components to address states unwilling to comply, or more problematic, states that publicly endorse diplomatic measures and accept inducements, but secretly continue weapons development. The recent failure of the 1994 Framework Agreement between the United States and North Korea illustrates the limited utility of diplomatic measures to constrain a state determined to develop nuclear weapons.

A robust prevention strategy requires mechanisms to address both cooperative and uncooperative potential proliferators. Programs like CTR have continued utility in helping control the unwitting transfer of weapons from generally cooperative states like Russia and Ukraine to less cooperative states like Iran and Syria, and provide viable policy alternatives where the diffusion of responsibility makes deterrence completely ineffective as a strategy. The critical dilemma is how to develop active programs that adequately deal with uncooperative nations that seek WMD, and are potential proliferators.

In general, the quiver of active mechanisms includes diplomatic sanction, economic sanction, and military intervention. It can be assumed that diplomatic sanction has little utility in coercing an uncooperative state. Economic sanctions have some utility, but are problematic in several respects. First, they require near complete international cooperation to be effective—a rare circumstance in international politics. Even a few sympathetic nations can significantly undermine their effectiveness, and the shortages caused by embargoes create huge financial incentives to defect. Even if states cooperate, the ability of multinational corporations to use middlemen, cutouts, and brokers to evade sanctions makes monitoring compliance nearly impossible. Similarly, when applied to authoritarian states, sanctions tend to impact civilian populations significantly more than they alter the policies of their leaders. Iraq's capacity to evade the coercive effects of sanctions—while tolerating their humanitarian consequences—highlights the difficulty of economic coercion.[22] In the end, the most effective mechanism of active prevention remains military action.

The Best of Three Bad Options

Comparison of these three alternate strategies in isolation makes clear that each has both advantages and disadvantages. What remains is a side-by-side comparison to determine which option, if any, has a reasonable probability of successfully achieving the objective of stopping the handoff of WMD. Our focus remains strictly limited to the question of how best to prevent WMD from falling into the hands of groups that would employ them. There is no question that these strategies have significant international and domestic ramifications. In fact, much of the debate over the merits of preemption and prevention resides in the ripples these strategies create for international organizations.[23] However, emphasizing the second order effects of a strategy before asking the fundamental question: "Will it work?" is a bit like putting the proverbial cart before the horse. By highlighting the narrow operational difficulties associated with each strategy, we will demonstrate that only prevention offers a reasonable probability of achieving stated goals. Whether or not it is a politically viable strategic option is of secondary interest to this study.

Regardless of the strategic option under examination, the operational challenges associated with tracking WMD transfer are significant. Given the range of options available to a determined proliferator, one accepts a high level of risk in assuming that even the United States, with its sophisticated global intelligence apparatus, can confidently detect WMD transfers.[24] Our experiences with similar efforts, such as interdicting drug trafficking and stopping illegal immigration, have shown that a determined adversary can evade even our best efforts an alarming portion of the time.[25] Unfortunately, when even low success rates are extended to WMD handoff, where only one failure could result in catastrophic damage, these risks exceed acceptable levels.

While the intelligence requirements for a preventive strategy are significant, they are less than those required of the previous two strategies. A mature WMD production base requires infrastructure, raw materials, and highly specialized scientists operating clandestinely for an extended period of time. Once assembled, the location of such assets is difficult, though not impossible, to disguise.[26] Successful proliferation, however, requires only a working device and a covert way to transfer it from buyer to seller. The more likely case is a weapon assembled from dual-use components acquired from multiple sources through several, intentionally disguised transport means. In relative terms, the intelligence required for both deterrence and preemption dwarfs that needed for a policy of prevention.

A deterrent strategy for the problem of WMD handoff must satisfy two additional conditions. First, potential proliferators must believe that the chance they can evade responsibility for a handoff is prohibitively low. If states think they can transfer WMD and escape detection, then a strategy to deter such acts based on the threat of retribution founders at the outset. Second, proliferators must perceive that the deterrent threat is credible. It must promise to impose severe costs on a proliferator that outweigh any potential gains to be had through WMD handoff. States must also believe that the United States is willing and able to follow through with the threatened response.

There are significant problems with the credibility of any threat the United States might make to deter the handoff of WMD, distinct from the myriad ways states would seek to conduct such transactions covertly and escape punishment altogether. The credibility of a deterrent threat is greatest when "we get ourselves into a position where we cannot fail to react as we said we would… or where we would be obliged by some overwhelming cost of not reacting in the manner we had declared."[27] In the context of WMD handoff, this is cause for concern. The combination of an intelligent adversary determined to avoid detection and a deliberate strategy to diffuse responsibility make it extremely difficult to pin responsibility for proliferation on any one state. In light of this, there is some question in our mind whether potential proliferators would believe that the United States could actually carry out its deterrent threat and punish WMD handoff with nuclear attack.

Several prominent political scientists argued against a preemptive war in Iraq, advocating just such a deterrent policy. A central pillar in their position was the belief that a rogue leader such as Saddam Hussein would never risk the handoff of WMD to terrorist groups for fear of facing nuclear incineration even if it was "merely suspected that he had made it possible for anyone to strike the United States with nuclear weapons."[28] However, this greatly oversimplifies the situation that would confront the president in the face of evidence of a WMD handoff. As we have indicated, the transfer of WMD can take several forms. Critical components of a weapon can be sold off a piece at a time, through one or several front companies. Responsibility for proliferation might be traced to rogue elements within a military, as is speculated in the case of the former Soviet Republics, or to high-tech firms operating within the sovereign territories of multiple states. Assembly of a crude WMD device may involve the transfer of materials and technology from multiple sources, none of which in isolation could provide a functioning weapon. Even in the absence of collaboration, it seems reasonable to assume that non-state actors intent on acquiring WMD might be forced to work through multiple sources. This diffusion of responsibility cuts against the utility of deterrence by removing the target of any threat.

Furthermore, the logic of nuclear deterrence works by holding the core values of an adversary hostage. Deterrence prevents a nuclear first strike because any potential opponent understands that their most prized possessions, whether in the form of territory, military forces, or population, will be destroyed the instant that such an attack is launched. Such calculations cannot be assumed to apply in the case of WMD proliferation. There are many reasons why a president might not be able to muster domestic support for a strike against the population of a proliferator. Unlike a nuclear first strike, the time between a WMD handoff and use of the weapon could be considerable. The parties responsible for the transfer may not be operating with consent of their people, if they even remain in power when the time comes for American retribution.

In each of these cases, there is a diffusion of responsibility for the WMD handoff that makes any retaliation, much less a nuclear response, extremely challenging. Who exactly will be punished for the handoff? The difficulty associated with making that determination can hardly be lost on the potential proliferators of WMD. As such, it creates a second source of risk for a strategy based on deterrence. When combined with the operational challenges of tracking WMD handoffs, it is not altogether unreasonable to assume that risk-acceptant states might see a reasonable probability of success in transferring WMD and then avoiding punishment. Proponents of deterrence assume that in the aftermath of a WMD use against this country, the government will respond swiftly and surely against the state that provided such weapons to the terrorist attacker. They do not contemplate the case where there is not one smoking gun, but many. Nor do they acknowledge that the guns are purposely hidden from view.

A preemptive strategy of counterproliferation suffers from its own operational and theoretical challenges. As previously stated, preemption requires intelligence on the WMD capability of the potential proliferators, and operational knowledge of impending transfers to a third party actor. Relying on "just-in-time" interdiction creates a two-fold hurdle for the preempting nation, and the costs of failure are potentially catastrophic in two distinct ways.

First, preemption requires a clear knowledge of the location, types, and quantities of weapons every potential proliferator possesses—a similar challenge faced by a deterrent strategy. Absent this level of detail, the ability to identify the covert movement of weapons—a signal of impending handoff—becomes unlikely. Adding complexity to the intelligence problem, preemption requires more than simple knowledge of weapons transfers—a sufficient condition for deterrence. It requires detailed, *actionable* intelligence of precisely where weapons are stored, how they are transported, and to whom they are to be delivered. The "smoking gun" demanded by the recent coalition intervention in Iraq pales before the requirements of a true preemptive strike. Second, even if a preempting nation can successfully track weapons and detect a potential transfer, the preemptor now faces the prospect of military action against a WMD-capable adversary. This raises the stakes of preemption considerably, approaching the quandary faced by the Superpowers during the Cold War: a preemptive strike will result in a second strike by the aggrieved party. Against a WMD-capable opponent, preemption not only demands the ability to prevent a single imminent transfer, it likely requires the capability for a comprehensive first strike against an aggressor's *entire* arsenal—a significantly taller order.

Failing to detect a transfer in timely fashion could result in a potentially devastating attack. But even if the intelligence operates perfectly, a tactical failure in a preemptive attack would likely result in the very event preemption is designed to stop—a WMD attack against the United States or an ally. Facing the difficulty of a successful first strike against a nuclear-capable adversary, the preemptor is easily deterred.

As a policy, prevention relies on the standard realist premise that intentions are generally unknowable, and frequently changing: it is dangerous to presume that the future good will or stability of governments can be sufficiently anticipated to warrant tacit acceptance of WMD development. While nuclear weapons cannot be returned to Pandora's Box, it is still good policy to constrain their dissemination to the extent possible. Accordingly, a preventive strategy would discourage *any* further proliferation of WMD capability—particularly nuclear weapons. The tools of prevention should vary, however, based on the relationship with the potential proliferators in question. States can be generally categorized according to three groups—each demanding a different preventive strategy.

The first group involves generally friendly states that seek to develop WMD. It is quite feasible that states allied with the United States could decide that a nuclear capability is in their best interest. Given that U.S. intentions and future security guarantees are likewise unknowable, stable governments with a strong recent history of popular consent and the rule of law could still perceive a need for an independent nuclear deterrent. Japan is such a potential future nuclear power. They certainly have the technical capability to develop nuclear weapons, and have regional rivalry with a current nuclear power in China, and an emerging one in North Korea. In these cases, passive preventive measures are appropriate to discourage the further proliferation of WMD capability. However, regardless of the good will or stability of the state in question, determined diplomatic opposition for any new entrant into the nuclear club should be constant—even for nations friendly to the United States. When the concerns of these threatened states are legitimate, the United States must offer credible security guarantees—both conventional and nuclear deterrent. Financial and economic incentives are similarly suitable when confidence exists in the states involved have sufficient economic and political transparency to verify compliance with agreements. When coupled with peer-to-peer military cooperation and integration, diplomatic measures such as international treaties have significant utility in these cases.

The second group involves generally friendly states that either currently possess WMD capability, or that develop it despite passive measures to prevent it. These states similarly warrant passive measures to prevent handoff of weapons to third party actors. In these cases, the United States should pursue bilateral or international monitoring of WMD programs to verify appropriate security of sensitive technology and weapons components, and proper accountability of existing arsenals. However, a sound prevention strategy should not merely accept the status quo of gradual proliferation: continued diplomatic and financial incentives such as an expanded Cooperative Threat Reduction program should encourage these WMD-capable states to reduce their arsenals or eliminate them altogether.

The third group involves nations with a recognized hostility to the United States, its interests or its allies. Examples include the states recognized as known supporters of terrorism. Additionally, this list should include states that lack sufficient institutional stability to preserve the rule of law or adequately control their borders, resources, and weapons. These states demand active measures to prevent their development of WMD. As previously discussed, these measures can range in severity from political and economic sanctions, to military blockade and intervention.

After careful consideration of the risks and probabilities of success for each of these three strategic alternatives, we arrive at a rather unsettling conclusion. In most cases, rational decision-making is rightly centered on the most likely outcome instead of the most dangerous. However, as we have attempted to demonstrate, WMD handoff confronts the United States with a unique set of challenges. The costs of failing to sever the link between proliferating states and non-state actors determined to inflict mass casualties are potentially catastrophic. Both deterrence and preemption are hampered by enormous intelligence challenges, leave the initiative to potential adversaries, and rest on a causal logic that involves accepting dangerous levels of risk. Only a strategy of prevention provides something approaching certainty: adversaries cannot transfer items that they don't have.

This is not blind advocacy for a far-reaching military policy of preventive strikes. Simply declaring that potential adversaries bent on acquiring weapons of mass destruction face possible preventive attack from the United States on the grounds that they could hand off WMD to terrorist organizations may serve to strengthen international regulatory bodies and put teeth into existing treaty obligations. When coupled with a broader policy of security agreements and economic incentives, the mere declaration of a preventive policy may be sufficient to deter WMD handoff.[29] However, the sheer gravity of the threat posed by weapons of mass destruction in the hands of terrorists demands closer evaluation of the theoretical underpinnings and operational requirements of our current counterproliferation policy. While all three strategic options are theoretically sound, they differ greatly in terms of risks incurred and requirements for success. In our view, while prevention incurs the greatest costs in terms of international cooperation, it alone offers a reasonable chance of halting the proliferation of weapons of mass destruction from hostile states to terrorist organizations determined to acquire them.

Michael R. Eastman is assistant professor and course director of National Security Studies at the United States Military Academy at West Point. He is a doctoral candidate in political science from the Massachusetts Institute of Technology.

Robert B. Brown is assistant professor and course director of public policy at the United States Military Academy at West Point. He holds a Master of Public Affairs degree from the LBJ School of Public Affairs at the University of Texas, Austin.

Works Cited

Ackerman, Gary and Laura Snyder. "Would They If They Could?" *Bulletin of the Atomic Scientists* (May/June 2002): 1–9.

Albright, David and Khidzhir Hamza. "Iraq's Reconstitution of its Nuclear Weapons Program." *Arms Control Today* (October 1998).

Art, Robert. "A Defensible Defense: America's Grand Strategy After the Cold War." *International Security* 15 (Spring 1991): 3–43.

Betts, Richard. "Fixing Intelligence." *Foreign Affairs* (Jan/Feb 2002): 43-59.

Bush, George W. *National Strategy to Combat Weapons of Mass Destruction.* Washington, D.C.: December 2002.

_____. *The National Security Strategy of the United States of America.* Washington, D.C.: 17 September 2002.

Cirincione, John. "The International Non-Proliferation Regime." The Carnegie Non-Proliferation Project (2000): 283–290.

Cronin, Audrey. "Behind the Curve: Globalization and International Terrorism." *International Security* (Winter 2002): 30–58.

Downs, George. "The Rational Deterrence Debate." *World Politics* (January 1989): 225–237.

Freedman, Lawrence. "Prevention, Not Preemption." *The Washington Quarterly* (April 2003): 104–114.

Gaddis, John Lewis. "A Grand Strategy." *Foreign Policy* (November-December 2002): 50–57.

Hagerty, Dean. *The Consequences of Nuclear Proliferation.* Cambridge: The MIT Press, 1998.

Hoffman, Bruce. "Viewpoint: Terrorism and WMD: Some Preliminary Hypotheses." *The Nonproliferation Review* (Spring-Summer 1997): 45–53.

Huth, Paul and Bruce Russett. "What Makes Deterrence Work?" *World Politics* (July 1987): 496–527.

Lee, Rensselaer. "Nuclear Smuggling from the Former Soviet Union: Threats and Responses." *Foreign Policy Research Institute* (27 April 2001).

Levy, Jack. "Declining Power and the Preventive Motivation for War." *World Politics* 40 (October 1987): 82–107.

_____. "The Causes of War: A Review of Theories and Evidence." in *Behavior, Society and Nuclear War.* Ed. Paul Tetlock et al. New York: Oxford University Press, 1989. 209-333.

Mearsheimer, John. *Conventional Deterrence.* Ithaca: Cornell University Press, 1983.

Mearsheimer, John and Stephen Walt. "Can Saddam Be Contained? History Says Yes." *New York Times.* 12 November 2002.

_____ "Keeping Saddam in a Box." *New York Times.* February 2003.

McNair Paper Number 41. *Radical Responses to Radical Regimes: Evaluating Preemptive Counter-Proliferation.* May 1995

O'Hanlon, Michael, Susan Rice and James Steinberg. *The New National Security Strategy and Preemption.* Brookings Institution Policy Brief #113. January 2003.

Perkovich, George. "Bush's Nuclear Revolution." *Foreign Affairs* 81 (March/April 2003): 2–9.

Perry, William. "The Next Attack." *Foreign Affairs* (Nov/Dec 2001): 31–45.

Pollack, Kenneth. "Next Stop Baghdad?" *Foreign Affairs* 82 (March/April 2002): 32–47.

Potter, William and Leonard Specter. "The Real Sum of All Fears." *Los Angeles Times.* 11 June 2002.

Schelling, Thomas. *Arms and Influence.* New Haven, Connecticut: Yale University Press, 1966.

Sheridan, Ralph. "The Challenge of WMD Detection in Cargo." Seaport Security Conference. 11 June 2002.

Stern, Jessica. "Dreaded Risks and the Control of Biological Weapons." *International Security* (Winter 2002): 89–123.

Worley, D. Robert. "Waging Ancient War: The Preemptive Use of Force." *Strategic Studies Institute Special Report*. U.S. Army War College. 8 November 2001.

Zanders, Jean Pascal. "Assessing the Risk of Chemical and Biological Weapons Proliferation to Terrorists." *The Nonproliferation Review* (Fall 1999):17–34.

Notes

1. George W. Bush, *The National Security Strategy of the United States of America*, 17 September 2002.
2. George W. Bush, *National Strategy to Combat Weapons of Mass Destruction*, December 2002.
3. See Bruce Hoffman, "Terrorism and WMD: Some Preliminary Hypotheses," *The Nonproliferation Review* (Spring-Summer 1997): 45–53.
4. See, for example Thomas Schelling, "Thinking About Nuclear Terrorism." *International Security*. Robert Art also finds fears of nuclear terrorism overstated due to a belief that terrorists, in order to achieve their political objectives, would need to identify themselves and then risk falling prey to retaliation. This overlooks a shift in modern terrorism to the desire to inflict mass casualties as an end in and of itself or as part of a larger religious struggle. See Robert Art, "A Defensible Defense: America's Grand Strategy After the Cold War," *International Security* 15 (Spring 1991): 27.
5. Matthew Bunn, Anthony Wier, and John Holdren, *Controlling Nuclear Warheads and Materials*, Project on Managing the Atom (Cambridge: Harvard University, 2003): 11.
6. Thomas Schelling, *Arms and Influence* (New Haven: Yale University Press, 1966).
7. Ibid, 33–36.
8. Paul Huth and Bruce Russett, "What Makes Deterrence Work?" *World Politics* (July 1987): 497.
9. For a strong argument on the relevance of a deterrent strategy against WMD use by states, see Devin Hagerty, *The Consequences of Nuclear Proliferation* (Cambridge: The MIT Press, 1998).
10. Kenneth Waltz, "Spread of Nuclear Weapons Nothing to Fear, says Waltz." Accessed from http://www.columbia.edu/cu/news/media/03/kennethWaltz/index.html, available 4 March 2003.
11. John Mearsheimer and Stephen Walt, "Can Saddam Be Contained? History Says Yes," *Los Angeles Times*, 12 November 2002.
12. Bush, *National Security Strategy of the United States of America*, 5.
13. Jack Levy, "Declining Power and the Preventive Motivation for War," *World Politics* 40 (October 1987): 91.
14. John Lewis Gaddis, "A Grand Strategy of Transformation," *Foreign Policy* (November-December 2000): 51.
15. Michael O'Hanlon, Susan Rice and James Steinberg, "The New National Security Strategy and Preemption," Policy Brief #113, Brookings Institution (January 2003).
16. D. Robert Worley, "Waging Ancient War: The Preemptive Use of Force," *Strategic Studies Institute Special Report*, U.S. Army War College, 8 November 2001: 17.
17. There are significant challenges associated with dual-use technologies, and these will be addressed in some detail. That states can sell certain classes of WMD components and enablers to non-state actors and claim innocent motives is a significant problem. However, this is partially overcome if the organizational ties of the customer are known, as even the legitimate business interests of terrorist organizations are still tainted by their larger objectives.
18. Jack Levy, "The Causes of War: A Review of Theories and Evidence," in *Behavior, Society, and Nuclear War*, ed. Phillip Tetlock, et al., (New York: Oxford University Press, 1989): 253.
19. Larwrence Freedman, "Prevention, Not Preemption," *The Washington Quarterly* 26 (Spring 2003): 106.
20. Jessica Stern, "Dreaded Risks and the Control of Biological Weapons," *International Security* (Winter 2002): 96. While Stern argues that the production of biological weapons is extremely difficult to detect, particularly as most components are dual-use, she agrees that the infrastructure required for fissile material processing is detectable at long distances using chem-

ical sensors. Our contention is that weaponized biological weapons require a comparable infrastructure. Weapons developed in a home brewery, for instance, are simply not sufficiently hardy and virulent to survive and inflict mass casualties in all but the most unusual circumstances.

21. John Cirincione, "The International Non-Proliferation Regime," in *Repairing the Regime*, The Carnegie Non-Proliferation Project (2000): 283–290.

22. For a detailed critique of the effectiveness of economic sanctions, see Robert A. Pape, "Why Economic Sanctions Do Not Work," *International Security* (Fall 97): 90.

23. For example, see George Perkovich, "Bush's Nuclear Revolution: A Regime Change in Non-proliferation," *Foreign Affairs* 82 (March/April 2003): 2–9.

24. Ralph Sheridan, "The Challenge of WMD Detection in Cargo," Seaport Security Conference, 11 June 2002.

25. Even with dedicated efforts to interdict fast-boat drug smuggling, for example, success rates of 10 percent are cited by the U.S. Coast Guard. See *Statement of Rear Admiral Ernest Riutta, USCG, on Anti-Narcotics Efforts in the Western Hemisphere Before the Subcommittee on the Western Hemisphere, Committee on International Relations, U.S. House of Representatives*, 3 March 1999. The possibility of proliferators adopting these and other tactics to effect the clandestine transfer of WMD does not seem unreasonable.

26. For example, the difficulties the CIA had determining the location and scope of the Soviet Union's biological warfare program are well documented. See William Broad, "The Impossible Task for America's Spies," *New York Times*, 11 May 2003.

27. Schelling, 43.

28. John Mearsheimer and Stephen Walt, "Can Saddam Be Contained? History Says Yes," *Los Angeles Times*, 12 November 2002.

29. For one example of such a comprehensive proposal, minus the emphasis on prevention, see Richard Garwin, "The Technology of Megaterror," *Technology Review* (September 2002).

Bruce Hoffman, 2003

The Logic of Suicide Terrorism

First you feel nervous about riding the bus. Then you wonder about going to a mall. Then you think twice about sitting for long at your favorite café. Then nowhere seems safe. Terrorist groups have a strategy—to shrink to nothing the areas in which people move freely—and suicide bombers, inexpensive and reliably lethal, are their latest weapons. Israel has learned to recognize and disrupt the steps on the path to suicide attacks. We must learn too.

Nearly everywhere in the world it is taken for granted that one can simply push open the door to a restaurant, café, or bar, sit down, and order a meal or a drink. In Israel the process of entering such a place is more complicated. One often encounters an armed guard who, in addition to asking prospective patrons whether they themselves are armed, may quickly pat them down, feeling for the telltale bulge of a belt or a vest containing explosives. Establishments that cannot afford a guard or are unwilling to pass on the cost of one to customers simply keep their doors locked, responding to knocks with a quick glance through the glass and an instant judgment as to whether this or that person can safely be admitted. What would have been unimaginable a year ago is now not only routine but reassuring. It has become the price of a redefined normality.

In the United States in the twenty months since 9/11 we, too, have had to become accustomed to an array of new, often previously inconceivable security measures—in airports and other transportation hubs, hotels and office buildings, sports stadiums and concert halls. Although some are more noticeable and perhaps more inconvenient than others, the fact remains that they have redefined our own sense of normality. They are accepted because we feel more vulnerable than before. With every new threat to international security we become more willing to live with stringent precautions and reflexive, almost unconscious wariness. With every new threat, that is, our everyday life becomes more like Israel's.

The situation in Israel, where last year's intensified suicide-bombing campaign changed the national mood and people's personal politics, is not analogous to that in the United States today. But the organization and the operations of the suicide bombers are neither limited to Israel and its conflict with the Palestinians nor unique to its geostrategic position. The fundamental characteristics of suicide bombing, and its strong attraction for the terrorist organizations behind it, are universal: Suicide bombings are inexpensive and effective. They are less complicated and compromising than other kinds of terrorist operations. They guarantee media coverage. The suicide terrorist is the ultimate smart bomb. Perhaps most important, coldly efficient bombings tear at the fabric of trust that holds societies together. All these reasons doubtless account for the spread of suicide terrorism from the Middle East to Sri Lanka and Turkey, Argentina and Chechnya, Russia and Algeria—and to the United States.

To understand the power that suicide terrorism can have over a populace—and what a populace can do to counter it—one naturally goes to the society that has been most deeply affected. As a researcher who has studied the strategies of terrorism for more than twenty-five years, I recently visited Israel to review the steps the military, the police, and the intelligence and security services have taken against a threat more pervasive and personal than ever before.

I was looking at x-rays with Dr. Shmuel Shapira in his office at Jerusalem's Hadassah Hospital. "This is not a place to have a wristwatch," he said as he described the injuries of a young girl who'd been on her way to school one morning last November when a suicide terrorist detonated a bomb on her bus. Eleven of her fellow passengers were killed, and more than fifty others wounded. The blast was so powerful that the hands and case of the bomber's wristwatch had turned into lethal projectiles, lodging in the girl's neck and ripping a major artery. The presence of such foreign objects in the bodies of his patients no longer surprises Shapira. "We have cases with a nail in the neck, or nuts and bolts in the thigh…, a ball bearing in the skull," he said.

Such are the weapons of war in Israel today: nuts and bolts, screws and ball bearings, any metal shards or odd bits of broken machinery that can be packed together with home-made explosive and then strapped to the body of a terrorist dispatched to any place where people gather—bus, train, restaurant, café, supermarket, shopping mall, street corner, promenade. These attacks probably cost no more than $150 to mount, and they need no escape plan—often the most difficult aspect of a terrorist operation. And they are reliably deadly. According to data from the Rand Corporation's chronology of international terrorism incidents, suicide attacks on average kill four times as many people as other terrorist acts. Perhaps it is not surprising, then, that this means of terror has become increasingly popular. The tactic first emerged in Lebanon, in 1983; a decade later it came to Israel, and it has been a regular security problem ever since. Fully two thirds of all such incidents in Israel have occurred in the past two and a half years—that is, since the start of the second intifada, in September of 2000. Indeed, suicide bombers are responsible for almost half of the approximately 750 deaths in terrorist attacks since then.

Last December, I walked through Jerusalem with two police officers, one of them a senior operational commander, who were showing me the sites of suicide bombings in recent years. They described the first major suicide-terrorist attack in the city, which occurred in February of 1996, early on a Sunday morning—the beginning of the Israeli work week. The driver of the No. 18 Egged bus was hurrying across a busy intersection at Sarei Yisrael Street as a yellow light turned red. The bus was about halfway through when an explosion transformed it into an inferno of twisted metal, pulverized glass, and burning flesh. A traffic camera designed to catch drivers running stop lights captured the scene on film. Twenty-five people were killed, including two U.S. citizens, and eighty were wounded.

The early years of suicide terrorism were a simpler time, the officers explained. Suicide bombers were—at least in theory—easier to spot then. They tended to carry their bombs in nylon backpacks or duffel bags rather than in belts or vests concealed beneath their clothing, as they do now. They were also typically male, aged seventeen to twenty-three, and unmarried. Armed with these data, the authorities could simply deny work permits to Palestinians most likely to be suicide bombers, thus restricting their ability to cross the Green Line (Israel's pre-1967 border) into Israel proper from the West Bank or the Gaza Strip.

Today, though, suicide bombers are middle-aged and young, married and unmarried, and some of them have children. Some of them, too, are women, and word has it that even children are being trained for martyrdom. "There is no clear profile anymore—not for terrorists and especially not for suicide bombers," an exasperated senior officer in the Israel Defense Forces told me last year. Sometimes the bombers disguise themselves: male *shaheed* (Arabic for "martyrs") have worn green IDF fatigues; have dressed as *haredim* (ultra-Orthodox Jews), complete with yarmulkes and tzitzit, the fringes that devout Jews display as part of their everyday clothing; or have donned long-haired wigs in an effort to look like hip Israelis rather than threatening Arabs. A few women have tried to camouflage bombs by strapping them to their stomachs to fake pregnancy. And contrary to popular belief, the bombers are not drawn exclusively from the ranks of the poor but have included two sons of millionaires. (Most of the September 11 terrorists came from comfortable middle- to upper-middle-class families and were well educated.) The Israeli journalist Ronni Shaked, an expert on the Palestinian terrorist group Hamas, who writes for *Yedioth Ahronoth*, an Israeli daily, has debunked the myth that it is only people with no means of improving their lot in life who turn to suicide terrorism. "All leaders of Hamas," he told me, "are university graduates, some with master's degrees. This is a movement not of poor, miserable people but of highly educated people who are using [the image of] poverty to make the movement more powerful."

Buses remain among the bombers' preferred targets. Winter and summer are the better seasons for bombing buses in Jerusalem, because the closed windows (for heat or air-conditioning) intensify the force of the blast, maximizing the bombs' killing potential. As a hail of shrapnel pierces flesh and breaks bones, the shock wave tears lungs and crushes other internal organs. When the bus's fuel tank explodes, a fireball causes burns, and smoke inhalation causes respiratory damage. All this is a significant return on a relatively modest investment. Two or three kilograms of explosive on a bus can kill as many people as twenty to thirty kilograms left on a street or in a mall or a restaurant. But as security on buses has improved, and passengers have become more alert, the bombers have been forced to seek other targets.

The terrorists are lethally flexible and inventive. A person wearing a bomb is far more dangerous and far more difficult to defend against than a timed device left to explode in a marketplace. This human weapons system can effect last-minute changes based on the ease of approach, the paucity or density of people, and the security measures in evidence. On a Thursday afternoon in March of last year a reportedly smiling, self-satisfied bomber strolled down King George Street, in the heart of Jerusalem, looking for just the right target. He found it in a crowd of shoppers gathered in front of the trendy Aroma Café, near the corner of Agrippas Street. In a fusillade of nails and other bits of metal two victims were killed and fifty-six wounded. Similarly, in April of last year a female suicide bomber tried to enter the Mahane Yehuda open-air market—the fourth woman to make such an attempt in four months—but was deterred by a strong police presence. So she simply walked up to a bus stop packed with shoppers hurrying home before the Sabbath and detonated her explosives, killing six and wounding seventy-three.

Suicide bombing initially seemed the desperate act of lone individuals, but it is not undertaken alone. Invariably, a terrorist organization such as Hamas (the Islamic Resistance Movement), the Palestine Islamic Jihad (PIJ), or the al Aqsa Martyrs Brigade has recruited the bomber, conducted reconnaissance, prepared the explosive device, and identified a target—explaining that if it turns out to be guarded or protected, any crowded place nearby will do. "We hardly ever find that the suicide bomber came by himself," a police officer explained to me. "There is always a handler." In fact, in some cases a handler has used a cell phone or other device to trigger the blast from a distance. A policeman told me, "There was one event where a suicide bomber had been told all he had to do was to carry the bomb and plant explosives in a certain place. But the bomb was remote-control detonated."

The organizations behind the Palestinians' suicide terrorism have numerous components. Quartermasters obtain the explosives and the other materials (nuts, bolts, nails, and the like) that are combined to make a bomb. Now that bomb-making methods have been so widely disseminated throughout the West Bank and Gaza, a merely competent technician, rather than the skilled engineer once required, can build a bomb. Explosive material is packed into pockets sewn into a canvas or denim belt or vest and hooked up to a detonator—usually involving a simple hand-operated plunger.

Before the operation is to be launched, "minders" sequester the bomber in a safe house, isolating him or her from family and friends—from all contact with the outside world—during the final preparations for martyrdom. A film crew makes a martyrdom video, as much to help ensure that the bomber can't back out as for propaganda and recruitment purposes. Reconnaissance teams have already either scouted the target or received detailed information about it, which they pass on to the bomber's handlers. The job of the handlers, who are highly skilled at avoiding Israeli army checkpoints or police patrols, is to deliver the bomber as close to the target as possible.

I talked to a senior police-operations commander in his office at the Russian Compound, the nerve center of law enforcement for Jerusalem since the time when first the Turks and then the British ruled this part of the world. It was easy to imagine, amid the graceful arches and the traditional Jerusalem stone, an era when Jerusalem's law-enforcement officers wore tarbooshes and pressed blue tunics with Sam Browne belts rather than the bland polyester uniforms and blue baseball-style caps of today. Although policing this multi-faith, historically beleaguered city has doubtless always involved difficult challenges, none can compare with the current situation. "This year there were very many events," my host explained, using the bland generic noun that signifies terrorist attacks or attempted attacks. "In previous years we considered ten events as normal; now we are already at forty-three." He sighed. There were still three weeks to go before the end of the year. Nineteen of these events had been suicide bombings. In the calculus of terrorism, it doesn't get much better. "How easy it has become for a person to wake up in the morning and go off and commit suicide," he observed. Once there were only "bags on buses, not vests or belts" to contend with, the policeman said. "Everything is open now. The purpose is to prove that the police can do whatever they want but it won't help."

This, of course, is the age-old strategy of terrorists everywhere—to undermine public confidence in the ability of the authorities to protect and defend citizens, thereby creating a climate of fear and intimidation amenable to terrorist exploitation. In Jerusalem, and in Israel as a whole, this strategy has not succeeded. But it has fundamentally changed daily behavior patterns—the first step toward crushing morale and breaking the will to resist.

The terrorists appear to be deliberately homing in on the few remaining places where Israelis thought they could socialize in peace. An unprecedented string of attacks in the first four months of last year illustrated this careful strategy, beginning at bus stops and malls and moving into more private realms, such as corner supermarkets and local coffee bars. In March, for example, no one paid much attention to a young man dressed like an ultra-Orthodox Jew who was standing near some parked cars as guests left a bar mitzvah celebration at a social hall in the ultra-Orthodox Jerusalem neighborhood of Beit Yisrael. Then he blew himself up, killing nine people, eight of them children, and wounding fifty-nine. The tight-knit religious community had felt that it was protected by God, pointing to the miraculous lack of injury a year before when a booby-trapped car blew up in front of the same hall. Using a strategy al Qaeda has made familiar, the terrorists revisited the site.

Less than a month after the Beit Yisrael attack the suicide bombers and their leaders drove home the point that Israelis cannot feel safe anywhere by going to the one large Israeli city that had felt immune from the suspicion and antipathy prevalent elsewhere—Haifa, with its successful mixture of Jews, Christian and Muslim Arabs, and followers of the Bahai faith. The University of Haifa has long had the highest proportion of Arab students of any Israeli university. The nearby Matza restaurant, owned by Jews but run by an Israeli Arab family from Galilee, seemed to embody the unusually cordial relations that exist among the city's diverse communities. Matza was popular with Jews and Arabs alike, and the presence of its Arab staff and patrons provided a feeling of safety from attack. That feeling was shattered at two-thirty on a quiet Sunday afternoon, when a suicide bomber killed fifteen people and wounded nearly fifty.

As we had tea late one afternoon in the regal though almost preternaturally quiet surroundings of Jerusalem's King David Hotel, Benny Morris, a professor of history at Ben Gurion University, explained, "The Palestinians say they have found a strategic weapon, and suicide bombing is it. This hotel is empty. The streets are empty. They have effectively terrorized Israeli society. My wife won't use a bus anymore, only a taxi." It is undeniable that daily life in Jerusalem, and throughout Israel, has changed as a result of last year's wave of suicide bombings. Even the police have been affected. "I'm worried," one officer told me in an aside—whether in confidence or in embarrassment, I couldn't tell—as we walked past Zion Square, near where some bombs had exploded. "I tell you this as a police officer. I don't come to Jerusalem with my children anymore. I'd give back the settlements. I'd give over my bank account to live in peace."

By any measure 2002 was an astonishing year for Israel in terms of suicide bombings. An average of five attacks a month were made, nearly double the number during the first fifteen months of the second intifada—and that number was itself more than ten times the monthly average since 1993. Indeed, according to a database maintained by the National Security Studies Center, at Haifa University, there were nearly as many suicide attacks in Israel last year (fifty-nine) as there had been in the previous eight years combined (sixty-two). In Jerusalem alone there were nine suicide attacks during the first four months of 2002, killing thirty-three and injuring 464. "It was horrendous," a young professional woman living in the city told me. "No one went out for coffee. No one went out to restaurants. We went as a group of people to one another's houses only."

Again, terrorism is meant to produce psychological effects that reach far beyond the immediate victims of the attack. "The Scuds of Saddam [in 1991] never caused as much psychological damage as the suicide bombers have," says Ami Pedahzur, a professor of political science at Haifa University and an expert on political extremism and violence who manages the National Security Studies Center's terrorism database. As the French philosopher Gaston Bouthoul argued three decades ago in a theoretical treatise on the subject, the "anonymous, unidentifiable threat creates huge anxiety, and the terrorist tries to spread fear by contagion, to immobilise and subjugate those living under this threat." This is precisely what the Palestinian terrorist groups are trying to achieve. "The Israelis... will fall to their knees," Sheikh Ahmad Yassin, the spiritual leader of Hamas, said in 2001. "You can sense the fear in Israel already; they are worried about where and when the next attacks will come. Ultimately, Hamas will win." The strategy of suicide terrorists is to make people paranoid and xenophobic, fearful of venturing beyond their homes even to a convenience store. Terrorists hope to compel the enemy society's acquiescence, if not outright surrender, to their demands. This is what al Qaeda hoped to achieve on 9/11 in one stunning blow—and what the Palestinians seek as well, on a more sustained, if piecemeal, basis.

After decades of struggle the Palestinians are convinced that they have finally discovered Israel's Achilles' heel. Ismail Haniya, another Hamas leader, was quoted in March of last year in *The Washington Post* as saying that Jews "love life more than any other people, and they prefer not to die." In contrast, suicide terrorists are often said to have gone to their deaths smiling. An Israeli policeman told me, "A suicide bomber goes on a bus and finds himself face-to-face with victims and he smiles and he activates the bomb—but we learned that only by asking people afterwards who survived." This is what is known in the Shia Islamic tradition as the *bassamat al-farah*, or "smile of joy"—prompted by one's impending martyrdom. It is just as prevalent among Sunni terrorists. (Indeed, the last will and testament of Mohammed Atta, the ringleader of the September 11 hijackers, and his "primer" for martyrs, *The Sky Smiles, My Young Son*, clearly evidence a belief in the joy of death.)

This perceived weakness of an ostensibly powerful society has given rise to what is known in the Middle East as the "spider-web theory," which originated within Hizbollah, the Lebanese Shia organization, following a struggle that ultimately compelled the Israel Defense Forces to withdraw from southern Lebanon in May of 2000. The term is said to have been coined by Hizbollah's secretary general, Sheikh Hassan Nasrallah, who described Israel as a still formidable military power whose civil society had become materialistic and lazy, its citizens self-satisfied, comfortable, and pampered to the point where they had gone soft. IDF Chief of Staff Moshe "Boogie" Ya'alon paraphrased Nasrallah for the Israeli public in an interview published in the newspaper *Ha'aretz* last August.

> The Israeli army is strong, Israel has technological superiority and is said to have strategic capabilities, but its citizens are unwilling any longer to sacrifice lives in order to defend their national interests and national goals. Therefore, Israel is a spider-web society: it looks strong from the outside, but touch it and it will fall apart.

Al Qaeda, of course, has made a similar assessment of America's vulnerability.

A society facing such a determined foe can respond. Israel, with its necessarily advanced military and intelligence capacities, was able in the first four months of last year to meet the most concerted effort to date by Palestinian terrorists to test the resolve of its government and the mettle of its citizens. Twelve Israelis were killed in terrorist attacks in January, twenty-six in February, 108 in March, and forty-one in April. The population of the United States is roughly forty-seven times that of Israel, meaning that the American equivalent of the March figure would have exceeded 5,000—another 9/11, but with more than 2,000 additional deaths. After April of 2002, however, a period of relative quiet settled over Israel. The number of suicide attacks, according to the National Security Studies Center, declined from sixteen in March to six in April, six in May, five in June, and six in July before falling still further to two in August and similarly small numbers for the remainder of the year. "We wouldn't want it to be perceived [by the Israeli population] that we have no military answers," a senior IDF planner told me. The military answer was Operation Defensive Shield, which began in March and involved both the IDF's huge deployment of personnel to the West Bank and its continuing presence in all the major Palestinian population centers that Israel regards as wellsprings of the suicide campaign. This presence has involved aggressive military operations to pre-empt suicide bombing, along with curfews and other restrictions on the movement of residents.

The success of the IDF's strategy is utterly dependent on regularly acquiring intelligence and rapidly disseminating it to operational units that can take appropriate action. Thus the IDF must continue to occupy the West Bank's major population centers, so that Israeli intelligence agents can stay in close—and relatively safe—proximity to their information sources, and troops can act immediately either to round up suspects or to rescue the agent should an operation go awry. "Military pressure facilitates arrests, because you're there," one knowledgeable observer explained to me. "Not only do you know the area, but you have [covert] spotters deployed, and the whole area is under curfew anyway, so it is difficult for terrorists to move about and hide without being noticed, and more difficult for them to get out. The IDF presence facilitates intelligence gathering, and the troops can also conduct massive sweeps, house to house and block to block, pick up people, and interrogate them."

The IDF units in West Bank cities and towns can amass detailed knowledge of a community, identifying terrorists and their sympathizers, tracking their movements and daily routines, and observing the people with whom they associate. Agents from Shabak, Israel's General Security Service (also known as the Shin Bet), work alongside these units, participating in operations and often assigning missions. "The moment someone from Shabak comes with us, everything changes," a young soldier in an elite reconnaissance unit told me over coffee and cake in his mother's apartment. "The Shabak guy talks in Arabic to [the suspect] without an accent, or appears as an Arab guy himself. Shabak already knows everything about them, and that is such a shock to them. So they are afraid, and they will tell Shabak everything." The success of Defensive Shield and the subsequent Operation Determined Way depends on this synchronization of intelligence and operations. A junior officer well acquainted with this environment says, "Whoever has better intelligence is the winner."

The strategy—at least in the short run—is working. The dramatic decline in the number of suicide operations since last spring is proof enough. "Tactically, we are doing everything we can," a senior officer involved in the framing of this policy told me, "and we have managed to prevent eighty percent of all attempts." Another officer said, "We are now bringing the war to them. We do it so that we fight the war in *their* homes rather than in *our* homes. We try to make certain that we fight on their ground, where we can have the maximum advantage." The goal of the IDF, though, is not simply to fight in a manner that plays to its strength; the goal is to actively shrink the time and space in which the suicide bombers and their operational commanders, logisticians, and handlers function—to stop them before they can cross the Green Line, by threatening their personal safety and putting them on the defensive.

Citizens in Israel, as in America, have a fundamental expectation that their government and its military and security forces will protect and defend them. Soldiers are expected to die, if necessary, in order to discharge this responsibility. As one senior IDF commander put it, "It is better for the IDF to bear the brunt of these attacks than Israeli civilians. The IDF is better prepared, protected, educated." Thus security in Israel means to the IDF an almost indefinite deployment in the West Bank—a state of ongoing low-level war. For Palestinian civilians it means no respite from roadblocks and identity checks, cordon-and-search operations, lightning snatch-and-grabs, bombing raids, helicopter strikes, ground attacks, and other countermeasures that have turned densely populated civilian areas into war zones.

Many Israelis do not relish involvement in this protracted war of attrition, but even more of them accept that there is no alternative. "Israel's ability to stand fast indefinitely is a tremendous advantage," says Dan Schueftan, an Israeli strategist and military thinker who teaches at Haifa University, "since the suicide bombers believe that time is on their side. It imposes a strain on the army, yes, but this is what the army is for." Indeed, no Israeli with whom I spoke on this visit doubted that the IDF's continued heavy presence in the West Bank was directly responsible for the drop in the number of suicide bombings. And I encountered very few who favored withdrawing the IDF from the West Bank. This view cut across ideological and demographic lines. As we dined one evening at Matza, which has been rebuilt, a centrist graduate student at Haifa University named Uzi Nisim told me that Palestinian terrorists "will have the power to hit us, to hurt us, once [the IDF] withdraws from Jenin and elsewhere on the West Bank." Ami Pedahzur, of Haifa University, who is a leftist, agreed. He said, "There is widespread recognition in Israel that this is the only way to stop terrorism." I later heard the same thing from a South African couple, relatively new immigrants to Israel who are active in a variety of human-rights endeavors. "Just the other day," the husband told me, "even my wife said, 'Thank God we have Sharon. Otherwise I wouldn't feel safe going out.'"

Nevertheless, few Israelis believe that the current situation will lead to any improvement in Israeli-Palestinian relations over the long run. Dennis Zinn, the defense correspondent for Israel's Channel 1, told me, "Yes, there is a drop-off [in suicide bombings]. When you have bombs coming down on your heads, you can't carry out planning and suicide attacks. But that doesn't take away their motivation. It only increases it."

Given the relative ease and the strategic and tactical attraction of suicide bombing, it is perhaps no wonder that after a five-day visit to Israel last fall, Louis Anemone, the security chief of the New York Metropolitan Transit Authority, concluded that New Yorkers—and, by implication, other Americans—face the same threat. "This stuff is going to be imported over here," he declared—a prediction that Vice President Dick Cheney and FBI Director Robert Mueller had already made. In March, Secretary of Homeland Security Tom Ridge also referred to the threat, saying in an interview with Fox News that we have to "prepare for the inevitability" of suicide bombings in the United States. Anemone even argued that "today's terrorists appear to be using Israel as a testing ground to prepare for a sustained attack against the U.S." In fact, Palestinians had tried a suicide attack in New York four years before 9/11; their plans to bomb a Brooklyn subway station were foiled only because an informant told the police. When they were arrested, the terrorists were probably less than a day away from attacking: according to law-enforcement authorities, five bombs had been primed. "I wouldn't call them sophisticated," Howard Safir, the commissioner of police at the time, commented, "but they certainly were very dangerous." That suicide bombers don't need to be sophisticated is precisely what makes them so dangerous. All that's required is a willingness to kill and a willingness to die.

According to the Rand Corporation's chronology of worldwide terrorism, which begins in 1968 (the year acknowledged as marking the advent of modern international terrorism, whereby terrorists attack other countries or foreign targets in their own country), nearly two thirds of the 144 suicide bombings recorded have occurred in the past two years. No society, least of all the United States, can regard itself as immune from this threat. Israeli Foreign Minister Benjamin Netanyahu emphasized this point when he addressed the U.S. Congress nine days after 9/11. So did Dan Schueftan, the Israeli strategist, when I asked him if he thought suicide terrorism would come to America in a form similar to that seen in Israel this past year. He said, "It is an interesting comment that the terrorists make: we will finish defeating the Jews because they love life so much. Their goal is to bring misery and grief to people who have an arrogance of power. Who has this? The United States and Israel. Europe will suffer too. I don't think that it will happen in the U.S. on the magnitude we have seen it here, but I have no doubt that it will occur. We had the same discussion back in 1968, when El Al aircraft were hijacked and people said this is your problem, not ours."

The United States, of course, is not Israel. However much we may want to harden our hearts and our targets, the challenge goes far beyond fortifying a single national airline or corralling the enemy into a territory ringed by walls and barbed-wire fences that can be intensively monitored by our armed forces. But we can take precautions based on Israel's experience, and be confident that we are substantially reducing the threat of suicide terrorism here.

The police, the military, and intelligence agencies can take steps that work from the outside in, beginning far in time and distance from a potential attack and ending at the moment and the site of an actual attack. Although the importance of these steps is widely recognized, they have been implemented only unevenly across the United States.

- Understand the terrorists' operational environment. Know their *modus operandi* and targeting patterns. Suicide bombers are rarely lone outlaws; they are preceded by long logistical trails. Focus not just on suspected bombers but on the infrastructure required to launch and sustain suicide-bombing campaigns. This is the essential spadework. It will be for naught, however, if concerted efforts are not made to circulate this information quickly and systematically among federal, state, and local authorities.

- Develop strong, confidence-building ties with the communities from which terrorists are most likely to come, and mount communications campaigns to eradicate support from these communities. The most effective and useful intelligence comes from places where terrorists conceal themselves and seek to establish and hide their infrastructure. Law-enforcement officers should actively encourage and cultivate cooperation in a nonthreatening way.

- Encourage businesses from which terrorists can obtain bomb-making components to alert authorities if they notice large purchases of, for example, ammonium nitrate fertilizer; pipes, batteries, and wires; or chemicals commonly used to fabricate explosives. Information about customers who simply inquire about any of these materials can also be extremely useful to the police.

- Force terrorists to pay more attention to their own organizational security than to planning and carrying out attacks. The greatest benefit is in disrupting pre-attack operations. Given the highly fluid, international threat the United States faces, counterterrorism units, dedicated to identifying and targeting the intelligence-gathering and reconnaissance activities of terrorist organizations, should be established here within existing law-enforcement agencies. These units should be especially aware of places where organizations frequently recruit new members and the bombers themselves, such as community centers, social clubs, schools, and religious institutions.

- Make sure ordinary materials don't become shrapnel. Some steps to build up physical defenses were taken after 9/11—reinforcing park benches, erecting Jersey barriers around vulnerable buildings, and the like. More are needed, such as ensuring that windows on buses and subway cars are shatterproof, and that seats and other accoutrements are not easily dislodged or splintered. Israel has had to learn to examine every element of its public infrastructure. Israeli buses and bus shelters are austere for a reason.

- Teach law-enforcement personnel what to do at the moment of an attack or an attempt. Prevention comes first from the cop on the beat, who will be forced to make instant life-and-death decisions affecting those nearby. Rigorous training is needed for identifying a potential suicide bomber, confronting a suspect, and responding and securing the area around the attack site in the event of an explosion. Is the officer authorized to take action on sighting a suspected bomber, or must a supervisor or special unit be called first? Policies and procedures must be established. In the aftermath of a blast the police must determine whether emergency medical crews and firefighters may enter the site; concerns about a follow-up attack can dictate that first responders be held back until the area is secured. The ability to make such lightning determinations requires training—and, tragically, experience. We can learn from foreign countries with long experience of suicide bombings, such as Israel and Sri Lanka, and also from our own responses in the past to other types of terrorist attacks.

America's enemies are marshaling their resources to continue the struggle that crystallized on 9/11. Exactly what shape that struggle will take remains to be seen. But a recruitment video reportedly circulated by al Qaeda as recently as spring of last year may provide some important clues. The seven-minute tape, seized from an al Qaeda member by U.S. authorities, extols the virtues of martyrdom and solicits recruits to Osama bin Laden's cause. It depicts scenes of *jihadists* in combat, followed by the successive images of twenty-seven martyrs with their names, where they were from, and where they died. Twelve of the martyrs are featured in a concluding segment with voice-over that says, "They rejoice in the bounty provided by Allah. And with regard to those left behind who have not yet joined them in their bliss, the martyrs glory in the fact that on them is no fear, nor have they cause to grieve." The video closes with a message of greeting from the Black Banner Center for Islamic Information.

The greatest military onslaught in history against a terrorist group crushed the infrastructure of al Qaeda in Afghanistan, depriving it of training camps, operational bases, and command-and-control headquarters; killing and wounding many of its leaders and fighters; and dispersing the survivors. Yet this group still actively seeks to rally its forces and attract recruits. Ayman Zawahiri, bin Laden's chief lieutenant, laid out a list of terrorist principles in his book, *Knights Under the Prophet's Banner* (2001), prominent among them the need for al Qaeda to "move the battle to the enemy's ground to burn the hands of those who ignite fire in our countries." He also mentioned "the need to concentrate on the method of martyrdom operations as the most successful way of inflicting damage against the opponent and the least costly to the mujahideen in terms of casualties." That martyrdom is highlighted in the recruitment video strongly suggests that suicide attacks will continue to be a primary instrument in al Qaeda's war against—and perhaps in—the United States. Suleiman Abu Gheith, al Qaeda's chief spokesman, has said as much. In rhetoric disturbingly reminiscent of the way that Palestinian terrorists describe their inevitable triumph over Israel, Abu Gheith declared, "Those youths that destroyed Americans with their planes, they did a good deed. There are thousands more young followers who look forward to death like Americans look forward to living."

Bruce Hoffman is an authoritative analyst of terrorism and a recipient of the U.S. Intelligence Community Seal Medallion, the highest level of commendation given to a nongovernment employee. He is currently the director of the Washington, D.C., office of the RAND Corporation, where he heads the terrorism research unit, and he regularly advises both governments and businesses throughout the world.

Kelly J. Hicks, 2003

How Business Can Defeat Terrorism
Global Financial Firms Battle the SARS Outbreak in Hong Kong

The two main entities that battled SARS in Hong Kong consisted of the Hong Kong government and the "commercial sector." Within each of these, especially in the commercial sector, there were multiple players. In order to present the story about SARS consistently, this paper more narrowly defines the commercial sector as the financial sector (of which there are hundreds of firms, with similar structures, that dealt with the outbreak along similar paths).

Imagine a terrorist group has just deployed a deadly, highly infectious disease in a densely populated financial "capital city." It starts through means of a vector, an infected human "drone," whose itinerary includes key landmarks, such as exchanges and major public buildings. To cause further confusion as to the source, he stays in an international hotel among guests—mostly businessmen—from twenty foreign countries. By the time three days pass, hundreds of people worldwide are infected with and dying from being infected by a virus of an unknown type, which has no cure. Take away the terrorist intrigue, and *you have the current SARS global pandemic that is now threatening the Asian economy and the global business environment.*

The Challenges

SARS, or Severe Acute Respiratory Syndrome, hit Hong Kong in March 2003, with 350 infected cases and 13 deaths (91 cases in Singapore with 2 deaths and 10 cases with no deaths in Taiwan) by the 30th of the month. Hospitals, that were fighting to understand the disease and its causes became spreading mechanisms for SARS. The virus hit medical staff particularly hard, impacting the their ability to respond effectively. The intensive care unit capacity in all of Hong Kong at the time was only 3,000 beds, and there were only a limited number of SARS respirators and related equipment. This fact, coupled with the direct threat to health care workers, brought the dreadful realization to the community's leaders that if the daily infection rate continued at the same pace, Hong Kong's hospitals would be at full capacity by June.

By late March highly sensational reports about the disease began appearing in the press. The causes of infection by SARS were not clear, and with the press conjecturing about the disease being airborne (it was not), people began to panic. When a rumor circulated about an infection in a nearby building, part of a trade floor in a famous brokerage firm grabbed their belongings and headed home. Management realized at this moment that they were facing a possibly catastrophic major business disruption if an infection broke out in that firm, or if just the fear of an outbreak caused people to refuse to come to work. As this ball begins to roll in the financial markets, the consequences can be dramatic. For example, in a margin call, say a firm has a number of futures positions on its books, which require payment due to an external factor that affects the price. If that firm fails to make its margin payment, the reaction from the rest of the trading community is severe. Thinking that firm is out of cash, they stop trading with it, and they go against that firm in other ways as well, creating a domino effect. This can break a financial institution quickly. If the stock exchange falls victim to an outbreak or mass panic, the financial impact to the greater community is worse. Once this happens enough times, a regional economy is threatened. This incidentally, underscores one of the main aims of bioterrorism—to wreck the economy and thus the society of an adversary.

As the number of cases in Hong Kong increased, sometimes dramatically as in the case of almost the entire housing estate of Amoy Gardens with several hundred infections in a matter of days, the pressure on management of major corporations and financial institutions became intense. Medical restrictions imposed locally and internationally meant that people could not travel without special medical clearance, or in many cases, without prior quarantine for a period of days. This meant that bankers could no longer see clients in certain locations (compounding this, there were reports that SARS could be easily caught onboard aircraft). This inability to travel effectively posed another potential threat to business, especially in terms of reputation.

Also, information about the treatment of SARS revealed an especially grave threat to the survival of unborn children, the solution to which was involuntary abortion under a certain gestational age. Given this threat to pregnant women, expectant mothers and their spouses were sent home from work. This posed another threat not only to business but also to morale of the workforce. To top it all off, Hong Kong's lucrative tourism ceased, schools closed, restaurants and other public places closed, and there was a run on grocery stores. By the beginning of April, Hong Kong was in serious distress.

The Responses

At the financial sector level. Major banks and other multinational businesses in Hong Kong took an aggressive approach in dealing with the threats posed by SARS to their people and their business. The most important theme to stress here is that the *fear* of the disease was much greater than the actual possibility of infection. This meant that people were physically afraid of coming out in public places, commuting to work on public transportation, and sitting near coworkers in crowded offices. Firms had to creatively determine approaches to instill confidence in the employees so as to avoid workplace panic and possibly a major business disruption.

Very early in the outbreak, many firms formed SARS taskforces, composed of members from human resources, security, business divisions, legal, head office, public relations, technology and the business continuity. Firms also communicated among one another to make sure of the most appropriate practices and share information. These SARS taskforces were linked globally with their sister offices so that senior management could stay abreast of the developing situation.

SARS taskforces began the process of tackling health and psychological issues. They developed approaches such as management toolkits designed to enable managers to completely brief their people on all medical developments, as well on as how to respond to an outbreak in the firm. From the beginning, it was evident that decisive leadership and information from the very top were essential in managing the growing fear of the disease among employees.

Fear actually became more of a threat than the chances of contracting the disease itself. The fear of the disease presented a continuity threat to business, but if managed decisively and openly, a "come to work" environment could be maintained. The human resources–wellness departments of the member firms of the financial sector provided surgical masks to all employees for use in the office on a nonmandatory basis, as well as to wear while commuting to and from work. The building management departments increased the number of cleanups daily in the workplace, adding bleach cleaning to all surfaces per government advisories. The SARS taskforces of the various financial firms also published a daily bulletin to all employees, helping them to stay abreast of accurate medical information, infection statistics, where to receive medical advice, and so on (as a lesson learned, there was a balance struck between providing complete versus excessive information. An example of this was that some of the medical information in circulation was not confirmed. It was therefore necessary to limit communications to just the known facts so as to avoid having to go back and repeatedly adjust the bulletins).

The daily bulletin also provided useful information about checking for symptoms of SARS, key phone numbers to call at the taskforce, and so on. Another confidence building measure put in place by firms was to authorize a taxi subsidy for employees who routinely take public transportation to and from work. This also decreased the risk of exposure of firm employees to ill persons, thereby reducing the risk to the workforce. Firms also brought in medical experts such as local and International SOS doctors, to provide daily medical advice and prescreening for travelers, and to address all employees in English and Cantonese on a frequent basis. Again, the psychological impact of the disease was worse than the disease itself; it created a level of tension and fear that required extraordinary measures to contain.

As part of risk management and business continuity, businesses pre-positioned executives in other regional offices in order to prequarantine them so they could effectively meet with clients or pick up trading from a desk that has visibility on that data. Even after quarantine and other measures, however, some clients still refused to meet with people from Hong Kong. Again, the fear of the disease was greater than the disease itself—giving way to illogical reactions.

While the human resources–wellness and executive office personnel worked to manage the people side of the threat, technology worked behind the scenes to bolster and upgrade the firm's capability to support the contingencies put in place in case of an outbreak within the office. Many firms have global technology architectures, allowing businesses to share data globally. With a disease being carried to hotels and public buildings— as it would in a bioterror attack—and the local populace in fear of coming to work, the contingency plan was to get assistance from other regional offices to provide handoff on trade settlements and other vital functions for financial firms.

The fear of SARS created the need for the employees potentially to work from home or from other offsite locations, including other regional offices.

If the disease spread widely within the community, the strict quarantine and lack of access to public buildings would severely impact the ability to conduct business. Therefore, dial-in capacity was increased to be able to handle about 30 percent of the workforce, concentrating on the key personnel and working downward. Offsite locations proved to be an effective means of prequarantining a segment of the workforce. Mingling of the workforce could be controlled or prevented, enabling certain business functions to continue in the event of an outbreak in the main campus (corporate headquarters).

Many firms have a business continuity off-site facility. Off-sites normally consist of a data center specially built in a location on a redundant power grid and with backup database servers, in case of a failure of the main campus data center. Normally a data center for a financial institution has a scaled-down version of a dealing floor, complete with the traders' personalized desktops and a settlement and funding team co-located in the same facility. Firms that invested in an offsite center had the added safety net of being able to operate or manage risk if an outbreak occurred in their main facility (this is also a lesson learned).

At the Hong Kong government level. The local government in Hong Kong began a public campaign of personal hygiene awareness, as well as implementing cleaning of streets and public facilities. One of the first actions the Hong Kong government took was to close all schools in late March. Schools remained closed for more than one month. When schools resumed on 28 April, strict daily temperature-taking procedures were implemented to ensure students' safety. The Hong Kong airport authority implemented a 100 percent temperature taking for all departing travelers. Anyone with a temperature above 38 degrees Celsius was refused boarding and further medically screened. The airport also installed infrared screeners for all arriving passengers, to detect elevate body temperatures. These measures were implemented at the border crossing points between Hong Kong and Shenzhen, China. Hospitals set up SARS-only wards, strictly sealing them off from the rest of hospitals. Moreover, the only hospitals authorized to treat SARS victims were government hospitals—no suspected SARS case could go to a private hospital. In this manner, the disease was localized to the extent possible within the centers best suited to treat it. Medical staff who were retired or privatized were also invited to return to medical duty in SARS hospitals. This helped reduce the tremendous stress on the already stretched medical staff in the government hospitals.

The health department worked in conjunction with local universities' biological research departments, as well as the World Health Organization (WHO) and the Centers for Disease Control (CDC). Aggressively, these entities cooperated and coordinated their efforts toward isolating the suspected virus that causes SARS. The WHO and CDC assisted Hong Kong, Singapore, and Canada in their efforts against SARS. Unfortunately, China refused to cooperate for nearly a month, covering up their seriously high number of cases, and blocking WHO support to Taiwan for political reasons (China's massive failure to safeguard its people by dealing with SARS head-on will cost dearly in the attraction of business investment from abroad—this is more a conclusion and a knock-on effect).

Conclusion: Lessons Learned—*Can Bioterrorism Be Defeated?*

Bioterrorism can be defeated. Large-scale acts of bioterrorism, such as SARS-like outbreaks, can be effectively contained if the appropriate measures are put in place quickly. SARS has not gone away and will be endemic in some areas until there is a vaccine discovered that is effective against it. (In the case of some bioterror diseases, there are vaccines or anti-bacterials, which can be brought to bear along with other public and commercial measures to combat it. Therefore, terrorists will likely try to obtain and use unusual diseases that would be more difficult to contain.) But SARS has been greatly reduced in Hong Kong and Singapore, where aggressive measures were put in place early on to combat its spread. Because of this, the WHO lifted travel restrictions to these locations relatively quickly. After the WHO dropped Hong Kong, Singapore, and China from the list of affected countries, business began to resume, and air travel volumes rose surprisingly quickly. (Another key factor in containing or defeating a bioterror attack, as the SARS epidemic proved, is the ability to conquer the fear of the disease within the community. This is emphasized repeatedly throughout this paper, because it is probably the greatest lesson learned and is of future value to authorities and businesses if they have to face a bioterror attack.)

There are examples in the SARS pandemic of how bioterrorism can have a more deadly impact. Nations with weak political systems or a weak national health care infrastructure are prime candidates for a devastating hit. The two most vivid examples are China and Taiwan. SARS continues to affect China, where the government delayed admitting facts about the disease for months and did not begin taking measures against it until it had become a serious health threat and an international embarrassment. Many feel that a healthy China translates into robust global business growth. The mishandling of SARS in China had a serious effect on international confidence. Economists predict a slowing of the Chinese economy for 2003 as a result.[1]

Taiwan is still struggling to contain SARS, where the infections and deaths continue to occur. Although the Taiwan government actively quarantined suspected cases from the beginning, the infection spread by more than 50 cases per day. The reason for the difficulty in containing the disease seems to be that Taiwan lacks the means to prevent cross-infection within its hospitals. If WHO had had early access to Taiwan health authorities, they may have been able to help prevent some medical mistakes with the disease. Further compounding the difficult situation in Taiwan, some doctors and other medical staff refused to come to work for fear of infection. (Again, the reaction to just the fear of the disease showed how damaging even a small-scale breakout from a bioterror attack could be.)

In closing, the SARS pandemic provided the world with a stark lesson in how a bioterrorist attack could unfold, as well as how nations, cities, and the financial sector could respond—and hopefully, recover. Equally stark—and unsettling—SARS gave terrorist groups a direct insight as to where weaknesses exist in security, government, policy, medical infrastructure and financial resilience of many nations and regions. So in combating bioterrorism, success depends on two key things: nations must have a robust medical infrastructure and the political will to be transparent and cooperate internationally.

Kelly J. Hicks has served in officer positions in Korea, Okinawa, and Hong Kong, as well as with the United States Army in many departments in Asia. He currently serves as head of the Business Continuity Program for Goldman Sachs in Hong Kong and Non-Japan areas of Asia.

Note

1. "Japan Strategy Flash," SARS Scenarios and Sector Implications, Goldman Sachs Group, 28 April 2003.

Russell D. Howard, 2003

Preemptive Military Doctrine
No Other Choice Against Transnational, Non-State Actors

In a speech delivered June 1, 2002, to graduating cadets at the U.S. Military Academy at West Point, President George W. Bush asserted his administration's intention to carry out preemptive military attacks if necessary to protect American interests.[1]

The implications of the speech signaled a historic shift from the long-accepted Cold War applications of the use of force. "For much of the last century," the president said, "America's defense relied on the Cold War doctrines of deterrence and containment. In some cases, those strategies still apply." However, the president contended, "new threats also require new thinking."

> Deterrence—the promise of massive retaliation against nations—means nothing against shadowy terrorist networks with no nation or citizens to defend. Containment is not possible when unbalanced dictators with weapons of mass destruction can deliver those weapons on missiles or secretly provide them to terrorist allies.[2]

More recently, President Bush reinforced his use-of-force-position in the "The National Security Act of the United States of America." According to the document, deterrence and containment, the previous foundations of U.S. strategy, are no longer valid. According to the president, the United States must instead identify and destroy the terrorist threat before it reaches our borders," and, if necessary, act alone and use preemptive force.[3]

This paper agrees with the president's assertion that a preemptive strategy is necessary in a post–Cold War security environment, in which America's most dangerous adversaries are transnational, non-state actors who have access to weapons of mass destruction and intend to use them. I argue that the United States must have a preemption doctrine that enables decision-makers to face the unique security threat posed by transnational, non-state actors such as al Qaeda. This paper does not engage in the debate regarding the use of military preemption or "preventive war" against sovereign states. Military preemption against a sovereign state may be an acceptable tactic in certain situations, particularly if the state is threatening the use of weapons of mass destruction. However, in addition to preemption, other military means such as defense, deterrence, and coercion can be used to influence an adversarial state's behavior. Better yet, non-military means of persuasion such

---

as diplomacy and economic pressure can also be used. Unfortunately, at least in my opinion, these more acceptable means of persuasion are not viable when dealing with a hostile, non-state actor, such as al Qaeda.

During the Cold War, most international terrorism was part of the East versus West, left versus right confrontation—a small but dangerous side show to the greater, bipolar, Cold War drama. Terrorism in this era was almost always the province of groups of militants that had the backing of political forces and states hostile to American interests. What is new today is the emergence of terrorism that is not ideological in a political sense. Instead, it is inspired by religious extremists and ethnic separatist elements. These elements might be individuals akin to the Unabomber or other like-minded people working in cells, small groups, or larger coalitions.[4] They do not answer completely to any government, they operate across national borders, and they have access to funding and advanced technology.[5]

These new terrorist groups are not bound by the same constraints or motivated by the same goals as nation-states. Religious extremists, ethnic separatists, and lone Unabombers are not responsive to traditional diplomacy or military deterrence because there is no state to negotiate with or to retaliate against.

Today's terrorists are not concerned about limiting casualties. Under the old rules, as Brian Jenkins first noted, terrorists wanted a lot of people watching, not a lot of people dead.[6] They did not want large body counts because they wanted converts and they also wanted a seat at the table. Today's terrorists are not particularly concerned about converts, and rather than wanting a seat at the table, "they want to destroy the table and everyone sitting at it."[7] In fact, religious terrorists such as al Qaeda, in particular, want casualties—lots of them.[8]

Today's terrorism is not an ideological "ism" like communism or capitalism, with values that can be debated in the classroom or decided at the polls. Rather, it is the fanatical misuse of an ancient tactic and instrument of conflict. The only difference between modern terrorism and its ancient roots is that the "new terrorism" is better financed and has a global reach that it did not have before the advent of globalization and the information revolution. The new terrorism can ride the back of the Web and use advanced communications systems to move vast financial sums from Sudan to the Philippines or virtually any place on earth. And for $28.50, any Internet surfer, including terrorists, can purchase the book *Bacteriological Warfare: A Major Threat to North America,* which explains how to grow deadly bacteria that could be used in a weapon of mass destruction (WMD).

Terrorists and WMD

The prospect of terrorists using WMD (nuclear, biological, and chemical) weapons to attack the United States is the main reason the president has little choice but to add preemption to his menu of potential military power options. About this, the president has been very clear:

> When the spread of chemical and biological and nuclear weapons, along with ballistic missile technology occurs, even weak states and small groups could attain a catastrophic power to strike great nations. Our enemies have declared this very intention, and have been caught seeking these terrible weapons. They want the capability to blackmail us, or to harm us, or to harm our friends—and we will oppose them with all our power.[9]

Indeed, al Qaeda has threatened the United States with WMD. Recent discoveries in Afghanistan have confirmed that al Qaeda and other terrorist groups are actively pursuing the capability of using biological agents against United States and its allies.[10] According to David Kaye, this should not be a surprise:

> Only a blind, deaf and dumb terrorist group could have survived the last five years and not been exposed at least to the possibility of the use of WMD, while the more discerning terrorists would have found some tactically brilliant possibilities already laid out on the public record.[11]

Steven Miller, director of the International Security Program at the John F. Kennedy School of Government at Harvard University, agrees that policy makers should be concerned about terrorist access to nuclear weapons, too. Presently, Miller believes the opportunities for well-organized and well-financed terrorists to infiltrate a Russian nuclear storage facility are greater than ever.[12]

Miller further believes there have been more than two-dozen thefts of weapons-usable materials in the former Soviet Union in recent years. According to Miller, several suspects have been arrested in undercover sting operations, leaving doubt about those who may have gotten away.[13] It almost happened in 1994, says Miller, "when 350 grams of plutonium were smuggled on board a Lufthansa flight from Moscow to Munich. Fortunately, SWAT teams confiscated the material as soon as it arrived."[14]

Given the known goals of terrorists, the United States can no longer rely solely on a reactive, crisis-response military posture as it has in the past. The inability to deter a potential attacker, the immediacy of today's threats, and the catastrophic consequences of a WMD attack do not permit that option. The United States simply cannot allow its enemies to strike first with nuclear, radiological, biological, or chemical weapons.[15]

Arms Control Protocols and Westphalian Rules No Longer Apply

The inability of the United States to negotiate with non-state actors and its over-reliance on treaties and conventions limit the usefulness of diplomacy in reducing the likelihood of WMD attacks. For example, U.S. policy states that it will not negotiate with terrorists.[16] The rationale behind this policy is clear: Giving in to terrorist demands will prompt more terrorist activity. This is especially true in hostage situations because negotiations with terrorists could potentially force the U.S. to risk having to meet certain demands for ransom or safe passage.

However, it would be very beneficial to have a mechanism—most likely secret—that could enable an opportunity to dialogue with terrorists. This would be especially important in regard to transnational, non-state actors who have no formal diplomatic voice. The manner in which this dialogue might take place would depend on the situation. Discussions could be held in secret or through surrogates. Preferably, a dialogue—not necessarily negotiations—with terrorists could be established before an attack and prevent it from happening, thus avoiding the necessity of preemption. In addition to the aforementioned possibility, opening a dialogue is important if for no other reason than because understanding what is really on a terrorist's mind has intelligence value. More importantly, a terrorist who understands what our response to a hostile act will be has deterrent value.

Nuclear arms control and reduction treaties promulgated during the Cold War were, and still are, valuable assets for preventing conflict. They provided baseline agreements that fostered cooperation between the powers and led to greater transparency and confidence-building measures that still exist today. Unfortunately, treaties meant to control and reduce the number of chemical and biological weapons have not been as effective.

The Chemical Weapons Convention (CWC) entered into force on April 29, 1997. It has been signed by 120 states, and bans chemical weapons production and storage as well as use. The strength of the convention is that it calls for unprecedented and highly intrusive inspection provisions, including routine and challenge inspection mechanisms. The weakness of the convention is that several countries that pose concerns about chemical proliferation have not joined the CWC regime. These include Iraq, Libya, North Korea, and Syria.[17]

Biological weapons are also prohibited by a treaty, the Biological and Toxin Weapons Convention (BWC), which entered into force in 1975 and now comprises some 140 member states. The strength of the BWC is that it bans an entire class of weapons, prohibiting the development, production, stockpiling, or acquisition of biological agents or toxins of any type or quantity that do not have protective, medical, or other peaceful purposes. "The major shortfall of the BWC is its lack of any on-site verification mechanism."[18]

The chemical warfare and biological warfare conventions and nuclear arms control and reduction treaties only affect state behavior. They have no impact on the behavior of transnational and other non-state actors that might possess and use chemical, biological, or nuclear weapons, or on rogue states that are not signatories to the conventions.

The major problems the United States has in addressing international WMD threats are outdated military doctrine and the traditional way the U.S. employs military force. The traditional uses of military force are defense, deterrence, compellence, and presence. Defense against terrorist use of WMD is extremely difficult, especially in a democracy. Without compromising civil liberties in draconian ways—a goal of terrorists—no defense regime could come close to guaranteeing security against a terrorist intent on attacking the United States with WMD. Or, as Secretary of Defense Donald Rumsfeld reflected in a speech at the National Defense University in January 2002, "It is not possible to defend against every conceivable kind of attack in every conceivable location at every minute of the day or night. The best, and in some cases, the only defense is a good offense."

Deterrence against non-governmental actors would be also be extremely difficult to implement. For example, where exactly do you nuke Osama bin Laden if he launches a biological attack?

> Deterrence generally does not work against terrorists. Stateless and usually spread over wide regions or even among continents, terrorists do not present a viable target for retaliation. The death and destruction that can be visited upon a terrorist organization in a retaliatory attack is greatly exceeded by the damage even a small terrorist cell can inflict on civilian society.[19]

Presence would certainly help get U.S. forces to a crisis area more rapidly, but U.S. military presence overseas—other than those already committed to combat or peace enforcement roles—is declining, as is the number of military personnel in the United States who can be deployed. Therefore, using military force to stop adversaries before they act has more utility in the post–Cold War world.

Historically, the United States has employed its military to compel enemies to change their behavior after a crisis has occurred. In the past, the United States could take a massive blow such as Pearl Harbor, retreat, accept some risk while re-arming and building up power, then counterattack, defeat the enemy, declare victory, and demobilize. This was "the American way of war." Today, the risk and the opportunity to attack are before the blow, not afterward. After the blow today—from a dirty nuke, biological or chemical agent, or something worse like a super strain of flu that is resistant to all antibodies—what gets mobilized if there is anything left to mobilize? Who gets counterattacked, if the attacker is unknown? What defines victory?

Preemption—Not Fighting Fair?

The use of military force preemptively is a difficult concept for many Americans to accept. It defies American's sense of fairness and proportionality as well as the rules of warfare, as Brad Roberts points out:

> Moral philosophy establishes that wars of self-defense are just, whereas wars of aggression are not. But there has long been a healthy debate about precisely what constitutes a war of self-defense. A mid-sixteenth-century scholar of just war wrote, "There is a single and only just cause for commencing a war… namely, wrong received." In our day Michael Walzer has argued, "Nothing but aggression can justify war…. There must actually have been a wrong, and it must actually have been received (or its receipt must be, as it were, only minutes away)."[20]

> However, this view has not been held by all. In 1625, Hugo Grotius wrote, "The first just cause of war… is an injury, which even though not actually committed, threatens our persons or our property."[21] Grotius emphasized that to safeguard against wars of aggression, it was essential to be certain about the enemy's intent to attack.

In 1914, Elihu Root said that international law did not require the aggrieved state to wait before using force in self-defense "until it is too late to protect itself."[22] Interestingly, in his book *Just Wars*, Michael Walzer seems to contradict earlier statements referenced by Brad Roberts by arguing that, "states can rightfully defend themselves against violence that is imminent but not actual."

Roberts contends, and I agree, that there can be, "no blanket reply to the question, is there a moral case for preemption? Some acts of preemption will be deemed just, others unjust." In the case of preemption against WMD threats, Roberts further argues that the strongest moral case for U.S. strategy of preemption exists under the following conditions:

> (1) an aggressor has actually threatened to use his WMD weapons, has taken steps to ready the means to do so, and has specifically threatened the United States (including its territory, citizens, or military forces); (2) those WMD weapons have been built in violation of international law; (3) the aggressor's threatened actions invoke larger questions about the credibility of security guarantees or the balance of power within a region; (4) the president has secured the approval of the U.S. Congress; and (5) the United

States has secured the backing of the U.N. Security Council and any relevant regional organization. The prudential tests of last resort, proportionality, and reasonable chance of success must also be met.[23]

I agree with the first four tenets of Roberts's argument but not with the last. The backing of the UN and regional organizations would strengthen the moral argument for preemption, but may be impossible to obtain given China's reluctance to violate sovereignty under any circumstances and Russia's recurring, post-Kosovo intervention habit of siding with rogue states like Iraq and Iran. Also, the United States must never forgo the option to act unilaterally.

Domestic Political Support

The commonly held view that Americans disapprove of preemption is simply not true. A good example of this is the 1998 bombing of a Sudanese chemical plant that was suspected of having ties to Osama bin laden. After the attack, even when it was revealed that the plant was probably making nothing sinister, U.S. public opinion was still strongly in favor of the attacks.[24] In fact, two-thirds of Americans approved of the military strike, while only 19 percent were opposed.[25]

More recent data show that Congress is in favor of preemption under certain conditions, particularly when conducted against non-state actors intent on harming the United States. Dr. Scott Silverstone, a professor and researcher at the United States Military Academy, has categorized data from congressional hearings, memos, media articles, and personal statements that show that members of the Senate and House are nearly unanimous in their support for preemption as a strategy. In fact, Silverstone's 2002–2003 data show that 90 percent of the Senate favored a preemption strategy against non-state actors. The figure in the House was 81 percent. Interestingly, not one elected official in the House or Senate explicitly rejected the notion of preemptive warfare directed against non-state actors.[26]

Preemption and International Law

According to Anthony Clark Arend, "Under the regime of customary international law that developed long before the UN Charter was adopted, it was generally accepted that preemptive force was permissible in self-defense."[27] If a state could demonstrate necessity—that another state was about to engage in armed attack—and act proportionately, preemptive self-defense was an acceptable, and legal, action.[28]

In the post–UN Charter world, Article 2(4) stipulates that states were to refrain from the threat or use of force against another state unless—as stipulated in Article 39—the Security Council authorizes the use of force against offending states due to a threat to peace, breach of the peace, or an act of aggression. However, Article 51 confirms that the Charter will not impair the inherent right of individual or collective self-defense if an armed attack occurs against a UN member.[29]

Two divergent interpretations of Article 51 prevent the UN from wholly accepting the preemptive use of force as an acceptable national strategy. Restrictionists interpret Article 51 to mean that a state can only respond if attacked, while counter-restrictionists believe states can use anticipatory self-defense, for many of the same reasons that self-defense was acceptable prior to the UN Charter.

My view is that neither "customary" nor "post–UN Charter" international law addresses the issue of preemptive self-defense against transnational, non-state actors with access to weapons of mass destruction who are intent on committing acts of terrorism. Therefore, preemption as defined by President Bush is as valid as any other interpretation of "preemptive self-defense."

Conclusion

I was on the dais at West Point when President Bush gave his "preemption speech" and was taken with one of his statements, which I include as part of my concluding remarks. He told the audience that "The gravest danger to freedom lies at the perilous crossroads of radicalism and technology. When the spread of chemical and biological and nuclear weapons, along with ballistic missile technology… when that occurs, even weak states and small groups could attain a catastrophic power to strike great nations.… Our enemies have declared this very intention, and have been caught seeking these terrible weapons. They want the capability to blackmail us, or to harm us, or to harm our friends—and we will oppose them with all our power."

In my view, "opposing them with all our power," must include the preemptive use of force to defeat terrorists before they can inflict pain on the United States.

Traditional applications of American power—economic, political, diplomatic, and military—used to leverage and influence states in the past are not effective against non-state actors. Whom do you sanction or embargo? With whom do you negotiate? How do you defend against or deter Osama bin Laden? You don't. The only effective way to influence the Osama bin Ladens of the world is to preempt them before they can act.

Colonel Russell D. Howard is professor and head of the Department of Social Sciences at the United States Military Academy at West Point. He is a career Special Forces officer, who has served at every level of unit command in Special Forces, including command of the 1st Special Forces Group from 1994 to 1996.

Notes

1. President George W. Bush, June 1, 2002, West Point, New York.
2. Ibid.
3. Karen DeYoung and Mike Allen, "Bush Shifts Strategy From Deterrence to Dominance," *Washington Post*, September 21, 2002, P. A01.
4. Stephen A. Cambone, *A New Structure for National Security Policy Planning*, Washington D.C.: Government Printing Office, 1996, p. 43.
5. Gideon Rose, "It Could Happen Here—Facing the New Terrorism," *Foreign Affairs*, March–April 1999, p. 1.
6. Frequently quoted remark made by Brian Jenkins in 1974.
7. Quote attributed to James Woolsey, 1994.
8. Bruce Hoffman, *Inside Terrorism*, New York: Columbia University Press, 1998, p. 205.
9. George W. Bush, June 1, 2002.
10. Judith Miller, "Lab Suggests Qaeda Planned to Build Arms, Officials Say," *New York Times*, September 14, 2002, p. 1.

11. David Kay, "WMD Terrorism: Hype or Reality," in James M. Smith and William C. Thomas, ed., *The Terrorism Threat and U.S. Government Response: Operational and Organizational Factors* (U.S. Air Force Academy: INSS Book Series, 2001), p. 12.

12. Doug Gavel, "Can Nuclear Weapons Be Put Beyond the Reach of Terrorists," *Kennedy School of Government Bulletin*, Autumn 2002, p. 43.

13. Ibid., p. 45.

14. Ibid., p. 48.

15. See the National Security Strategy of the United States.

16. Stansfield Turner, *Terrorism and Democracy*, (Boston: Houghton Mifflin, 1991), p. xii. Actually Admiral Turner makes the argument that the United States will negotiate with terrorists. See Chapter 26, *We Will Make Deals*.

17. "Weapons of Mass Destruction," *Great Decisions*, 1999, p. 51.

18. Ibid., p. 52.

19. James Wirtz and James A. Russell, "U.S. Policy on Preventive War and Preemption," *The Nonproliferation Review*, vol. 10, number 1, Spring 2003, p. 116.

20. Brad Roberts, "NBC-Armed Rogues: Is there a Moral Case for Preemption?" *Close Calls: Intervention, Terrorism, Missile Defense, and 'Just War' Today*, Ed. Elliott Abrams, (EPPC-March, 1998), p. 11.

21. Hugo Grotius, *The Law of War and Peace*, book 2, chapter 1, section 2.

22. Elihu Root, "The Real Monroe Doctrine," *American Journal of International Law* 35 (1914), p. 427.

23. Roberts, p. 13.

24. "Excerpts: U.S. Editorials Assess Impact of Anti-Terrorist Strikes," *USIS Washington File*, www.fas.org/man/dod-101/ops/docs/98082307_tpo.html, June 14, 2000, p. 1–6.

25. John Diamond, "U.S. Strikes Tougher Stance Against Terrorism," *Cnews*, www.canoe.ca/CNEWSStrikeAtTerrorism/aug20_us.html, August 21, 1998.

26. Multiple conversations with Dr. Scott Silverstone.

27. Anthony Clark Arend, "International Law and Preemptive Use of Military Force," *Washington Quarterly*, Spring 2003, p, 90.

28. Ibid., p. 91.

29. Ibid.

Brian Michael Jenkins, 2002

Countering Al Qaeda

Summary

Since the terrorist attacks of September 11, 2001, the United States has achieved significant successes in its war on terrorism. Removing the Taliban government in Afghanistan, thereby eliminating al Qaeda's sanctuary and training camps, has broken an important link in the process that once provided al Qaeda's leadership with a continuing flow of recruits. Toppling the Taliban also demonstrated American resolve and international support, and it underscored the considerable risk run by governments that provide assistance to terrorists.

Having achieved its initial goals in Afghanistan, the United States is now in a second, more complex phase of the war, where it must continue its efforts to destroy al Qaeda and at the same time attempt to combat terrorism as a mode of conflict. Al Qaeda, along with its associates and its successors, will fight on, drawing upon a deep reservoir of hatred and a desire for revenge. It must be presumed that al Qaeda will exploit all of its ability to cause catastrophic death and destruction—there will be no self-imposed limits to its violence. It can also be presumed that the organization will continue its efforts to acquire and use weapons of mass destruction (WMD); that it will attack U.S. targets abroad where possible; and that it will attempt to mount attacks within the United States. Al Qaeda constitutes the most serious immediate threat to the security of the United States.

Although some measure of success has been achieved in uncovering terrorist plots, the ability of U.S. agencies to detect and prevent future terrorist attacks is limited. Al Qaeda, however, must now operate in a less-permissive environment. If al Qaeda can be kept on the run, the numbers it can train will decline. And declining numbers eventually will result in a corresponding qualitative decline in terrorist operations. However, it is possible that al Qaeda will adapt to the more difficult post–September 11 operational environment by morphing into an even looser network, devolving more initiative and resources to local operatives.

The greatest challenge in the second phase of the campaign against terrorism is that as military operations move beyond a single theater, the more complex tasks will be dispersed among numerous departments, agencies, and offices, and the focus on the overall U.S. strategy will be lost, along with the nation's ability to coordinate operations. The American campaign must continue to emphasize the following central elements:

- The destruction of al Qaeda remains the primary aim.
- The pursuit of al Qaeda must be single-minded and unrelenting.
- The campaign against terrorism will take time, possibly decades.
- The fight in Afghanistan must be continued as long as al Qaeda operatives remain in the country.
- Pakistan must be kept on the side of the allies in efforts to destroy the remnants of al Qaeda and the Taliban and dilute Islamic extremism.

- New networks must be created to exploit intelligence across frontiers.
- The goals of the war on terrorism cannot be accomplished unilaterally —international cooperation is a prerequisite for success.
- This is a war against specific terrorists, the larger goal of which is to combat terrorism.
- The strategy should include political warfare, aimed at reducing the appeal of extremists, encouraging alternative views, and discouraging terrorists' use of WMD.
- Deterrent strategies may be appropriate for dealing with the terrorists' support structures.
- It must be made clear that terrorist use of WMD will bring extraordinary responses.
- Homeland security strategies must be developed that are both effective and efficient.
- The war against the terrorists at home and abroad must be conducted in a way that is consistent with American values.

Finally, it is necessary to be determinedly pragmatic. America's goal is not revenge for the September 11 attacks. The goal is not even bringing individual terrorists to justice. It is the destruction of a terrorist enterprise that threatens American security and, by extension, the security of the world.

Introduction

Since the terrorist attacks of September 11, 2001, the United States has achieved significant successes in its war on terrorism. Removing the Taliban government in Afghanistan, thereby eliminating al Qaeda's sanctuary and training camps, has broken an important link in the process that once provided al Qaeda's leadership with a continuing flow of recruits. Toppling the Taliban also demonstrated American resolve and international support, and it underscored the considerable risk run by governments that provide assistance to terrorists.

The United States has avoided portraying its campaign against al Qaeda and the Taliban as a crusade against Islam (an accusation made by al Qaeda's leaders), and it has successfully brought about a fundamental change in Pakistan's policy. Once a Taliban supporter, Pakistan has become an ally in the campaign against Islamic extremism. U.S. diplomacy has also turned the international outrage and concern prompted by the September 11 attacks into a global commitment to combat terrorism, confirmed in United Nations Resolution 1373. Through its military presence in Uzbekistan, its diplomatic intervention in the confrontation between Pakistan and India over Kashmir, and its direct military assistance to the Philippines and Georgia, the United States has limited al Qaeda's ability to exploit other conflicts and develop new bases.

Despite these successes, the United States still faces a serious terrorist threat. Public warnings of possible attacks continue to rattle nerves and impede economic recovery, and September 11 signaled a fundamental and permanent change in the security environment. But while Americans are apprehensive, still in shock over the attacks on the World Trade Center and the Pentagon, they appear reluctant to accept that this was not a one-time anomaly. Despite the continuing issuance of new warnings, Americans are capable of lapsing into a dangerous complacency.

The tasks of reorganizing government, investigating perceived failures in intelligence, implementing new security measures, dealing with new crises abroad, and addressing important domestic matters inevitably distract government and public attention from the very real threat posed by al Qaeda. In this environment, one can understand the relentless determination of the otherwise unappealing ancient Roman Senator Cato, who reportedly concluded every speech with the reminder that "Carthage must be destroyed."

Having achieved its initial goals in Afghanistan, the United States is now in a second, more complex phase of the war, where it must continue its efforts to destroy al Qaeda and at the same time attempt to combat terrorism as a mode of conflict. This will require the orchestration of intelligence collection, the pursuit of traditional criminal investigations leading to trials, the imposition of financial controls and economic sanctions as well as offers of material reward, the application of conventional military power, the use of covert and special operations, the provision of military assistance, and psychological warfare to disrupt terrorist operations and destroy terrorist groups. Greater international coordination will be required. Without a clear exposition of strategy, the focus of the campaign could easily be lost.

Understanding the Enemy

The Emergence of al Qaeda

Al Qaeda was a product of the struggle to eject the Soviet Union from Afghanistan. Portrayed as a holy war, that campaign brought together volunteers and financial contributors from throughout the Islamic world. Muslims from Algeria, Egypt, Saudi Arabia, Southeast Asia, and beyond fought side by side, forging relationships and creating a cadre of veterans who shared a powerful life experience, a more global view, and a heady sense of confidence underscored by the Soviet Union's ultimate withdrawal and subsequent collapse, for which they assumed credit. Instead of being welcomed home as heroes, however, the returning veterans of the Afghan campaign were watched by suspicious regimes who worried that the religious fervor of the fighters posed a political threat. Isolated at home, they became ready recruits for new campaigns.

There were ample reasons and opportunities to continue the fight: the Gulf War and the consequent arrival of American troops in Saudi Arabia; the continued repression of Islamic challenges to local regimes; armed struggles in Algeria, Egypt, the newly independent Muslim republics of the former Soviet Union, Kashmir, the Philippines, and Bosnia; the forces of globalization that seemed threatening to all local cultures; and the continuing civil war in Afghanistan. Organizational survival, the natural desire to continue in meaningful activity, and the rewards of status and an inflated self-image contributed powerful incentives to continue the fight. The subsequent victories of a like-minded Taliban guaranteed safe haven for the militants and their training camps, which graduated thousands of additional volunteers.

What Osama bin Laden and his associates contributed to this potent but unfocused force was a sense of vision, mission, and strategy that combined twentieth century theory of a unified Islamic polity with restoration of the Islamic Caliphate that, at its height, stretched from Spain to India. This vision had operational utility. It recast the numerous local conflicts into a single struggle between an authentic Islam and a host of corrupt satraps who would collapse without the backing of the West—the United States in particular. It thereby provided a single, easily agreed-upon enemy, whose fate, when confronted with a unified Islamic struggle, would be the same as that of the Soviet Union. By erasing the boundaries between individual countries and their conflicts, al Qaeda could draw upon a much larger reservoir of human resources for the larger battle. In addition to the thousands of veterans of the war against the Soviet Union, al Qaeda now had thousands of new recruits to train.

Quantity ultimately translates into quality. It enables organizers to identify and exploit specialized talent that would be scarce or not available in a smaller enterprise. This is key to al Qaeda's operational capabilities. Amply funded, protected in Afghanistan, supported by Pakistan, motivated by a powerful vision, al Qaeda became the banner carrier of Islam's response to past defeats, frustration, humiliation, resentment, and fear. Al Qaeda's spectacular terrorist blows against the United States in Africa and the Middle East and America's feeble response, despite its vigorous denunciations, made Osama bin Laden a heroic leader. Everything seemed to confirm al Qaeda's calculations.

Process, Planning, and Mission

Al Qaeda is more than just an organization; it is also a process, and its principal resource is its human capital. Al Qaeda's future ability to grow and continue operations depends most strongly on its ability to gather new recruits.

On the basis of what we know about the September 11 attackers and the limited testimony of captured al Qaeda operatives, al Qaeda appears to function like many cults. Frustrated immigrants in Europe and America, drifters living on the margins of society, seekers of absolute truth or greater meaning in their lives, lonely souls with varying levels of education show up—on their own or invited by friends—at mosques and prayer groups, a few of which offer radical interpretations of faith. Fiery sermons identify common enemies, the obstacles to political and personal achievement. Recruiters watch for resonance and select promising acolytes for more intense indoctrination and training.

Prior to September 11, the training camps in Afghanistan provided a way of testing commitment. In Afghanistan, volunteers faced hardship and sacrifice, as well as opportunities for combat. With practical training came further indoctrination. The recruits became part of a secret international brotherhood that superseded all other affiliations and loyalties.

Fulfillment of the radical Islamic vision of heroic deeds leading to the restoration of a utopian Islamic empire on earth—or, if God wills, eternal reward in the hereafter—requires embracing an aggressive interpretation of jihad. Exhortations to kill in quantity underscore the teaching that there are no innocents in this war. The most intelligent and dedicated volunteers receive further training and indoctrination, and they return to the world with a sense of mission and power. Of course, not all are Mohammed Attas, fanatics capable of planning and executing complex operations. Some are "acorns," buried at random to be dug up when needed for an operation.

Most of the proposals for terrorist operations appear to come from the operatives in the field, rather than from the center. Approval from above, however, brings resources that elevate such plans to a deadlier realm. The provision of technical advice, money, documents, and additional manpower to the self-selected warriors suggests the existence of an underground bureaucracy—al Qaeda has middle management. Some operations seem to receive little central support, but a plan for an attack on the scale of September 11 would certainly have significant central control and could well have been initiated by al Qaeda's command.

An attack that carries the al Qaeda brand, duly credited in the news media to Osama bin Laden, thus enhances his reputation. Each attack becomes a recruiting poster, demonstrating the power of al Qaeda's interpretation of Islam, attracting more recruits.

Changed Perceptions of the Terrorist Threat

The September 11 attack destroyed America's sense of invulnerability and illustrated the limits of its intelligence infrastructure. It demonstrated that foreign terrorists were capable of mounting major attacks on U.S. soil without being detected. Preparations for earlier terrorist attacks, including the 1996 bombing of Khobar Towers in Saudi Arabia, the bombings of the American embassies in Kenya and Tanzania, and the attack on the U.S.S. *Cole*, had also gone undetected, but those incidents took place in areas where U.S. authorities had limited opportunities to obtain intelligence firsthand. Preparations for the 1993 bombing of the World Trade Center and the 1995 bombing of the federal building in Oklahoma City had also gone undetected, but these were the work of small domestic conspiracies (although there was some foreign participation in the 1993 World Trade Center bombing). The fact that at least 20 operatives from a terrorist organization that was already being closely watched by American intelligence services could enter the United States, remain in the country for months while training to carry out multiple terrorist attacks of unprecedented scale, receive instructions and hundreds of thousands of dollars from abroad, even travel out of the country and return, all without being detected by the authorities, raised questions about the adequacy of American intelligence that are still being debated.

September 11 also raised the lethality of terrorism to a new level. The terrorists clearly were determined to cause catastrophic casualties—tens of thousands of casualties—confirming a long-term trend toward increasingly large-scale, indiscriminate attacks. Tens died in the worst incidents of terrorism in the 1970s, hundreds in the 1980s and 1990s, but thousands died on September 11. The September 11 attacks involved an imaginative plan (although no exotic weapons), and they indicated a mindset that would not preclude the use of weapons of mass destruction (WMD) if the terrorists could somehow acquire them. Subsequent discoveries in al Qaeda's training camps showed that the use of chemical, biological, and nuclear weapons certainly was an aspiration, even if the organization lacked the actual capabilities.

Fears of bioterrorism increased when a still unidentified perpetrator sent letters contaminated with anthrax to target recipients in the news media and government. No evidence directly connects the anthrax attacks to al Qaeda's September 11 attack, but the coincidence in timing led to a convergence of concerns. Regardless of who was responsible for the anthrax attacks, bioterrorism had become a deadly and disruptive reality.

The Aftermath of September 11: Al Qaeda's View

From the terrorists' perspective, the September 11 attacks dealt a massive blow to the most prominent symbols of American economic and military might, a dramatic demonstration of what could be achieved through commitment to the Islamic extremists' vision of jihad. Al Qaeda's leadership probably anticipated that the attack would provoke a major military response, which it could then portray as an assault on Islam. This would inspire thousands of additional volunteers and could provoke the entire Islamic world to rise up against the West. Governments that opposed the people's wrath, quislings to Western imperialism, would fall. The West would be destroyed.

If this was al Qaeda's rapture, it repeated the folly of terrorists past. The strategy of carrying out spectacular attacks to deliberately provoke an overreaction by government authorities which, in turn, would provoke a popular uprising has seldom worked, and it didn't work this time either. To be sure, the attacks on the World Trade Center and the Pentagon were popular on Arab streets, where they were met with spontaneous celebrations and reportedly made Osama a popular name for new babies. But when the United States launched its attack on Afghanistan, careful not to portray it as an assault on Islam despite bin Laden's efforts to do so, there were no visible rivers of recruits streaming toward al Qaeda's banner, nor were there any uprisings or organized resistance.

More than nine months after the attacks, the Taliban have been removed from government, although not eliminated from Afghanistan entirely, and al Qaeda has lost its sanctuary and training camps. The "business continuity" plans that al Qaeda probably had in place before September 11 may have permitted many of its leaders and operatives to escape, but some have been killed, others have been captured, and the rest are on the run. Pakistan, once a source of support and recruits, has reversed its policy and cracked down on Taliban and al Qaeda sympathizers. Other governments in the Middle East and beyond have rounded up al Qaeda suspects and have committed themselves to cooperation in combating terrorism, although they still cannot agree on a definition of what terrorism is. Whatever appreciation Palestinians might have owed Osama bin Laden for opportunistically including their cause on his broader agenda has been offset by the vicissitudes of their own struggle. Its operatives forced deeper underground and its financial supporters forced to be more circumspect, al Qaeda's balance sheet does not look so favorable. However, we have not seen the last of al Qaeda.

Al Qaeda will not quit. Terrorist groups seldom quit, and al Qaeda did not retire on September 12. Growing evidence acquired since September 11 suggests that in addition to taking steps to protect its finances, instructing some of its key operatives to disappear, and making preparations to protect its leadership, al Qaeda has vowed to carry out further attacks. And indeed, terrorist attacks have occurred in Pakistan, Tunisia, and Saudi Arabia, and other terrorist plots have been discovered before they could be carried out. Some of the plots originated prior to September 11, but others were set in motion afterwards. Not all of the plots are directly linked to al Qaeda, although some clearly are. Some of the attacks may have simply been provoked by America's war on terrorism and Pakistan's decision to support it, as well as by other events in the Middle East.

Al Qaeda's leaders may have underestimated the American response, just as they may have overestimated the readiness of their sympathizers to rise up against the West. They now must adapt their organization and strategy to this new reality, but they will continue their campaign.

Religious conviction gives them strength, but the armed struggle is what holds them together. Violence is their *raison d'être*. The enterprise of terrorism provides status, power, and psychological satisfaction. It attracts new recruits. It demonstrates their devotion and gives them historical importance. Without terrorism, al Qaeda would collapse into just another exotic sect.

Terrorists understand when they suffer setbacks, but they operate in a clandestine world, a closed universe cut off from normal discourse and competing views. They measure success differently: They define death and destruction as achievements in themselves. Terrorists do not feel that it is necessary to translate these into political progress, and they have a high tolerance for cognitive dissonance. Adversity is seen as a test of their commitment. Compromise equals apostasy, so leaders counseling restraint risk accusations of betrayal. In an association of extremists, it is perilous to be less than the most extreme. Successes are seen to derive from violence, and setbacks thus call for greater violence. Individual terrorists may become disillusioned, but there is no easy way for them to leave the organization. A few groups have officially suspended their campaigns of violence, but their leaders were denounced, while splinter and rival groups vowed to fight on.

Other groups have faded with the death or capture of charismatic and effective leaders (e.g., Peru's Shining Path and Turkey's PKK), the loss of state sponsors or the imposition of state control that left their tongues but removed their teeth (the Palestinian rejectionists currently residing in Damascus), or the drying up of their reservoir of support (America's Weathermen Underground). In some cases, circumstances changed, making the terrorists' struggle less relevant (e.g., Germany's Red Army Faction). Other groups have disappeared when a generation passed without successors. The evolution of terrorist organizations is a long process, measured in decades.

Sources of al Qaeda's strength. Although al Qaeda has been damaged by the American-led campaign, it continues to benefit from its image as a powerful Islamic force that is capable of inflicting devastating blows on its foes. Osama bin Laden's mystique survives, even if his personal fate is in doubt. Al Qaeda's key figures remain at large, and there may be others who have not yet been identified.

It is more difficult to assess the capability of al Qaeda's global network. We know that as of September 11, 2001, it was extensive, reportedly in place in at least 60 countries. More than 2,000 suspected al Qaeda operatives have been captured or arrested, but others have disappeared underground. Since September 11, terrorist attacks carried out or thwarted in Singapore, Pakistan, Saudi Arabia, Lebanon, Tunisia, Morocco, Macedonia, Bosnia, Italy, France, and the United States indicate that al Qaeda's operational capability still exists. It is able to communicate, reconnoiter targets, plan operations, travel, meet clandestinely, and obtain finances.

Al Qaeda also still benefits from a large reservoir of recruits. While many have been dispersed or perhaps temporarily demoralized, at least some fighters remain dedicated and willing to carry out attacks, including suicide missions. That some attacks have been prevented by intelligence, alert police, or simply good luck is fortunate. At the same time, there remains the nagging fear that another catastrophic attack is being prepared somewhere and that it will be revealed only when it occurs, days, months, or years from now.

Terrorist organizations benefit from having virtually unlimited targets, as homeland defense planners are discovering. Al Qaeda's strategy playbook, however, shows certain preferences. Commercial aviation, diplomatic facilities, and American (or allied) servicemen recur as targets. Naval vessels in port (or in narrow straits), government buildings, monuments, and symbolic landmarks also figure prominently. Finally, al Qaeda enjoys a large constituency that accepts and applauds extreme violence against the West in general and the United States in particular.

Operating environment. While al Qaeda clearly continues to benefit from certain strengths, it must now operate in a less-permissive environment. The loss of the supportive Taliban government, its easily accessible safe haven, and its training camps may not be felt immediately, as al Qaeda will be able to draw upon its reserves for some time while it tries to establish new centers. But these are likely to be smaller and less accessible. Moreover, the pilgrimage to Afghanistan, the experience in the training camps, and participation in Afghanistan's armed conflict served an important role in attracting and indoctrinating volunteers to the cause and in providing future terrorist operatives. Televised videotapes and virtual realms on the Internet may not suffice to maintain a high level of devotion. If al Qaeda can be kept on the run, the numbers it can train will decline. And declining numbers eventually will result in a corresponding qualitative decline in terrorist operations.

Pakistan's withdrawal of support for the Taliban and its promised crackdown on the extremist religious schools that supplied volunteers for al Qaeda's training camps will also reduce the flow of recruits. Poorly educated Pakistani youth were never likely to become sophisticated international operatives. On the other hand, they will pose a continuing danger within Pakistan.

Financial contributors may also be constrained by international efforts to limit terrorist finances. The new measures will not prevent the financing of terrorist operations, which require relatively small amounts, but they could reduce al Qaeda's welfare and proselytizing efforts. The new laws also provide additional sources of intelligence about terrorist organizations.

Finally, increased surveillance and intelligence gathered from captured al Qaeda members and documents will further increase al Qaeda's risks.

Adapting to new circumstances. The greatest threat posed by al Qaeda is that it will attempt another attack as catastrophic as the September 11 attacks or even more so. None of the terrorist plots uncovered since then have been that ambitious, but we know now that the planning for the September 11 attacks was under way for several years, overlapping planning for other major attacks and undetected by the authorities.

An attack on the scale of September 11 could have profound political, social, and economic consequences for the United States. It could inspire widespread anxiety, anger at the government for failing in its primary mission of providing security, and popular demand for draconian measures that could shake the American political system and fundamentally alter the American lifestyle. The economic effects of such an attack, the subsequent disruption, and the need for even greater security measures could be devastating to the economy. But that level of destruction can be achieved only with coordinated conventional attacks, multidimensional assaults calculated to magnify the disruption, or the use of chemical, biological, or nuclear weapons. These, in turn, are likely to need the kind of organization that requires some participation on the part of al Qaeda's central command. We are uncertain whether al Qaeda's key leaders are still alive or able to "do" strategy. Wild-eyed recruits may be plentiful. Brains are precious. Thus, the immediate goal of the war on terrorism must be to destroy al Qaeda's ability to operate at this level.

It is also possible that al Qaeda will adapt to the more difficult post–September 11 operational environment by morphing into an even looser network, devolving more initiative and resources to local operatives. This does not appear to be inconsistent with al Qaeda's current operational philosophy, which seems to invite local initiative. A looser al Qaeda network would be better able to survive the intense worldwide surveillance of authorities, but it might not be able to operate at the level required for a catastrophic attack. The failed attempt to sabotage an American airliner last December might be characteristic of this level of organization.

Continuing, but uncoordinated, acts of terrorism may be waged by al Qaeda cells, unconnected supporters, and even individuals, inspired by al Qaeda's call or provoked by America's war on terrorism. It may be difficult to distinguish these from isolated acts of violence unconnected with any terrorist organization. Such attacks could be lethal and capable of inspiring terror among an already apprehensive population, but they are likely to remain sporadic events. The anthrax letters and the recent bombings in Pakistan are characteristic of this level of terrorism.

Prospects for the use of weapons of mass destruction. Much of the concern about the current terrorist threat relates to the possible employment of WMD. These include chemical and biological weapons, radioactive dispersal devices, and, potentially, stolen nuclear weapons or improvised nuclear devices. Such concerns are not new; they have been debated at least since the early 1970s.[1] Participants in that debate could appropriately be described in theological terms, since the arguments reflected beliefs more than evidence. "Apocalyptians" believed that terrorist escalation to mass destruction was inevitable, while disbelievers pointed to the absence of any evidence indicating that terrorists were moving in this direction. In the middle were "prudent agnostics," who remained uncertain about whether chemical, biological, or nuclear terrorism was inevitable but nonetheless argued for increased security.

Skeptics found support in the fact that terrorists at that time clearly did not operate at the upper limits of their capabilities if mayhem was their goal. Terrorists who did not understand technically challenging chemical, biological, or nuclear weapons certainly knew how to build large conventional bombs, which they could have set off in public areas to kill far more people than they did. The fact that they did not do so, therefore, had to indicate that they operated under self-imposed constraints. Subsequent research showed that terrorists argued about the proper level of violence. Some believed that wanton killing could jeopardize group cohesion. They also did not want to alienate their perceived legions of supporters. Terrorists wanted publicity and to create alarm; they did not necessarily want to provoke public backlashes that would support government crackdowns that the terrorists themselves might not survive.

In the 1980s, the constraints appeared to erode as terrorists escalated their violence, especially in the Middle East. By the 1990s, terrorists turned to large-scale, indiscriminate attacks calculated to kill in quantity. Part—but only part—of the reason could be found in the changing motives that drove conflict in the final decade of the twentieth century. Whereas terrorism in the 1970s and 1980s had been driven mostly by political ideology— terrorists had secular motives, political agendas, and therefore constituents, real or imaginary, on whose behalf they fought—terrorism in the 1990s was increasingly driven by ideologies that exploited religion. The conviction that they had God's sanction freed religious fanatics from ordinary political or moral constraints. But the religious angle should not be overstated, as some of the most deadly terrorist attacks, in terms of fatalities, were carried out by agents of Libya, who sabotaged PanAm and UTA flights in 1988 and 1989, or North Koreans, who brought down a Korean airliner in 1987. Nor should the frequency of large-scale attacks be overestimated. According to RAND's chronology of international terrorism, between 1968 and September 11, 2001, only 14 of more than 10,000 international terrorist incidents resulted in 100 or more fatalities, although there appear to have been more attempts to kill in quantity.

At the same time the terrorists seemed to be escalating their violence, the fall of the Soviet Union raised concerns about the security of the Soviet weapons research program and its vast nuclear arsenal. In an environment of poverty, increasing corruption, and growing organized crime, would Soviet weapons remain secure? Would impoverished Soviet weapons designers and builders find employment in the clandestine weapons research programs of would-be proliferators or state sponsors of terrorism? Might Russia or other republics of the former Soviet Union, desperate for hard currency, willingly provide the materiel and expertise that could accelerate nuclear weapons development by terrorist organizations? Further anxiety derived from the realization that Iraq was further along in developing WMD than had been imagined.

The 1995 sarin attack on Tokyo's subways seemed to confirm the darker view of the apocalyptians. At the direction of their very human god, Aum Shinrikyo's members fit the pattern of religious fanatics willing to kill thousands. This attack reminded us that organizations other than identified terrorist groups could carry out significant acts of terrorism. It showed that a group was capable of clandestinely acquiring and experimenting with both chemical and biological weapons for years without detection, despite numerous suspicious incidents. But the attack also demonstrated the difficulties of developing and deploying biological or chemical devices. Although it had months of experimentation and an ample budget, the Aum Shinrikyo cult developed only a crude version of nerve gas, which it dispersed in a primitive manner that reduced its effectiveness so that casualties were limited. Within weeks of the attack, Aum Shinrikyo was destroyed, its leaders under arrest. More than seven years later, no terrorist organization has yet tried to duplicate the attack.

There is no inexorable escalation from truck bombs or even suicide air attacks to WMD. Nonetheless, terrorist desires to use WMD cannot be discounted. On September 11, al Qaeda terrorists were trying to kill tens of thousands. They succeeded in killing thousands. Captured documents and interrogations of captured al Qaeda members have revealed the organization's aspirations to acquire chemical, biological, and nuclear capabilities, although there is no indication that it has such capabilities today. If it had those capabilities, al Qaeda would undoubtedly be willing to use them.

There is distance between ambition and achievement. Chemical, biological, and radiological weapons will not necessarily cause mass destruction—worst-case scenarios are planning vehicles, not forecasts. In the most plausible scenarios, the psychological effects of chemical, biological, or radiological attacks are likely to vastly exceed the actual death and destruction, but we are on the frontier of a new, more dangerous domain.

Some Realistic Assumptions

Strategy must be based upon realistic assumptions about the current situation. Al Qaeda, its associates, and its successors will fight on. It draws upon a deep reservoir of hatred and a desire for revenge, and U.S. efforts have reduced, not eliminated, its ability to mount significant terrorist operations.

It must be presumed that al Qaeda will exploit all of its ability to cause catastrophic death and destruction—there will be no self-imposed limits to its violence. Attempts to cause massive death and destruction using conventional or unconventional weapons are likely. It can also be presumed that al Qaeda will continue its efforts to acquire and use WMD; that it will attack U.S. targets abroad where possible; and that it will attempt to mount attacks within the United States. Al Qaeda constitutes the most serious immediate threat to the security of the United States.

Although some measure of success has been achieved in uncovering terrorist plots, the ability of U.S. agencies to detect and prevent future terrorist attacks is limited. There will not be sufficient intelligence to provide adequate warning in every case, and while security is being increased around likely targets of terrorist attack, terrorists can attack anything, anywhere, anytime, while it is not possible to protect everything, everywhere, all the time. Some attacks will occur.

Strategy for the Second Phase of the War on Terrorism

The United States has formulated and carried out a coherent first-phase strategy in the war on terrorism. But what next? The campaign has now entered a more difficult phase. The greatest challenge is that as military operations move beyond a single theater, the more complex tasks will be dispersed among numerous departments, agencies, and offices, and the focus on the overall U.S. strategy will be lost, along with the nation's ability to coordinate operations. That strategy must continue to emphasize the key elements outlined below.

The destruction of al Qaeda must remain the primary aim of the American campaign. Al Qaeda will adapt to new circumstances; it may disperse, change names, merge with other entities, or be absorbed into its own successors, but as long as its leadership, structure, operatives, relationships, financing, and ability to recruit survive in any form, it will seek to repair damage, reestablish connections, issue instructions, and mobilize resources to support further terrorist operations. The al Qaeda enterprise itself cannot easily be deterred. It can be disabled only by permanently disrupting the process that provides it with human and material resources. Further terrorist attacks must be kept within the level of tolerable tragedy; another catastrophe on the scale of September 11 must not be allowed to occur.

The pursuit of al Qaeda must be single-minded and unrelenting. The episodic nature of terrorism (long periods of time elapse between major attacks), the heavy burden of security, and the public's impatience for closure can tempt the United States into dangerous complacency. Distracting events, including the conflict between Israel and the Palestinians, the confrontation between India and Pakistan over Kashmir, and America's determination to deal with other threats to national security must be addressed in the context of the immediate and continuing threat posed by al Qaeda.

The United States cannot inflict upon its dispersed and amorphous terrorist foe the immediate destruction that would serve as a deterrent to other terrorist entities contemplating alliance with it or replication of its war on America. However, assured destruction can be pursued over time—years, if necessary—without letup, without amnesty, as an ongoing reminder to others of the consequences of provoking the United States.

The campaign against terrorism will take time. Wars against terrorists throughout history have been long, even when the terrorists operate on the national territory of the government they oppose and are accessible to its authorities. Italy's Red Brigades fought from the late 1960s to the early 1980s, and after years of quiet, they may now be reemerging. Germany's Red Army Faction survived from the early 1970s to the 1990s. The Provisional Wing of the Irish Republican Army emerged in the late 1960s and laid down its arms only at the end of the 1990s. Spain's ETA is approaching its fifth decade in the field. Colombia's guerrillas can find their origins in armed struggles that began more than a half-century ago.

Al Qaeda itself represents more than a decade of organizational development built upon relationships that were first established in the 1980s. Its active planning for a terrorist war on the United States began not later than the mid-1990s, and its planning for September 11 began three or possibly four years before the actual attack, starting with plots elaborated in the first half of the 1990s. The thoroughness of al Qaeda's planning suggests that it has prepared for a long campaign, one that inevitably will involve setbacks. It is probably prepared to lie low indefinitely. The battle against al Qaeda could last decades.

The fight in Afghanistan must be continued as long as al Qaeda operatives remain in the country. There may be differences within al Qaeda between those who wish to make their last stand in Afghanistan (and have no other options) and those who would disperse to reconstitute new versions of the organization elsewhere. Although some analysts argue that the United States has only complicated its task by chasing al Qaeda out of Afghanistan, I believe that it is preferable to destroy al Qaeda operatives in Afghanistan rather than hunting for them elsewhere. Continued pressure in Afghanistan will consume al Qaeda's resources and distract its leadership. Premature withdrawal—historically, the American tendency—would be dangerous. Only when al Qaeda is completely destroyed or when the new Afghan government can effectively exercise authority throughout its territory can withdrawal be risked.

Long-term operations in Afghanistan will require carefully controlling the application of violence in order to avoid the errors and collateral damage that will fuel Afghan hostility and pressure to depart. If Americans accept the commitment to remain in Afghanistan for a very long haul, the mode of operations can be altered to reduce the risks of counterproductive incidents. It may be prudent to place more emphasis on Special Forces operations, longer tours of duty, and the creation of specially trained combined Afghan-American hunter units. It may also be necessary to tighten the rules governing the use of American air power. With time, it will be increasingly beneficial to ensure that military successes are seen as those of Afghan warriors rather than American air power.

The continued U.S. presence in Afghanistan must not be seen as an occupation by foreign predators. Positive benefits of America's involvement —the reconstruction of infrastructure, assistance for health care and education, the restoration and preservation of Afghanistan's cultural heritage—can temper the country's natural resistance to outsiders.

Pakistan must be kept on the side of the allies in efforts to destroy the remnants of al Qaeda and the Taliban and dilute Islamic extremism. The government of Pervez Musharraf faces a potential coalition of Taliban supporters, militant Muslim groups committed to a continuation of the war in Kashmir, and Sunni extremists who for years have waged terrorist campaigns against Shi'ites and political opponents, principally in Karachi. The loss of

Pakistan's support could reverse America's victory in Afghanistan. It could provide al Qaeda with a new sanctuary in the turbulent tribal frontier areas that border Afghanistan, leaving the United States and its allies with the dismal prospect of large-scale military operations in Pakistan. If a new Pakistani government were hostile to the West, the United States could find itself faced with military action against Pakistan itself. The most likely successor to the present government is not a more liberal, democratic, pro-Western regime, but one that is at the very least less accommodating. A more radical Islamic Pakistan could emerge, one that is more sympathetic to the extremists, more belligerent on the issue of Kashmir, and in possession of nuclear weapons.

The United States must be firm in ensuring that President Musharraf fulfills his pledges, especially those that involve constraining the activities of the extremists and halting infiltration into Kashmir, which could provoke a dangerous war with India. This will demand much of a weak government: that it check the activities of extremists in Pakistan and Kashmir; shut down the religious academies that feed recruits to extremist groups; cooperate with the allies in rooting out and running down al Qaeda operatives; and implement political reforms that ultimately will deliver democracy, while confronting religious extremism, sectarian violence, separatist sentiments, and hostile neighbors. The United States needs to provide political and economic support that will enable the Pakistani government to demonstrate the positive benefits of the alliance while checking popular bellicose sentiments in Kashmir. Without destabilizing the country, the United States should also try to nudge Pakistan toward the political reforms that are prerequisite to democracy and development.

New networks must be created to exploit intelligence across frontiers. Suspected al Qaeda operatives arrested worldwide since September 11 are providing some information about the terrorist network. The capture of documents found at al Qaeda safe houses and training camps will add to the picture, but this material must be effectively exploited to support the continued identification and pursuit of al Qaeda's remaining cells and the successful prosecution of those arrested. Rapid and accurate translation, analysis, and dissemination to investigators and prosecutors in the United States and abroad will require an unprecedented level of multinational coordination between intelligence services and justice departments. Magistrates and prosecutors abroad must receive intelligence in a form that is both useful and legally admissible within their varying systems of law. And the United States must understand the legal and political concerns of each of its allies and adapt its strategy accordingly. Not every suspected terrorist need be in U.S. custody, nor can information flow only in the direction of Washington.

U.S. agencies still have great difficulty sharing intelligence among themselves, although the situation is improving. Only recently have intelligence efforts and criminal investigations been orchestrated to enable successful prosecution of foreign terrorists. Achieving even better cooperation and coordination internationally will require structures that exist today only in embryonic form. It may require the creation of a U.S. task force dedicated to the coordination, collection, and dissemination of vital material to justice departments and intelligence services abroad. It may require the creation of bilateral and multilateral task forces focused on dismantling the al Qaeda network and the deployment of liaison personnel abroad for the duration of the campaign.

The crucial second phase of the war on terrorism cannot be accomplished unilaterally—international cooperation is a prerequisite for success. Full cooperation will be limited to a few governments. The British, with whom some of the mechanisms for close intelligence cooperation are already in place, will continue to be America's closest allies. NATO and other traditional allies also can be expected to cooperate closely. The cooperation of the French is especially important, although it brings with it a unique set of challenges. France has global intelligence resources, vast area knowledge, and valuable historical experience in dealing with the threat posed by terrorists operating in North Africa and the Middle East.

Russian cooperation is also important, for both political and technical reasons. Although Russian intelligence today may not match the capabilities of the Soviet intelligence infrastructure during the Cold War, and the Russian leadership tends to see terrorism exclusively through the lens of its conflict in Chechnya, Russia nonetheless has valuable knowledge and experience in Central and South Asia and can be a major contributor to ongoing international efforts to combat terrorism. Although they have significant differences in approach, Russia and the United States are natural allies on this issue.

Israel, America's closest ally in the Middle East, has vast knowledge and a strong political agenda. Historically, intelligence cooperation is close and will continue to be so, even as the two countries occasionally have differences on how to address the Palestinian issue.

Moderate Arab regimes will also contribute to the intelligence pool. Diplomacy can create new coalitions that extend beyond those of traditional allies. The United States should be flexible enough to exploit opportunities for cooperation among governments it previously has penalized for their support of terrorism. Both Libya and Sudan are anxious to normalize relations, and Sudan has offered outright cooperation in the fight against bin Laden. The United States need not seek the political endorsement of those countries on every issue, but it could be operationally and politically useful to have strong nationalist governments—even those critical of the United States— seen to be cooperating against al Qaeda's terrorism.

It is not natural for intelligence agencies to share. The CIA, with more experience in the give and take of international intelligence collection and diplomacy, is better at it than the FBI, whose organizational culture derives from the prosecution of crime. Sharing intelligence with foreign services is never easy, but unlike the Cold War era when there were understandable concerns about Soviet penetration, there is far less concern today that al Qaeda or other terrorists have burrowed into the intelligence services of America's traditional allies, and no one is concerned about keeping the terrorists' secrets. Except as intelligence-sharing is limited by the requirement to protect sources, methods, and ongoing operations, exposure rather than withholding should be the aim.

This is a war against specific terrorists—the goal is to combat terrorism. The president has said that we are at war, and the Congress has passed a joint resolution authorizing military action against al Qaeda and the Taliban as well as future actions against other nations, organizations, or persons found to have participated in the September 11 attacks. Although it may still fall short of a declaration of war, this formal expression of belligerency against terrorists and those who assist them enables the United States to more easily keep the initiative. Previous uses of military force against terrorists were limited to the framework of retaliation, although U.S. officials shunned that specific term. The United States on occasion struck back against terrorists and their state sponsors to disrupt or discourage further attacks, but the initiative remained in the hands of the terrorists. Moreover, retaliatory strikes had to be timely and seen as proportionate to the attacks that provoked them. While it might have been hoped that terrorists would fear that the United States would attack them a second time, this never happened. The president's declaration and subsequent Congressional resolution clearly signal an intent to attack terrorists whenever, wherever, and with whatever methods the United States chooses. It facilitates covert operations, and it creates a requirement for a specific plan of action.

The use of the term *war* does not carry any recognition of terrorist outlaws as *privileged combatants* entitled to treatment as prisoners of war, although, of course, the United States will not mistreat captives. It does not end American efforts to bring terrorists to justice through the legal system, either the American system or that of other countries with capable authorities who are willing to enforce the law. In countries without such authorities, the United States may take appropriate measures to defend itself. Such a declaration does not oblige the United States to run down every terrorist or attack every nation identified as a state sponsor of terrorism. Sensible diplomacy will prevail.

President Bush has correctly portrayed the war on terrorism as likely to be a long war, but it has finite aims: the removal of the Taliban government; the destruction of al Qaeda's training bases in Afghanistan; putting Osama bin Laden and his associates on the run; and rounding up al Qaeda's operatives around the world. The United States is not going to destroy every terrorist group or pursue every terrorist in the world, but as a matter of self-defense, it will wage war against terrorists capable of causing casualties on the scale of September 11. The targets are specific.

But America is not "at war" with terrorism, which is a phenomenon, not a foe. It is trying to *combat* terrorism. To make terrorism an unattractive mode of conflict, the United States will collect and exchange intelligence with allies. It will conduct criminal investigations. It will seek to expand international conventions and cooperation. It will assist in resolving conflicts that may produce terrorism and will address the causes of the deep hatred that terrorists are able to exploit. This is consistent with U.S. actions for the 30 years since the creation in 1972 of the Cabinet Committee to Combat Terrorism.

The distinction between *war* on terrorism and *combating* terrorism may also be useful in dealing with allies who attempt to enlist the United States in their wars. As counterterrorism becomes a new basis for American foreign policy, local conflicts are being presented or relabeled to enlist American political and material support. In some cases, the United States may go along in order to gain the support of other nations for its own efforts. But America is not at war with everyone's terrorists, and not all nations need be front-line participants in America's war against al Qaeda. Nevertheless, all nations should cooperate in combating terrorism, an obligation that has been formally recognized in United Nations Resolution 1373. Efforts to deal with root causes of terrorism fall under the rubric of combating terrorism, not the war against al Qaeda. Dealing with terrorist events below the threshold of catastrophe falls within the realm of combating terrorism; events above that threshold provoke war. For the foreseeable future, the United States will be dealing with both.

The current U.S. strategy should be amended to include political warfare. There appears to be a curious bias in America: The nation endorses death to terrorists but is loath to use influence. This bias has been perpetuated in bureaucratic in-fighting and deliberate misrepresentation. But it is not sufficient to merely outgun the terrorists. The enemy here is an ideology, a set of attitudes, a belief system organized into a recruiting network that will continue to replace terrorist losses unless defeated politically. At a tactical level, the campaign should include efforts to discredit al Qaeda, create discord, provoke distrust among its operatives, demoralize volunteers, and discourage recruits. At a strategic level, political warfare should be aimed at reducing the appeal of extremists, encouraging alternative views that are currently silenced by fear and hostile policy, and discouraging terrorists' use of WMD. The United States invested a great deal in this type of activity in the early years of the Cold War with some success, but its growing military superiority has led to this vital component of warfare being discarded. Changes in public attitudes and in communications technology will not permit a return to the sometimes brilliant but often risky operations of a half-century ago, nor would this be desirable. But political warfare is an arena of battle that should be subjected to rational inquiry.

Deterrent strategies may be appropriate for dealing with the terrorists' support structures. The very nature of the terrorist enterprise makes the traditional strategy of deterrence difficult to apply to terrorist groups. In traditional deterrence, the adversaries do not exceed mutually understood limits and will not employ certain weapons, although their continued existence is accepted. Deterrence worked in the Cold War, where central decisionmakers were in charge and in control on both sides. The limits and the consequences were mutually understood. Coexistence was acceptable. Deterrence regulated the conflict; it did not end the struggle.

Deterring terrorism is an entirely different matter. Here, there are diverse foes, not a single enemy with different goals and values. Terrorist leaders are not always in complete control, and they often have difficulty constraining their own followers. Coexistence is not a goal, on either side. Would the United States accept the existence of al Qaeda and any form of freedom for its current leaders, even with credible promises that they will suspend operations against this country? As individual "repentants" ready to cooperate in the destruction of the organization, perhaps; as leaders of al Qaeda, never. Nor are there any acceptable limits to continued terrorist violence.

Still, the notion of deterrence should not be too hastily abandoned. The existence of self-imposed constraints in the past—and for most groups, today—suggests decision-making that calculates risks and costs. Al Qaeda's unwillingness to attack Saudi targets despite its denunciation of the ruling family suggests that even bin Laden's lieutenants make political calculations. We do not know what these are or how they are weighted by the decisionmakers. Al Qaeda may be reluctant to kill fellow Arabs; or if attacked, the ruling Saudi family might push its Wahabi religious allies to denounce bin Laden—and the Saudi government does have clout in the worldwide Islamic community. Moreover, al Qaeda may deem attacking an Arab country to be inconsistent with its vision of focusing its violence on the United States. If any of these speculations is correct, then Saudi Arabia has achieved a level of deterrence. The United States may not be able (or may not want) to duplicate this situation with al Qaeda. It may prefer to demonstrate that large-scale attacks will bring unrelenting pursuit and ultimate destruction in order to deter future terrorist groups.

Deterrence might also be employed in targeting terrorists' support systems. Economic sanctions, although blunt instruments, have had some effect in modifying state behavior. The fate of the Taliban serves as a warning to state supporters of terrorism.

Financial contributors to terrorist fronts may also be deterred by threats of negative publicity, blocked investments, asset seizures, exposure to lawsuits, or merely increased scrutiny of their financial activities. Institutions that assist or tolerate terrorist recruiting may be deterred by the prospect of all members or participants coming under close surveillance. Communities supporting terrorists might be deterred by the threat of expulsions, deportations, selective suspensions of immigration and visa applications, or increased controls on remittances.

Stings may also be used as a deterrent to terrorists seeking WMD. Bogus offers of materials or expertise can be set up to identify and eliminate would-be buyers or middlemen, divert terrorists' financial resources, and provoke uncertainty in terrorists' acquisition efforts.

It must be made clear that terrorist use of WMD will bring extraordinary responses. As terrorists escalate their violence, it is necessary to create a firebreak that signals a different set of responses to terrorist attempts to use WMD. The term *weapons of mass destruction* is used deliberately, to distinguish these weapons from chemical, biological, radiological, or nuclear devices, which collectively may be referred to as *unconventional weapons*. Conventional weapons (from explosives to fully fueled airliners) may be used to create mass destruction—thousands of deaths—whereas chemical, biological, or radiological weapons may cause far less than mass destruction—12 people died in the 1995 Tokyo sarin attack, and the anthrax letters killed five people. The intent here is to focus on *mass destruction*, not *unconventional weapons*, although some ambiguity might not be unwelcome.

Even if attacks involving unconventional weapons do not result in mass casualties, their use could still cause widespread panic with enormous social and economic disruption. This would be true of radiological attacks and almost any deliberate release of a contagious disease. It is, therefore, appropriate to speak of weapons of mass effect as well as weapons of mass destruction. For purposes of response, the United States may decide to treat them as the same.

I have argued since 1977 that it should be a well-understood article of American policy that to prevent terrorist acquisition or use of WMD, the United States will take whatever measures it deems appropriate, including unilateral preemptive military action. In his speech at West Point on June 1, 2002, President Bush warned that "if we wait for threats to fully materialize, we will have waited too long." He went on to declare that the United States would take "preemptive action when necessary."

The United States may reassure its allies that preemptive action is unlikely in circumstances where local authorities have the capability of taking action themselves and can be depended upon to do so, but it is not necessary to precisely outline the circumstances in which U.S. action would be precluded. If preemptive military action is required, the government should be prepared to make a compelling public case *after the event* that such action was justified. The United States failed to do this after the American attack on Sudan in 1998. In the event of such an attack, the United States will be inclined to presume, or may choose to presume, state involvement. In a response to any terrorist attack involving WMD, all weapons may be considered legitimate.

Obviously, these warnings apply more to states than to autonomous terrorist groups who may acquire a WMD capability on their own and may find threats of possible unilateral preemption, unrelenting pursuit, and the possible use of any weapon in the U.S. arsenal to be unpersuasive. The warnings, however, may dissuade states, even hostile ones, from offering expertise or material support to terrorists moving toward WMD; such states may instead be persuaded to take steps to ensure that terrorist actions do not expose them to the danger of preemptive action or retaliation.

Another possible deterrent, perhaps more compelling to the terrorists' supporters and sympathizers than to the terrorists themselves, would be to widely publicize the fact that a major bioterrorism attack involving a highly contagious disease such as smallpox would almost certainly result in a pandemic that would spread beyond U.S. borders. Despite some weaknesses in its public health system, the United States, with its vast medical resources, would be able to cope with an outbreak, as would Europe. But with weak public health institutions and limited medical capabilities, the world's poorer nations would suffer enormously, perhaps losing significant portions of their populations. And if terrorists were to unleash some diabolically designed bug that even the United States could not cope with, the world would be doomed. This grim realization may not stop the most determined fanatic, but it may cause populations that currently find comfort in the illusion that only arrogant Americans will suffer from bioterrorism to come to the view that taboos against certain weapons are necessary to protect all.

Homeland security strategies must be developed that are both effective and efficient. The form future attacks by al Qaeda might take is impossible to predict, and areas of vulnerability both within the United States and abroad are infinite. Commercial aviation remains a preferred target for terrorists seeking high body counts; public surface transportation offers easy access and concentrations of people in contained environments; cargo containers have been identified as a means by which terrorists might clandestinely deliver weapons. Because of its size and complexity, the critical infrastructure of the United States is hard to protect; then again, terrorists have seldom attacked it, preferring instead to go after targets offering high symbolic value or killing fields. Blowing up bridges, pylons, and rail lines is more consistent with guerrilla and civil wars. Still, that does not mean that terrorists will not seek to carry out traditional sabotage in the future.

Security is costly and can be disruptive. A serious terrorist threat to the U.S. homeland may persist for years and indeed may become a fact of life in the twenty-first century; therefore, the security measures that are taken now will likely have to remain in place for a very long time. Terrorists are aware of the cascading economic effects of the September 11 attacks and may conclude that terrorism is an effective way of crippling America's economy.

Terrorists have learned to think strategically rather than tactically, to study and exploit specific vulnerabilities rather than to simply blast away until their opponent yields. If al Qaeda terrorists are allowed to successfully implement a strategy of economic disruption, America will lose the war. It can win only by removing the threat. But at the same time, the U.S. defense must be efficient.

It is therefore necessary not only to increase security but also to reduce the disruption that can be caused by future attacks, as well as the disruptive effects of the security measures themselves. America has just begun to formulate a homeland defense strategy. The current "castles and cops" approach may prove to be costly and disruptive. Priorities must be set. Instead of trying to protect every conceivable target against every imaginable form of attack, policymakers must explore strategies that accept a higher level of risk but offer greater strength or resiliency. The aging infrastructure may be replaced with more powerfully constructed facilities (a feature of some Cold War architecture) or with multiple facilities that provide continued service even if one goes down. This is not a new approach—terrorism simply has become a new ingredient in architecture and system design. There is ample room for research here.

The war against the terrorists at home and abroad must be conducted in a way that is consistent with American values. America cannot expect the world's applause for every action it takes in pursuit of terrorists abroad, but it is important not to squander the international support upon which the United States unavoidably will depend if it is to win the war. Military force is at times justified, but the violence should never be wanton, even if future attacks provoke American rage. The monument to those killed on September 11 and to those who may die in future terrorist attacks cannot be a mountain of innocent dead in some distant land.

At home, it is imperative that America play by the rules, although those rules may be changed. Every liberal democracy confronting terrorism has been obliged to modify rules governing intelligence collection, police powers, preventive detention, access to lawyers, or trial procedures. The United States has attempted to kill enemy commanders during times of war—the prohibition against assassination is a presidential directive, not a law. Captured terrorists may be tried in civilian courts or before military tribunals, but in either case, rules of evidence and the right to representation should apply. It is appropriate that any suspension of such rules be clearly set forth, widely discussed, and endorsed by legislation with time limits or renewal requirements to ensure that it does not become a permanent feature of the landscape. Measures that appear *ad hoc* and arbitrary should be avoided.

Finally, it is necessary to be determinedly pragmatic. America's goal is not revenge for the September 11 attacks. The goal is not even bringing individual terrorists to justice. It is the destruction of a terrorist enterprise that threatens American security.

Brian Michael Jenkins has devoted the last 25 years to an in-depth study of terrorism and international crime. Appointed in 1996 by President Clinton, Mr. Jenkins served on the White House Commission on Aviation Safety and Security. In 2000 he became a member of the U.S. Comptroller General's Advisory Board. He wrote his first monograph on the topic of terrorism in 1974. In addition, he has written several books and articles; over 100 articles have appeared in the RAND reports.

Note

1. I wrote my first monograph on the topic in 1974 (see Brian Michael Jenkins, *Will Terrorists Go Nuclear?* Santa Monica, CA: RAND, P-5541, 1975).

Wayne A. Downing, 2003

The Global War on Terrorism
Focusing the National Strategy

No group or nation should mistake America's intentions: We will not rest until terrorist groups of global reach have been found, have been stopped, and have been defeated.

—George W. Bush
November 6, 2001

The first thing soldiers must know when given a mission is the commander's intent. They need answers to the questions, "What does the boss really want to accomplish? What is the bottom line of this campaign?" The commander's intent is fundamental to any military operation, not because it provides step-by-step instructions, or elaborates every contingency, but because in a few short phrases it provides the most junior member of the team an idea of the desired end state to pursue in the face of confusion or ambiguity. It is the "why" more than the "how."[1] Such focus is as important to the current counter-terrorism operations as in any prior war. President Bush clearly articulated his intent for the U.S. Global War on Terrorism (GWOT) in the quotation above. The foot soldiers in the war, the diplomats, intelligence operatives and analysts, law enforcement officers, service members, and other federal agents in the field, fully understand the sense of urgency in the president's intent. As a result, I believe, they are energized and united in effort and purpose to a degree that we have not seen since World War II.

After September 11, I was asked to return to government service and advise the president on developing his intent into an overarching strategy to defeat an enemy that had dramatically demonstrated its capability to directly attack the U.S. homeland and kill our citizens. As the National Director and Deputy National Security Advisor for Combating Terrorism, I was responsible for closely coordinating the military, diplomatic, intelligence, law enforcement, and financial operations of our war on terror, and for developing and executing a strategy that integrated all elements of national power. It was a unique position in that I worked not only for the National Security Adviser, Condaleeza Rice, but also the Homeland Security Adviser, Governor Tom Ridge. The Office of Combating Terrorism (OCT) that I formed had the complete terrorist portfolio responsible for the threat both overseas and in the United States.

I found that just as the commander's intent helps the soldier operate in the fog of war, the president's intent also guided the U.S. government's understanding of the new security realities post-9/11. I observed an unprecedented sense of urgency to quickly confront and neutralize al Qaeda and unseat the Taliban in Afghanistan. The president made it very clear that he was willing to underwrite aggressive unconventional warfare operations and military action. For the first time in decades, the political will to act decisively and preemptively was

146

present. The policy makers, the intelligence community, and senior military commanders were not intimidated by the enormity and complexity of the task before them and most endorsed the notion that "sometimes the most difficult tasks are accomplished by the most direct means."[2] The forces in the field, a handful of CIA operatives and Special Operations troops supported by precision airpower and technical intelligence, reacted magnificently, achieving an incredible victory against the Taliban and al Qaeda in just six weeks.

But, tactical victories in the Afghan campaign, while viscerally satisfying to all, would not be enough. The president's National Security team recognized that the terrorist threat confronting us was indeed different from those we had faced in the past; well financed, technologically savvy, networked globally and more lethal than we had previously thought possible. While the threat was shadowy and diffuse, our national goals and plan for execution were clear from the start: stop further attacks against the United States and our friends and allies both here at home and overseas; create an international environment that was inhospitable to terrorists and those who support them; diminish the underlying causes that contribute to terrorism. The defense of the homeland, we recognized, began overseas. In order to meet these goals, the federal government would have to work together: harmoniously applying all elements of national power—diplomatic, intelligence, military, information, economic/financial, and law enforcement—to reduce terrorist scope and capability in order to realize the president's intent.

With this guidance, we began developing an overarching strategy for the U.S. government to contain and ultimately defeat the terrorist enemy. Our strategists were led by U.S. Navy SEAL Captain (now Rear Admiral) Bill McRaven. Bill assembled a broad range of experts from all U.S. government agencies and operational units as well as private experts in the field and academics to draft the National Strategy for Combating Terrorism, an elaboration of Section III of the National Security Strategy. The resultant strategy this group developed was actually implemented as we wrote it in late 2001 and early 2002 although it was not finally published formally for the American public until February 2003.[3]

The purpose of this chapter is to describe the U.S. strategy for the GWOT. In the following sections, I will discuss the new realities of terrorism and the national goals.[4] I will then outline how we intend to execute the strategy. I will close with some comments on the challenges we must address in order to achieve success.

The New Structure of Terrorism

Twenty-first century terrorism is distinctly different from the Cold War-era terrorism in Europe, the Middle East, Asia and Latin America. The structure of terrorism pyramid we developed for the National Strategy describes a terrorist threat with global reach that operates effectively with little or no formal state sponsorship (see Figure 1).

Underlying Conditions

The base of the pyramid reflects the broad social, political, and economic conditions that spawn today's terrorism. The menace facing the United States has its roots in radical Islam. A group of Muslim extremists, using their interpretations of the Koran, feel that they have been empowered by God to wage a holy and just war against the Great Satan—the United States and its allies—wherever and whenever they can.

Figure 1

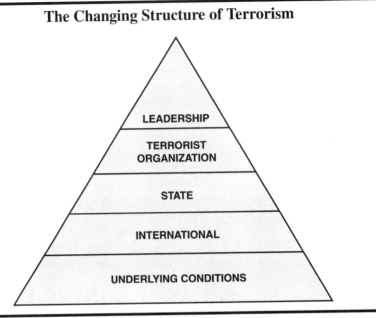

The Changing Structure of Terrorism

Source: National Strategy for Combating Terrorism, February 2003.

Many of these Muslims are disenfranchised citizens—people who feel they have no voice in how their country is run or its resources are expended. They span the social and the economic spectrum. Poverty by itself does not lead a person to terrorism but the squalid conditions in many countries have prompted some citizens, rich and poor, to seek violent redress and revolution. Oppressive regimes are a factor. It is no secret, for example, that Osama bin Laden's number one objective is to topple the Saudi royal family. The Israeli-Palestinian struggle is a major issue in every Islamic country (and in most of the world). As long as the United States is perceived as actively aiding and abetting the Israelis in suppressing the valid aspirations of the Palestinian people, more Muslims will be prompted to join the extremist ranks.

International Environment

The global economy and the boundary-less nature of information technologies allow terrorists to spread their message, to recruit, to organize, to plan, and to move money. Today, over 140 million people live and work outside of their countries of citizenship; the authors of the *National Strategy* noted that members of al Qaeda have traveled "with the ease of a vacationer or business traveler.[5] Lax enforcement and permissive laws and policies on immigration in many Western countries, including the United States, have made it easy for terrorists and their cells to "hide in plain sight."

Terrorists take full advantage of advanced technologies such as cell phones, encrypted e-mails, and the Internet. They raise funds through seemingly charitable organizations and non-governmental organizations, and they move money through banks and *hawalas*, largely unregulated money transfer systems in some immigrant communities. Organized criminal activity has also prospered in these conditions and there is often a nexus between terrorists and criminals. Some terrorist organizations are financing their local operations by low-level scams and alliances with common criminals.

Sanctuaries

We can no longer ignore failed states that cannot or will not exert control over significant portions of their territory. This is as much a selfish concern as a moral imperative, even though our efforts will ultimately result in a better world. Afghanistan is an excellent example. The United States and our allies probably spent over $7 billion to assist the Mujahidin in defeating the Soviets. Yet when the Afghan war was over in 1992, the flow of aid ceased, contributing directly to the resumption of the civil war and the rise of the Taliban government that seized Kabul in 1996.[6] If we had taken just one percent of those $7 billion and used it to rebuild Afghanistan following the war, there is a good chance that the Taliban would not have been able to found the first radical Wahabbi state that would later grant haven to Osama Bin Laden and al Qaeda when they were expelled from Sudan.

It would be overly simplistic to suggest that nation building is a panacea, necessary and sufficient to stop all terrorism, but order, stability, and state legitimacy are preconditions for reducing the recruitment and freedom of terrorist organizations. The National Strategy recognizes this, explaining "Whether through ignorance, inability, or intent, states around the world still offer havens—both physical (for example, safe houses, training grounds) and virtual (for example, reliable communication and financial networks)—that terrorists need to plan, organize, train, and conduct their operations."[7]

The United States officially identifies seven state sponsors of terrorism: Iran, Iraq, Syria, Libya, Cuba, North Korea, and Sudan but this list is not complete nor is it completely accurate. Some states just cannot control vast areas of their domains, resulting in safe havens for terrorist groups. Countries such as Pakistan, Indonesia, Thailand, the Philippines and areas like the Caucuses, the Horn of Africa and others have major problems. The United States is willing to offer assistance and incentives to encourage states to gain control of their territory or to cease abetting terrorism. When incentives do not work, the United States is also capable of applying disincentives to ensure that uncooperative states change their behavior even to the point of taking unilateral action. The good news is that most of these states recognize the problem and are cooperating with the United States in gaining control of ungoverned territories and in addressing other conditions that facilitate terrorist operations.

Terrorist Organizations

The terrorist organizations themselves are decentralized and difficult to penetrate. As radical Islamic organizations, they have common values, social rites, sense of justice, identity, and sense of self. Since many of them fought in Afghanistan in both recent wars, or in Chechnya, or the Balkans, or were trained in the same camps, they have shared hardships and dangers. Their brotherhood is tight and almost impenetrable to outsiders.

With perhaps as many as 3,000 al Qaeda members in jails in 30-plus countries, we now know a lot more about these organizations than we did pre-9/11. These terrorists are dedicated and willing to die for the cause. Very few of the ones we have captured have "turned" and those we have gotten to know well in interrogation have impressed us with their devotion and fanaticism. They have global reach and are very adaptive. While al Qaeda still finances and directs some operations like the May 2003 bombings in Saudi Arabia, other splinter groups or franchises, such as Jemaah Islamiyah in Southeast Asia and Ansar al Islam in Iraq, are conducting semi-independent operations to complement these attacks. Despite their losses of top leadership, al Qaeda is adapting and morphing into new cells and forms.

Leadership

Charismatic and smart leaders such as Osama bin Ladin and Ayman al Zawahiri, his number two, have attracted, in some cases, a near-cult following. These figures become emblematic of the larger phenomena. In 2002, CBS News asked a sample of Americans, "If Osama bin Laden is not captured or killed, then do you think the United States will have won the war in Afghanistan, or not?" Twenty-three percent of the sample said yes, but 67 percent said that bin Laden's capture was critical to the success of the war.[8] Successful operations in Thailand have recently captured the Southeast Asia al Qaeda chief, Riduan Isamuddin (better known as Hambali) in Thailand where authorities suspect he was preparing to attack world leaders, including President Bush, at this October's Asia-Pacific Economic Conference. Abu Baakir Baasyir, the radical Islamic preacher, was just convicted on lesser charges in an Indonesian court and will be imprisoned for a few years. All four men retain a strong voice and influence in the Islamic world and will remain spiritual leaders and, perhaps martyrs someday when they are killed or imprisoned.

The Principal Threat

The principal terrorist threat to the United States remains a weakened, but dangerous, al Qaeda. Though our efforts since 2001 have critically damaged the organization, al Qaeda is like a wounded animal, and just because we have inflicted great pain on it does not mean it cannot strike again as it demonstrated in May in Riyadh and most recently in Iraq. Al Qaeda's goals are unchanged as it seeks to promote conflict between Islam and the West, weaken U.S. and Western influence in the Islamic world, and topple "corrupt" and oppressive Islamic regimes. Their tactics have not changed either. They continue to plan large-scale, 9/11-like attacks on U.S. soil with WMD if possible. Al Qaeda's targeting criteria appears to remain consistent: attack targets of symbolic significance that have an economic impact, and inflict mass casualties. They have a penchant for returning to targets they have attacked before or have missed in the past. If we rebuild the twin towers, I believe that they will try to reattack that site. I also believe that they will attempt to attack the White House and the Capitol as well as Wall Street and other locations in New York. Other key American cities like Philadelphia, Boston, Atlanta, Chicago, St Louis, Los Angeles, San Francisco, and Seattle are likely on their list.

Based on interviews with key incarcerated al Qaeda leaders and captured computers, manuals, writings, and manuscripts, there are indications that al Qaeda has experimented with different forms of weapons of mass destruction to include chemical weapons, biological, and perhaps a radiological dispersal device. They are fascinated with nuclear weapons. Obtaining weapons of mass destruction is a high on their priority list. Al Qaeda makes no distinction between weapons of mass destruction and other, less lethal, weapons. They are fighting a total war, which makes these terrorists very innovative, unpredictable, and dangerous!

While al Qaeda is the most immediate and dangerous terrorist threat, there are other "wild cards" to watch. Groups like Hezbollah have not engaged the United States directly post-9/11, but are capable of doing so.[9] Using a sports analogy, al Qaeda is a junior varsity team, compared to Hezbollah, which is the first team—a mature organization with a very strong political and benevolent wing and a tough military wing that is well trained and supplied by the Iranians. They are very capable with global reach. We must never forget that prior to 9/11 Hezbollah killed more Americans then any other terrorist group. We have indictments against several key Hezbollah leaders and we must bring them to justice some day. Our advantage against Hezbollah is one of intelligence, as we know a lot about them. When we do move against the top Hezbollah leaders, however, and our counterterrorist forces in the military, FBI, and CIA bring the responsible people to justice, the United States should be prepared for a coordinated and potentially bloody reaction.

Global Networking

After the Cold War, active state sponsorship of terrorist groups declined. New terrorists, facilitated by permissive Western societies, global communications, and easy travel described earlier, were able to organize, proliferate, and conduct operations without this support. As the National Strategy points out, "The terrorists adapted to this new international environment and turned the advances of the twentieth century into the destructive enablers of the twenty-first century."[10] It is not uncommon for terrorists today to move from Islamic countries where they have traditionally assimilated and found employment, to the long-established Islamic diasporas in other countries where they can network through religious and social systems.

Terrorist groups are taking advantage of freedom of information to increase their geographic reach. Al Qaeda, for example, has inspired groups such as Abu Sayyaf in the Philippines and Jemmah Islamiyah in Southeast Asia to become franchises by sharing resources, information, people, and ideology. Not surprisingly, their agendas are similar.

Networking also permits decentralized command and control as today's terrorists operate under their own version of the commander's intent. Many terrorist groups do not respond to direct orders from al Qaeda or any other higher headquarters. Instead, they are guided by military-style mission orders to attack targets of opportunity using all available methods. Actions are often not coordinated, and terrorist plans may be sloppy or hastily executed. Regardless of their success or failure, the effect of these attacks is to bring the fight to the United States and our allies and force us to react. The recent increase in terrorist attacks in Iraq illustrate this phenomenon.

Networking allows terrorists to translate their intentions into action. As the United States has increased its efforts against terrorism and has successfully stopped them from attacking U.S. targets, al Qaeda and its franchises have shifted operations to new geographic locations in order to exploit easier prey and softer targets. The outbreaks of violence around the world in 2002 and thus far in 2003 in places such as North Africa, Africa, Southeast Asia, the Caucuses, and now Iraq reflect that changing focus.

Expanding the war in this manner is a risky course of action for the terrorists because it has reinforced alliances among some targeted states and prompted other states to energetically join with the United States for the first time to combat a mutual menace. Al Qaeda's attack in Saudi Arabia, for example, may well result in the terrorists losing an important safe haven in the kingdom. In the past, the Saudi government has been less than aggressive against al Qaeda. Many suspect that Saudi al Qaeda members often sent their families back home and some were even able to enjoy a low-key visit occasionally. Now that terrorists have killed Saudis and Westerners in brazen attacks, an awakened and embarrassed royal family has been forced to confront the threat. Saudi officials appear to be taking a much tougher stance against terrorism.

Currently, a vast amount of hatred and distrust is being spawned in an insidious pan-Islamic educational system. In the past 25 years, the radical Wahabbi sect from Saudi Arabia has sponsored religious schools or *madrassahs* throughout the Islamic world. The Indonesians have seminaries called *pesandren*. Most of these schools spread a message of hatred and intolerance, radicalizing young Muslims, and encouraging them to join the Holy War or Jihad. These *madrassahs* and *pesendren* are in no way a replacement for secular educational systems.[11] A student's curriculum in these schools rarely extends beyond rote memorization of the Koran and American/anti-Western diatribe.[12] These schools along with the radical mosques serve as a very effective terrorist assessment and selection program.

U.S. Goals in the Global War on Terrorism

The GWOT national strategy to combat the new global, networked terrorism has four goals—"The Four D's": *defend* against terrorism, *defeat* existing terrorist groups, *deny* state sponsorship and other forms of support, and *diminish* the underlying conditions that contribute to terrorism (Figure 2).

Defense of the homeland is the most immediate concern but we recognize that the best defense is a good offense and that defense of the homeland begins overseas. The United States is already committed to a multifaceted defense of its interests at home. The *National Strategy for Homeland Security*, the *National Strategy to Secure Cyberspace* and the *National Strategy for the Physical Protection of Critical Infrastructures and Key Assets* all address this need. The National Strategy for Combating Terrorism emphasizes a new "domain awareness" of all possible threats in the domains of air, land, sea and cyberspace. Homeland defense is also accomplished by working with neighboring nations and trading partners to secure critical infrastructure. A vital global economy requires free flow of what the National Strategy calls "low risk, high volume" people and goods.[13] The United States must support free trade, while still ensuring that containers, trucks and aircraft do not become "terrorist weapons" for the few and the malevolent.

The second goal is to defeat terrorists of global reach by attacking their finances, safe haven, command, control and communications. It is absolutely essential to work closely with allies and friends as we root out terrorist organizations and cells overseas.

The third goal is to deny groups support from other nations. The National Strategy is clear on this point: "The United States has a long memory and is committed to holding terrorists and those who harbor them accountable for past crimes."[14] Accomplishing this goal will require the establishment of an international standard of accountability, based on current international counterterrorism conventions and protocols, the UN Security Council Resolution 1373, and international rights to collective and self defense. An effective denial of support also requires joint intelligence and law enforcement efforts, sanctions against nations that sponsor terrorism and assistance to nations that lack law enforcement resources. While the United States will stand with old allies like Britain, it

Figure 2

Fundamental Goals: The Four D's

- ❖ Defend U.S. citizens and interests at home and abroad
- ❖ Defeat/destroy terrorist organizations
- ❖ Deny sanctuary and support to terrorist organizations
- ❖ Diminish the underlying causes

Source: National Strategy for Combating Terrorism, February 2003.

will also benefit from recasting its relationships with nations such as Russia, Pakistan, India, Indonesia, and China. New alliances have been formed that appeared unlikely prior to 9/11 with nations such as Yemen and the former Soviet Republics in the Caucuses. When the United States and the Soviet Union fought the Cold War, international conflicts were often characterized as zero-sum games. Today, the opportunity exists for mutually beneficial, "win-win" outcomes. Every nation can commit to combating terrorism and benefit from a safer world.

Finally, diminishing terrorism requires that, at some point, we address the underlying social and economic causes of terrorism by "winning the war of ideas," promoting freedom and democracy, delegitimizing terrorism, and supporting moderate governments. To this end, the United States must pursue mutually beneficial alliances with moderate Muslims. Many Muslims state that they feel backed into a corner because of a perceived anti-Islamic U.S. foreign policy. This global war on terrorism must not be viewed as an anti-Islamic campaign. We should work with moderate and modern Muslim governments to turn back totalitarianism and extremism and continue the U.S. record of assisting Islamic states such as Afghanistan, Kuwait, Jordan, Bosnia, Kosovo, and Iraq. This will take years, but unless we start now we will never stop the endless terrorist cycle of dissatisfaction, radicalization, recruitment, jihad, and martyrdom.

Executing the Strategy

Key to this strategy is the use of all elements of national power (Figure 3). The president recognized the importance of the interagency effort when he addressed the Joint Session of Congress following 9/11: "We will direct every resource at our command—every means of diplomacy, every tool of intelligence, every instrument of law enforcement, every financial influence, and every necessary weapon of war—to the disruption and to the defeat of the global terror network."[15] As the president suggests, this war is not solely a military fight. While the military has a role to play, it will likely become less significant as the GWOT continues. The front lines of this conflict appear to be diplomatic, intelligence, and law enforcement fought side by side and in close coordination with our allies.

Contrary to conventional wisdom, the present war on terrorism has not been unilateral. The primary reason for our current success (for example, close to over 4,000 terrorists arrested and up to 3,000 in jail with 50 percent of the al Qaeda leadership off the street) is

Figure 3

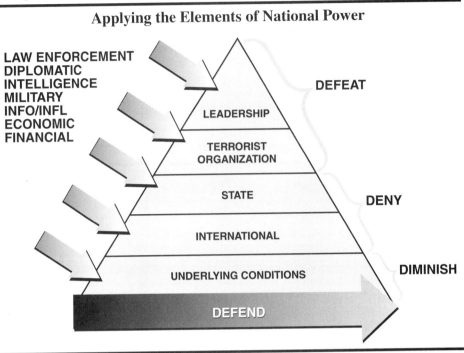

Applying the Elements of National Power

LAW ENFORCEMENT
DIPLOMATIC
INTELLIGENCE
MILITARY
INFO/INFL
ECONOMIC
FINANCIAL

LEADERSHIP

DEFEAT

TERRORIST
ORGANIZATION

STATE

DENY

INTERNATIONAL

UNDERLYING CONDITIONS

DIMINISH

DEFEND

Source: National Strategy for Combating Terrorism, February 2003.

the high degree of cooperation with our allies in the Middle East, Europe, Asia and Africa. After 9/11, NATO invoked Article V of the NATO Treaty, Australia invoked Article IV of the ANZUS treaty and over 37 nations provided military, law enforcement, intelligence, or humanitarian support in the GWOT.[16] Most of these successful and relatively unpublicized operations have taken place overseas, conducted by host-nation police, military and intelligence organizations with whom we enjoy trust and confidence.

The war on terrorism must also be supported by a strategic information campaign that can win the war of ideas. Thus far in the GWOT, U.S. efforts to sell our antiterrorism message overseas has been largely unsuccessful. For the first six to nine months after 9/11 we were able to maintain a level of international empathy and consensus, but even that support was qualified. From September 14 to 17, 2001, Gallup surveyed people in 14 foreign countries on whether they thought that the United States should attack the country (or countries) serving as a base for the 9/11 terrorists "once the identity of the terrorists is known." While well over half of the respondents in almost all the countries supported extradition and trial for suspected terrorists, only Israel and India supported a military attack.[17] We have seen a further erosion of support since the war in Iraq. America is failing to get its message across, nowhere more so than in the Islamic world and on the Arab street.

The United States and its allies must exert unrelenting pressure on the terrorists affording them no safe haven, respite, or place to hide. Operations must be continuous to disrupt planned attacks, kill or imprison the leaders, dry up financing and, over time, degrade and destroy the organizations. Alliances are essential to reinforce existing relationships and build new ones. Finally, as the scope of terrorism is localized, unorganized, and relegated to the criminal domain, we must rely upon and assist sovereign states in eradicating the vestiges of terrorism.

In my judgment, no lasting solution is possible until the United States addresses the Israeli-Palestinian conflict. The National Strategy recognizes that "No other issue has so colored the perception of the United States in the Muslim world."[18] The United States has been severely criticized not only in Islamic nations, but also in much of the world, for our lack of involvement in solving the Palestinian problem. The United States will need to stand by its commitment to an independent and democratic Palestine living beside Israel in peace. Moreover, we have to reassess our relationships with illegitimate regimes that oppress their people. If we want to succeed in a long-term campaign against terrorism, then words and deeds must match.

What is the best way then to apply the four strategic goals to the current pyramid of terrorism? The world will never be free of all terrorism. A more realistic goal is to eliminate terrorists' global reach, render them less lethal and reduce their capabilities to the point that they are a regional threat, then a state threat, then a provincial or local threat that can be controlled as ordinary crime by local law enforcement. Studies of past successful counter-terrorism campaigns indicate that intensive, sustained police action is the most successful strategy for disrupting and halting terrorist violence especially in areas where the terrorist does not depend on host country tolerance or sponsorship.

While strategic information may someday reduce the success of recruitment efforts, the United States must acknowledge that we will not change the minds of the hard-core terrorists. Some of our interrogators, consistent with their training, have formed close relationships with captured terrorist suspects, and their observations are telling. The interrogators report that the al Qaeda will is unbending. Detainees say, "You may as well kill me, because if you let me out of this camp, I will come back to attack you." We cannot change such a mind. We will not win their "hearts and minds." Our only alternative is to give them no place to hide and take them out of the conflict—by death or incarceration.

Figure 4 shows how we intend to execute this strategy by compressing terrorist scope and isolating terrorist networks so that global threats become regional or state threats and further become localized in specific communities. It is also necessary to reduce terrorist capabilities so that terrorists who may have sought WMD in the past now must use small arms and improvised explosives. Once a group is forced into the lower left quadrant of this figure, with short reach and limited capabilities, the United States and the host country cannot ease the pressure. The Abu Sayyaf Group (ASG) serves as a cautionary tale of how independent, networked groups can quickly reconstitute following a setback. The Philippine military reported that the leader Abu Sabaya was killed in June 2002 by a combined Filipino/U.S. operation. The Philippine and U.S. governments congratulated themselves and declared the group mortally wounded. But the ASG recovered. In February 2003, the de facto operations officer of the group, Abu Soliman, announced plans for a "welcome party" for U.S. troops on a military exercise.[19] ASG backed up this threat with action and continue to kill Americans and Filipinos and take hostages. America and our allies can ill afford to take pressure off these types of groups.

Finally, we must commit to a long-term strategy against terrorism, and avoid turning the GWOT into a domestic political issue. Americans sometimes want policy fast, sequentially, and in sound bites. The National Strategy must span administrations with broad

Figure 4

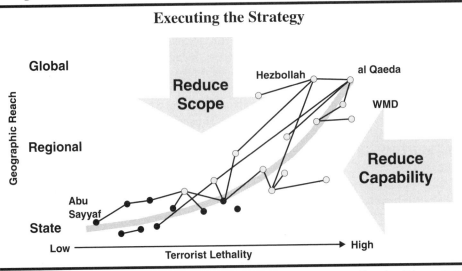

Executing the Strategy

Source: National Strategy for Combating Terrorism, February 2003.

public and bipartisan support, avoiding at all costs major policy reversal as we execute the strategy. The National Strategy best summarizes this challenge: "We will be resolute. Others might flag in the face of the inevitable ebb and flow of the campaign against terrorism. But the American people will not. We understand that we cannot choose to disengage from the world, because in this globalized era, the world will engage us regardless."[20]

Challenges

The GWOT has been very successful thus far. We have successfully prevented further attacks on the U.S. homeland. We have killed and captured large numbers of the enemy. And, we have assembled an impressive coalition to carry on the long-term struggle. But our successes have led the enemy to shift attacks to other geographic regions against softer targets that have killed and injured Americans and our friends. The war in Iraq did not eliminate the threat. In fact, it may have energized and coalesced our enemies. More terrorist attacks at home and abroad are likely and WMD will be employed if available. Time does not appear to be on our side. As the scope and intensity of the conflict increases, it is clear that the United States must drive a wedge between the extremists and the rest of the Islamic world before Osama bin Laden and company persuade Muslims that the United States is the common enemy and that they must join the fight. The failure to stabilize both Afghanistan and Iraq undermines the perception of U.S. power and resolve.

The United States has unsought opportunities to shape the future. The task is great: conduct a worldwide global war on terrorism with complex, diverse campaigns with old allies and new friends. We must seize opportunities to do things better, with ingenuity, innovation and the strength of the American people. Our actions will likely set conditions for the remainder of the twenty-first century.

Wayne A. Downing is presently chair at the Combating Terrorism Center at West Point, and additionally assists on several boards in the private sector. He has served as the national director and deputy national security adviser for Combating Terrorism. His role there included close coordination among the intelligence, military, diplomatic, law enforcement, and financial operations for the war on terror.

Notes

1. For a more detailed discussion of the history and doctrine of the commander's intent, see Lawrence G. Shattuck, "Communicating Intent and Imparting Presence," *Military Review*, March–April 2000: 66–72.
2. National Strategy for Combating Terrorism, February 2003, p. 2.
3. Formal approval of the strategy by the interagency was time consuming and difficult. The USG bureaucracy remains formidable. While the foot soldiers understand the war and cooperate magnificently in the field, the agencies in Washington continue to squabble. It remains to be seen whether the ponderous federal bureaucracies will be able to work together to achieve the national goals. Immediately following 9/11, cooperation and sharing was better than I had ever experienced. As we commemorate the second anniversary of the 9/11 attack, there are signs that many USG agencies are returning to their bickering turf battles and protection of rice bowls.
4. For a concise summary of U.S. policy toward Afghanistan, see Courtney Draggon, "A Cautionary Tale: Lessons to Be Learned from Past Mistakes in Afghanistan," *Conflict Resolution Abroad* (Association for Conflict Resolution), 7 Feb 2002.
5. National Strategy for Combating Terrorism, February 2003, p. 7.
6. For a concise summary of U.S. policy toward Afghanistan, see Courtney Draggon, "A Cautionary Tale: Lessons to Be Learned from Past Mistakes in Afghanistan," *Conflict Resolution Abroad* (Association for Conflict Resolution), 7 Feb 2002.
7. National Strategy for Combating Terrorism, February 2003, p. 7.
8. Telephone poll of 647 American adults 13 May–14 May, 2002. Ten percent of respondents did not answer, selected both, or did not know. Lexis-Nexis Roper accession number 0404211.
9. There are recent, unconfirmed reports that Hezbollah may be joining the fight against the U.S.-led coalition in Iraq. If true, this would be a serious incursion and could widen that conflict to Syria, Lebanon, and ultimately Iran.
10. National Strategy for Combating Terrorism, February 2003, p. 7.
11. For a discussion of Pakistan's response to the spread of *madrassahs*, see Ilene R. Prusher, "Musharraf vs. the Mullahs: A Fight for Islamic Schools," *Christian Science Monitor*, 30 Jan 2002.
12. I attended the first meeting with President Bush and Pakistani President Musharraf in November 2001. The topic they most passionately discussed was the Pakistani education system and the need to replace *madrassahs* with schools that could better satisfy educational needs while producing productive, responsible citizens.
13. National Strategy for Combating Terrorism, February 2003, p. 26.
14. National Strategy for Combating Terrorism, February 2003, p. 17.
15. The White House Office of the Press Secretary, September 20, 2001, "Address to a Joint Session of Congress and the American People," as delivered by President Bush.
16. Jim Garamone, "International Coalition Against Terror Grows," *American Forces Press Service*, 23 May 2002.
17. Nations polled were Israel, India, United States, Korea, France, Czech Republic, Italy, South Africa, United Kingdom (excluding N. Ireland), Germany, Bosnia, Colombia, Pakistan, Greece and Mexico. The two nations with less than a majority supporting trial and extradition, Israel and India, overwhelmingly supported an attack (77% and 72%, respectively). As cited in: Peter Ford, "Why Do They Hate Us?" *Christian Science Monitor*, 27 Sep 2001.
18. National Strategy for Combating Terrorism, February 2003, p. 24.
19. Arlyn de la Cruz, "Abu Sayyaf Prepares 'Welcome' for U.S. Forces," *Philippine Daily Inquirer*, 19 Feb 03, www.inq7.net.
20. National Strategy for Combating Terrorism, February 2003, pp 29–30.

Acknowledgments

Foreword: Copyright © 2003 by Wayne A. Downing.

Preface: Copyright © 2003 by Russell D. Howard.

Rohan Gunaratna, "Defeating Al Qaeda—The Pioneering Vanguard of the Islamic Movements." Copyright © 2003 by Rohan Gunaratna.

Audrey Kurth Cronin, "Behind the Curve: Globalization and International Terrorism," *International Security*, vol. 27, no. 3 (Winter 2002/2003), pp. 30–58. Copyright © 2003 by The President and Fellows of Harvard College and The Massachusetts Institute of Technology. Reprinted by permission of MIT Press Journals.

Patrick D. Buckley and Michael J. Meese, "The Financial Front in the Global War on Terrorism." Copyright © 2003 by Patrick D. Buckley and Michael J. Meese.

Robert Mandel, "Fighting Fire with Fire: Privatizing Counterterrorism." Copyright © 2003 by Robert Mandel.

James S. Robbins, "Defeating Networked Terrorism." Copyright © 2003 by James S. Robbins.

Michael R. Eastman and Robert B. Brown, "Security Strategy in the Gray Zone: Alternatives for Preventing WMD Handoff to Non-State Actors." Copyright © 2003 by Michael Eastman and Robert Brown.

Bruce Hoffman, "The Logic of Suicide Terrorism," *The Atlantic Monthly*, vol. 291, no. 5 (June 2003). Copyright © 2003 by Bruce Hoffman. Reprinted by permission of the author.

Kelly J. Hicks, "How Business Can Defeat Terrorism: Global Financial Firms Battle the SARS Outbreak in Hong Kong." Copyright © 2003 by Kelly J. Hicks.

Russell D. Howard, "Preemptive Military Doctrine: No Other Choice Against Transnational Non-State Actors." Copyright © 2003 by Russell D. Howard.

Brian Michael Jenkins, *Countering Al Qaeda: An Appreciation of the Situation and Suggestions for Strategy* (RAND, 2002). Copyright © 2002 by RAND. Reprinted by permission of The RAND Corporation, Santa Monica, CA.

Wayne A. Downing, "The Global War on Terrorism: Focusing the National Strategy." Copyright © 2003 by Wayne A. Downing.